THE
GERMAN
U-BOAT BASE
at Lorient, France

VOLUME 3

AUGUST 1942 – AUGUST 1943

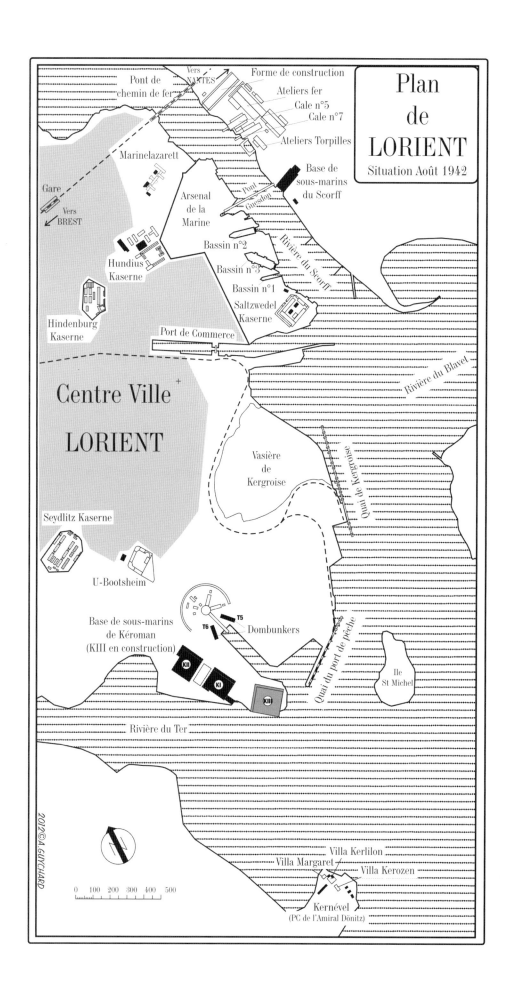

Plan de LORIENT
Situation Août 1942

Vers NANTES
Pont de chemin de fer
Forme de construction
Ateliers fer
Cale n°5
Cale n°7
Ateliers Torpilles
Marinelazarett
Base de sous-marins du Scorff
Gare
Vers BREST
Arsenal de la Marine
Pont Guesdon
Rivière du Scorff
Bassin n°2
Hundius Kaserne
Bassin n°3
Bassin n°1
Hindenburg Kaserne
Saltzwedel Kaserne
Port de Commerce
Rivière du Blavet
Centre Ville
LORIENT
Vasière de Kergroise
Quai de Kergroise
Seydlitz Kaserne
U-Bootsheim
Dombunkers
T5
T6
Base de sous-marins de Kéroman
(KIII en construction)
KII
KI
KIII
Quai du port de pêche
Ile St Michel
Rivière du Ter
2012 © A. GUYCHARD
Villa Kerlilon
Villa Margaret
Villa Kerozen
Kernével
(PC de l'Amiral Dönitz)

0 100 200 300 400 500

AUGUST 1942 – AUGUST 1943

THE GERMAN U-BOAT BASE

at Lorient, France

VOLUME 3

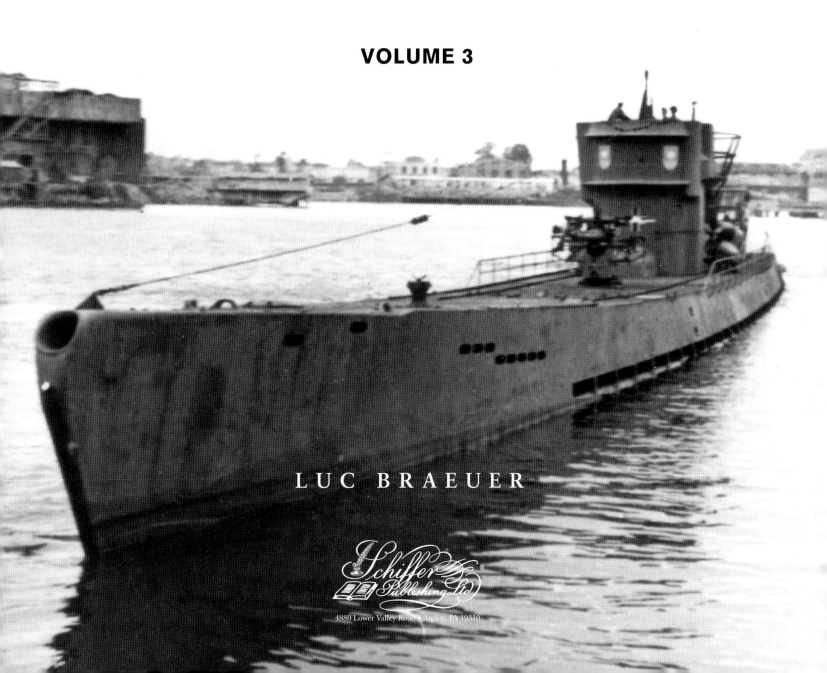

LUC BRAEUER

Schiffer Publishing Ltd
4880 Lower Valley Road • Atglen, PA 19310

THIS BOOK IS DEDICATED
TO THE VICTIMS OF
THE BOMBARDMENTS
OF LORIENT.

Type set in Sabon & Akzidenz

ISBN: 978-0-7643-4832-7
Printed in China

Published by Schiffer Publishing, Ltd.
4880 Lower Valley Road
Atglen, PA 19310
Phone: (610) 593-1777; Fax: (610) 593-2002
E-mail: Info@schifferbooks.com

For our complete selection of fine books on this and related subjects, please visit our website at www.schifferbooks.com. You may also write for a free catalog.

This book may be purchased from the publisher. Please try your bookstore first.

We are always looking for people to write books on new and related subjects. If you have an idea for a book, please contact us at proposals@schifferbooks.com.

Schiffer Publishing's titles are available at special discounts for bulk purchases for sales promotions or premiums. Special editions, including personalized covers, corporate imprints, and excerpts can be created in large quantities for special needs. For more information, contact the publisher.

CONTENTS

ACKNOWLEDGMENTS

I would like to thank everyone who helped me with the creation of this book, the fruit of over two years of study, research, and contacts in several European countries.

Firstly, Mr. Horst Bredow, the founder and director of the *Deutsches U-Boot Museum*: a unique and major archive where all the technical information on this subject is centralized for researchers. The foundation functions without official subventions, but by donations from the people who use the archives. For further information, contact: Friends of the Deutsches U-Boot Museum-Archiv: Freundeskreis Traditionsarchiv Unterseeboote, Lange Strasse 1, D-27478 Cuxhaven/Altenbruch, Germany.

For their historical and technical help: my two friends, research, and voyage companions Anthony Guychard (who also drew the plans in this book), and Benoît Senne, along with my brother Marc; Frans Beckers and Walter Cloots in Belgium who sent me the result of over fifteen years research on submarine war diaries; Robert Briet veteran of the merchant navy for his research on the agent disembarked by U-66; Bernard Disdier, Alain Durrieu for their proof-reading; Bruno Jaffre, British contact; Peter Jowitt who regularly sends me information about the Battle of the Atlantic; Patrice Thebrun for his advice; Olivier le Cabellec who took part in our research on the vestiges; Lucien le Pallec retired helmsman in the navy for his historical knowledge of Lorient; Captain (retired) of the USN Jerry Mason, who put the German submariners' interrogations by the Americans, conserved in the National Archives in Washington, or the Internet; Axel Niestlé the diver; Jean-Louis Mourette about U-171; Thierry Nicolo for his advice on photographic documents; the National Archives in London and Wast in Berlin.

For lending their photos: Jacques Alaluquetas, Josef Charita in charge after the war of military identification at the Belgian Interior Ministry who lent his personal archives; Alain Chazette; Hans-Jürgen Drewitz son of the commander of U-525; Karl-Heinz Kanzler of U-993; Ariane Krause whose grandfather was on U-126; Achim Krüger whose grandfather was the engineer on U-154 and then of the 2nd Flotilla; Alain le Craver formerly of the National Navy; Robert Maschauer survivor of U-526; Ulf-Normann Neitzel son of U-510's first commander; Wolfgang Ockert; Michel Quettier; Pierre Rebeyrolle; Mathieu Rouxel; Pierre-Marie Rousseau; Dietmar Scholten; Uwe Stachelhaus who did ten years of research on the history of U-526 that his father had served aboard; Bernd Siepert; Sabine Turck daughter of Chief Engineer Ernst Turck on U-621 and Walter Wittig former radioman on U-518. I would also like to thank Mr. Ivry, in charge of ECPAD who gave me access to the photos taken by war correspondents of the era; the Photo Service at the Imperial War Museum in London, the National Archives in Washington, DC, and Maryland, and the American Coast Guard.

For giving authorization to photograph part of their collection: Hervé le Diagon; Andreas Dwulecki; Philippe Esvelin; Jean-Philippe Lamotte; Serge l'Hotellier; Eric Miquelon; Pierre Pennanech and Pascal Theffo.

Finally, thanks to my mother Monique for her precious re-reading, and to my wife Celine for her patience.

October 2011: Souvenir photo after a week working in the U-Boot-Archives in Cuxhaven. Lieutenant Benoit Senne, Anthony Guychard, and Luc Braeuer help Horst Bredow, the archive manager. *LB*

PROLOGUE

Summer 1942: the German submariners' rest camp *Lager Lemp* in the Caudan
commune. During a day of leave, members of the 2nd Flotilla's ground personnel
take a turn in a boat on Kersalo Lake. On the right: the young German marine who
conscientiously assembled three photograph albums about the history of the U-boat
corps in Lorient on which my series of books is based. *LB*

In 2005, when I was doing research on the German U-boats that stopped off in Lorient from 1940 to 1944, I didn't imagine that I'd be able to find so many photos and eyewitness accounts and so much information. I would like to thank the readers of my two previous books, which encouraged me to chase up the information for over two years that would result in this third volume. Thanks to several veterans and/or their families who helped me in my research, this book contains numerous eyewitness accounts that make it even more interesting to read.

Each U-boat is a story in itself. Some of them have already been the subjects of books. When I study a particular U-boat, I'm always surprised to discover an often-incredible fate and a real human adventure. The crews were composed of very young men, three quarters of whom have been lying at the bottom of the ocean for over seventy years. With their photos, where most of them are identified along with their stories, it is now possible to understand a little of their daily lives in that era. Their fate, usually dramatic, now seems closer and easier to understand.

Here is the history of the U-boats that stopped off in Lorient from August 1942 to August 1943, a difficult period for the citizens of Lorient with the terrible bombardments on their town, and for the German submariners completely overtaken by the Allies' technical innovations. Because of these, the U-boats, which had been the hunters during the first years of the war, became the prey of the Allied escort ships, sometimes operating in hunting groups, and the aircraft now equipped to destroy them. After March 1943, a U-boat out of Lorient had more chance of finding itself on the seabed than of returning home. The height being reached in April 1943: out of twenty departures, only five returned to port. ■

INTRODUCTION: GENERAL SITUATION OF THE BATTLE OF THE ATLANTIC ON AUGUST 1, 1942

British Admiral Sir Max K. Horton, appointed commander-in-chief of the Western Approaches on November 17, 1942, was to become one of Dönitz's principal adversaries. He was also a submariner in the Royal Navy during the First World War. In 1914, as commander of the submarine HMS E9, he sunk one German light cruiser, two destroyers, and several cargo ships before damaging an armored cruiser. In 1940, he was named chief of all submarines based in England, and was promoted to the rank of admiral on January 9, 1941. He was a great golf player, a sport he practiced each day during the war. However, this didn't keep him from being present every night at his headquarters in Liverpool, a period during which the attacks on convoys were at their height. His principal task aimed at increasing the efficiency of the escort ships by creating escort groups at the beginning of 1943. Sailing independently of the convoys, they were there to reinforce them in the event of attack then to chase the U-boats (whose diving-time was limited), and destroy them, leaving the convoy to continue with its initial escort. *IWM*

In July 1942, Admiral Dönitz made a long speech to the German press. He declared that the U-boat Corps was facing hard times. A total of eleven U-boats had been sunk during July alone, which represented half of the losses during the entire first half of 1942! Until now, his general staff had always been able to exploit the Allies' weaknesses: they found zones where traffic was heavy and little defended; they attacked heavily and then left the area before any defense could be organized. Attacking several points at the same time also forced the Allies to spread out their defense. In August 1942, chased from the coast of the USA, Dönitz dispersed his Type IX long-range U-boats based in Lorient to sectors still lightly defended, notably the Caribbean and the coast of South America, the Gulf of St. Lawrence, Canada, and then on the other side of the Atlantic off the African coasts, near Freetown, in the Gulf of Guinea to Cape Town, and the limits of the Indian Ocean. But the greater distance meant a fall in the U-boats'

daily results. While the Type IX U-boats were sent to far-flung oceans, the majority of the Type VII U-boats formed wolfpacks, mainly in the middle of the North Atlantic, where Allied planes couldn't reach them. To be able to attack with several wolfpacks at the same time, Dönitz counted on the massive arrivals of new U-boats that would be produced at a steady rhythm of twenty-five units a month during the second half of 1942. However, thanks to the Allies' aircraft manufacturers, who increased the range of certain planes, this "Mid-Atlantic gap" was slowly reduced. Up to the end of summer 1941, the planes could patrol a maximum of 500 miles from the coast, but by September 1941, a squadron of American B-24 Liberators, with a range of 750 miles, was delivered to the Coastal Command. From the beginning of the summer of 1942, the U-boats had another ten months, until the spring of 1943, before the Mid-Atlantic gap (which covered 300 miles of ocean),

was completely covered by Allied aircraft. After this, the Liberators, delivered in large numbers, and the escort aircraft carriers protected each convoy. However, even during this ten-month respite, with the growing Allied defense, and their superior technical equipment, the German U-boats never recaptured the favorable conditions of the first two years of the war. Admiral Dönitz was far from suspecting the enormous possibilities of the American shipyards that had planned the construction of six million tons of merchant ships for 1942. Two types of ships, standardized on the model of the car industry, were produced: The *Liberty Ships* cargo ships, 443-feet long and weighing 10,000 tons, the equivalent in merchandise to 300 railroad cars, and T2-SE-A1-type fuel tankers, 502-feet long and weighing 10,195 tons. The American shipping industry surpassed its already ambitious initial program by finally building eight million tons of shipping during 1942! ∎

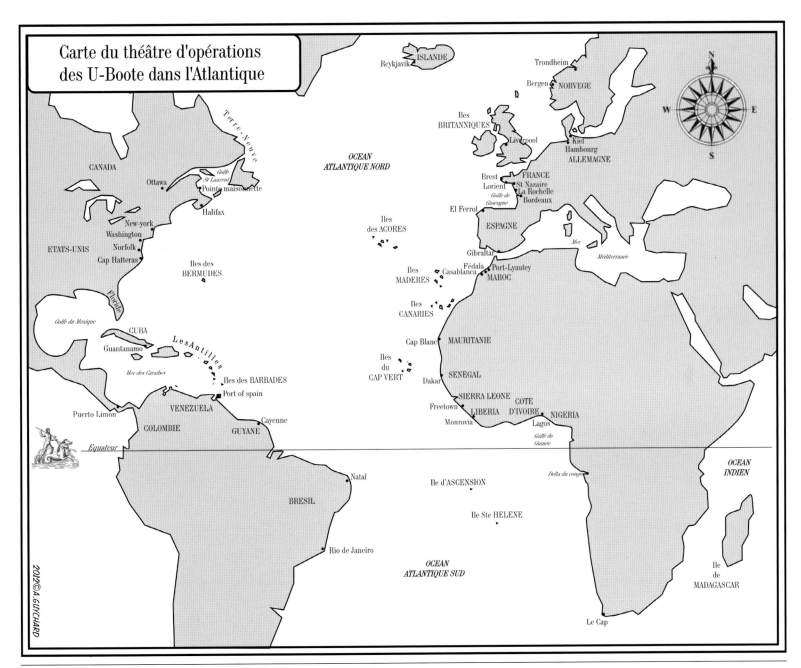

Carte du théâtre d'opérations des U-Boote dans l'Atlantique

Chart of the Atlantic with the location of the mentioned sites. *By Anthony Guychard*

SECOND HALF OF 1942: MISSIONS TO CANADA, THE ANTILLES, ALONG THE BRAZILIAN AND AFRICAN COASTS TO CAPE TOWN

August 1942: First Wave of Departures for Cape Town, and the Arrival of a Japanese Submarine

Movements: eight arrivals, six departures, passage of a Japanese submarine, number of U-boats present at the end of the month: fourteen. For the first time since July 1940, apart from the U-116 Type XB, there were only Type IXs in Lorient. In accordance with the expectations of the U-boat Corps Command, the Type VIIs were now housed in bases at Brest, St. Nazaire and La Pallice.

Observations: the results of the Germans U-boats in August 1942 increased by nearly 100,000 tons in relation to the preceding month with 114 ships sunk for 544,908 tons. The six Type IXs arrived in Lorient during the month, with twenty-nine cargos sunk in the Caribbean and off Florida, were responsible for a quarter of this figure; principally against ships sailing alone. But, after having five of her ships sunk by U-507 between August 16 and 17, Brazil declared war on Germany and Italy on August 22, 1942. This gave the Allies

the opportunity to use the country's airstrips, principally in Natal, which put the submarines operating in the north along the coasts of French Guiana and Venezuela in serious danger until the end of the year.

Between August 19 and 20, 1942, U-68, U-156, U-172 and U-504, forming the "*Eisbär*" (Polar Bear) Wolfpack, left Lorient for Cape Town, at the limit of the South Atlantic and the Indian Ocean. Dönitz hoped that their appearance in this remote sector at the beginning of October, still protected, would yield good results. Until then, this zone where the raiders and German blockade runners operated was out of bounds for the U-boats. To reach their far-flung objective, the *Eisbär* pack had to be re-supplied a month after leaving Lorient by the "milk cow" U-459 in the sector of St. Helena Island, 600 miles below the equator. On September 12, U-156 sank the

passenger ship *Laconia*. U-156 was damaged in turn four days later, and its place in the *Eisbär* Wolfpack was filled by U-159.

On August 5, 1942, the Japanese submarine I-30 arrived in Lorient. This arrival followed the German-Japanese military agreement signed in Berlin on January 18, 1942, in which the two countries agreed to exchange military equipment and technology. Meanwhile, on March 27, 1942, the Kriegsmarine, through the two countries' diplomats, had asked the Japanese Navy to send their submarines to the Indian Ocean. Numerous Allied ships crossed the ocean before passing through the Suez Canal, carrying supplies for the British in North Africa. Installing a base for the Japanese submarines on the French island of Madagascar was even considered, as it was the only possibility in the west of this ocean. To stop this, the British, aware of the plans thanks to decoding messages passed between the Axis

In August 1942, *Lager Lemp*, the 2nd Flotilla's large rest camp was ready to receive off-duty submariners. However, during the second half of 1942, the young submariners clearly preferred the lively streets of Lorient at night to the peaceful countryside. *LB*

embassies, decided to take Madagascar, which was faithful to the Vichy government. A large-scale attack with assault craft was carried out on the main port of Diego Suarez on May 5, 1942. The French resisted for two days before capitulating when their losses reached around 150 dead and 500 wounded. However, in the southern part of the island, isolated groups of French fighters continued the combat against the British until November 6. On May 30, the Japanese launched an attack against the British fleet based in Diego Suarez with two midget submarines, transported there on the bridge of I-16. The battleship HMS *Ramillies*, hit by a torpedo, was immobilized for a year, and the fuel tanker *British Loyalty* was sunk. This didn't stop the British from holding on to the island to keep the Japanese from using it as a base. In the context of technological exchange,

AUGUST 1942

U-BOAT	TYPE	FLOT.	COMMANDER	ARRIVAL	DEPART	NOTES
Departures						
U-68	IXC	2	Karl-Friedrich Merten		20	Departure for Cape Town, *Eisbär* Wolfpack.
U-103	IXB	2	Gustav-Adolf Janssen			Being repaired June 22 – October 21, 1942.
U-105	IXB	2	Heinrich Schuch			U-105 stayed for repairs June 30 – November 23, 1942, after serious damage during an aerial attack on June 23. The entire crew transferred to U-154 that returned from mission on August 24.
U-106	IXB	2	Hermann Rasch			Being repaired July 28 – September 22 after an air attack July 22.
U-107	IXB	2	Harald Gelhaus		15	Departure for the Freetown sector
U-124	IXB	2	Johann Mohr			Being repaired June 26 – November 25, 1942.
U-126	IXC	2	Ernst Bauer			In maintenance July 25 – 19 September 19, 1942.
U-128	IXC	2	Ulrich Heyse			In maintenance July 22 – 2 September 2, 1942.
U-156	IXC	2	Werner Hartenstein		20	Departure for Cape Town, *Eisbär* Wolfpack.
U-159	IXC	10	Helmut Witte		24	Departure for the South Atlantic, Congo Delta zone, rejoins the *Eisbär* Wolfpack direction Cape Town to replace U-156 damaged during an air attack September 16 after rescuing survivors from the *Laconia*.
U-172	IXC	10	Carl Emmermann		19	Departure for Cape Town, *Eisbär* Wolfpack.
U-504	IXC	2	Fritz Poske		19	Departure for Cape Town, *Eisbär* Wolfpack.
Arrivals						
I-30	Jap.		Shinobu Endo	5	22	First Japanese submarine in Lorient.
U-161	IXC	2	Albrecht Achilles	7		Return from the coast of Brazil where little traffic was spotted; then the Caribbean, where it sunk two ships and two sailing ships, notably by penetrating Puerto Limon Port in Costa Rica. It sank a third ship in a convoy on the way home, which caused it to be chased for nine hours by destroyers and damage to the conning tower.
U-67	IXC	2	Günther Müller-Stöckheim	8		Returning from a successful mission off Florida with eight pennants: six for petrol tankers. In truth, only four petrol tankers out of six were sunk, two were only damaged.
U-43	IXA	2	Hans-Joachim Schwantke	15		Returning from an unsuccessful patrol in the North Atlantic. Hans-Joachim Schwantke is the new commander of U-43 since April 1942, in Kiel. He had been watch officer since October 1940.
U-129	IXC	2	Hans-Ludwig Witt	21		Returning from a successful mission in the Caribbean where eleven ships were sunk for a total of 41,570 tons.
U-116	XB	1	Werner von Schmidt	23		This submarine minesweeper had acted like an attack submarine in the middle of the Atlantic against the OS-33 convoy where it damaged one ship and sunk one other before resupplying four U-boats west of Freetown. A change in commander, Werner von Schmidt, is named on November 2, 1942, chief of the 8th Training Flotilla and Danzig fortifications.
U-154	IXC	2	Walther Kölle	23		Return from the Caribbean where one cargo and one fishing ship were sunk. On July 13, while the U-boat was on the surface, a man who was in the toilet on the bridge found himself in the water when the submarine was forced to dive when a plane appeared; he was later picked up, swimming amidst sharks! Complete change of crew with U-105 in for repairs.
U-160	IXC	10	Georg Lassen awarded Knight's Cross on arrival.	24		Return from a two-month patrol off the coast of Venezuela: six ships were sunk and a seventh damaged.
U-505	IXC	2	Axel-Olaf Loewe	25		Early return from the Caribbean because the commander had appendicitis at the end of July; appendix was removed on his arrival in Lorient. Two cargo ships and one Colombian sailing ship were sunk. Change of commander, Axel-Olaf Loewe joined the *BdU's* general staff in December 1942.

the first Japanese submarine sent to France was I-30. It left Japan on April 11, 1942 and crossed the Indian Ocean in May, where it carried out aerial reconnaissance four times, using its onboard seaplane and observations at periscope depth. The results eased the operations for the first Japanese submarine campaign against Allied ships in this sector between June 5 and July 8, a period during which twenty-one cargo ships were sunk. The I-30 arrived in Biscay Bay on August 2, 1942. It was immediately protected by eight German Junkers Ju 88s, and then, three days later, by eight minesweepers and a *Sperrbrecher* that guided it to the entrance of Lorient Port. On August 5, a motorboat took helmsman Heinrich Lüdmann, second watch officer, aboard U-105, to act as pilot to berth the Japanese submarine at A4 ex-*Vaucluse*, in front of the *Saltzwedel Caserne*. The Kriegsmarine had organized an appropriate welcome for the arrival of the first Japanese submarine in France, with Admiral Dönitz accompanied by Admiral Otto Schultze, commander the German navy in France, and Japanese Naval attaché in Germany, Captain Yokoi Tadao, who arrived from Berlin. Once the welcome ceremony was over, the submarine was towed to the small base on the Scorff that it couldn't completely enter, because of its 167-meter length for a 99.50-meter pen. Unloading its cargo in the shelter of the pen began. There was 1,500 kg of mica in its holds, used during the manufacture of electrical components, and 660 kg of shellac, an element in the fabrication of bombs. The Japanese also brought plans of their Type 91 aerial torpedo. The same evening, the Japanese officers were invited to drink a toast in the large hall in Péristyle barracks. The next day, a meal for the entire crew of 110 men was organized in the *U-Bootsheim* gardens, where German submariners from U-105 were also invited. They were to accompany their Japanese guests during their stay in France. Heinrich Lüdmann tells of how they took the train together to Paris where a reception and a meal was held in a room in the Japanese embassy. Naturally, they visited the Eiffel Tower and the Champs Elysées. The

talks between the Germans and the Japanese were held in English! The Japanese were then received at the Chancellery in Berlin where Commander Endo was decorated with the *Verdienstkreuz vom Deutschen Adler*—the Order of the German Eagle. After these visits, the crew of I-30 was taken to spend their leave at Trevarez Château in Châteauneuf-du-Faou. During this time, the Japanese submarine was repainted light gray by the workers in *KMW Lorient*; a *Metox* radar detector was installed, with its wooden antenna and a double-barreled 20 mm DCA. Its new cargo, to be carried back to Japan, consisted of five torpedo firing systems, as well as five Type G7a torpedoes, three G7e electric torpedoes, 240 *Bold* sonar decoys, a hydrophone system, rockets and glide-bombs, anti-tank weapons, a Zeiss anti-aircraft control system, a *Würzburg* radar (and the plans for building one), and finally diamonds worth a million yen. So that communication between the two navies remained secret, Germany also ceded fifty Enigma coding machines which were also loaded. A Japanese engineer would also be a passenger returning to his country. On August 22, I-30 was towed to B6, and berthed on the ex-*Martinière*. The chief of the 2d Flotilla, Victor Schütze, said goodbye to the crew, while a woman offered flowers to Commander Endo. I-30 then left Lorient. After a six-week voyage across the Atlantic and then the Indian Ocean, the I-30 safely arrived at the base in Penang on October 8, 1942. After three days call while it was re-supplied, the submarine left on October 11 for Singapore where Rear-Admiral Zenshiro, chief of the Navy Logistics Section was based. He had asked for ten Enigma machines for his QG in Singapore. These were unloaded on October 13 and after a few hours in the port, I-30 left for Japan, but it suddenly hit a mine in Singaporian waters. Fourteen crewmembers, and the precious cargo, were lost. Divers were able to recover a part of it in the following weeks.

In August 1942, several battles around the convoys began; the best plan for the submarines was to silently track a convoy guiding other U-boats

toward it in the instant the convoy entered the "Mid-Atlantic gap." For the first time since the beginning of the war, the number of available U-boats and the presence of U-boat re-suppliers gave Dönitz the chance to create two U-boat packs, one west of the "gap," the other to the east. The decisive battle, postponed time and again, between the Allied escorts and the U-boats, finally began. The attack on the SL-118 convoy spotted in the Azores sector by U-653 on August 16, is an example: thanks to heavy maritime escort and aerial assistance, only four ships were sunk in four days, while four of the seven U-boats engaged were forced to turn back after having sustained serious damage. This pushed the U-boat Corps Command into stopping the attack. Most of the U-boats that took part in this battle were Type VIICs, seven of which had been heading to the Freetown sector, but which had stopped after spotting the convoy. In the North Atlantic, the situation was repeated for the attack on the ONS-122 convoy on August 24, by nine U-boats, where six were damaged for four ships sunk. The escorts were being equipped more and more with the high-frequency radio signal localization system called Huff/Duff, which allowed them to situate, almost exactly, a U-boat on the radar screen. Seventy escorts from the Royal Navy had already been equipped with Huff/Duff in August 1942; a year later all had them. A crossed-utilization of this machine permitted two similarly equipped escorts to crosscheck rather accurately the position of a U-boat. In the beginning, Huff/Duff systems had been installed on land on each side of the Atlantic. Since the spring, fourteen escort groups shared the difficult mission of protecting convoys in the Atlantic: the three American A1-A3 groups, the seven British B1-B7 groups and the four Canadian C1-C4 groups. Reunited in the MOEF (Mid-Ocean Escort Force) for nine and a half days, they escorted convoys in one direction across the Atlantic, with a week in the port before taking the route back the other way. Each escort group was made up of six or seven ships, half of them destroyers; the others were *Flower*-type corvettes.

The camp was composed of wooden huts built around Kersalo Lake. Trenches in the foreground as well as a tunnel dug in the rock offered safety for the submariners in case of an air raid. No concrete bunker was ever built in the camp. At the bottom on the left, one of the watchtowers, which, as well as barbed wire and mines outside, protected the approaches to the rest camp. Hermann Fritz, a thirty-year-old Austrian officer, considered to be rather obliging with the locals, was in charge of security. *LB*

Aerial photograph of *Lager Lemp*. Set up in the countryside around Kersalo in the Caudan commune about thirty kilometers to the north of Lorient, it was a long way from the risks of bombardment. *NA*

The highly detailed logbooks of U-68 and U-128 gave complete reports of movement in Lorient Port during August 1942 for maintenance. Arriving in Lorient on July 10, 1942, the U-68 had been unloaded the same day, then hoisted onto the slip-way in Kéroman I the next morning. After nearly a month of cleaning and repairs in the dry dock, it was put back into the water on August 7 and moored alongside *Psyché* serving as a platform in B4 two days later for stability tests. On August 10, it was placed at S2 in the U-boat base on the Scorff to be loaded with torpedoes and oil. The next day, test dives were carried out and following a problem, kept in the shipyards until the nineteenth. On August 12, it returned to S2 where the torpedoes and oil were unloaded. The next day it was hoisted onto the slipway until the fifteenth. On August 16, it returned to S2 to collect torpedoes and oil and for another stability test. On August 17, it was put at A4 berthed on the *Vaucluse* where supplies and equipment were loaded. Two days later, it was moved to A3 and berthed on the *Isère* where foodstuffs were loaded; the next day an additional fourteen days' worth of food was loaded. On August 20, it cast off at 1905 and left at 1925 with an escort to point *L2* that it reached at 2100. From there, it had an anti-aircraft escort by three minesweepers from the *2nd MS-Flotilla* to point *Kern*, which it reached at 0320. At 0444, it dived to cross Biscay Bay underwater. The U-128's logbook is even more precise as it gives the names of the seven tugs from *KMW Lorient* used to change its place: arrival in Lorient position A3 on July 22, 1942, unloaded the next day between 0900 and 1700. On July 24, the tugs *Carpe*, *Beatrix* and *Niederbronn*, took it from A3 to the slipway in Kéroman I. After nearly a month being cleaned and repaired, on August 23, it was towed by *Carpe*, *Tanche* and *Rosheim* to S3 in the U-boat base on the Scorff. During the day of August 25, it was towed by the tugs *Yonne*, *Carpe* and *Tanche* to B6 (*La Martinière*) then taken back to S3. On August 28, it was towed from the U-boat base on the Scorff by the tugs *Tanche*, *Carpe* and *Lohic*, it spent an afternoon at sea for tests; after test dives, it went to the demagnetization station and then returned to S3. On August 31, the tugs *Carpe* and *Lohic* took it from S3 to A3.

Allied reactions: between July 13 and 20, the Coastal Command carried out three mine laying operations with three or four devices, each dropping one mine for the *Hampden* (first two operations) and two for the *Wellington*. ∎

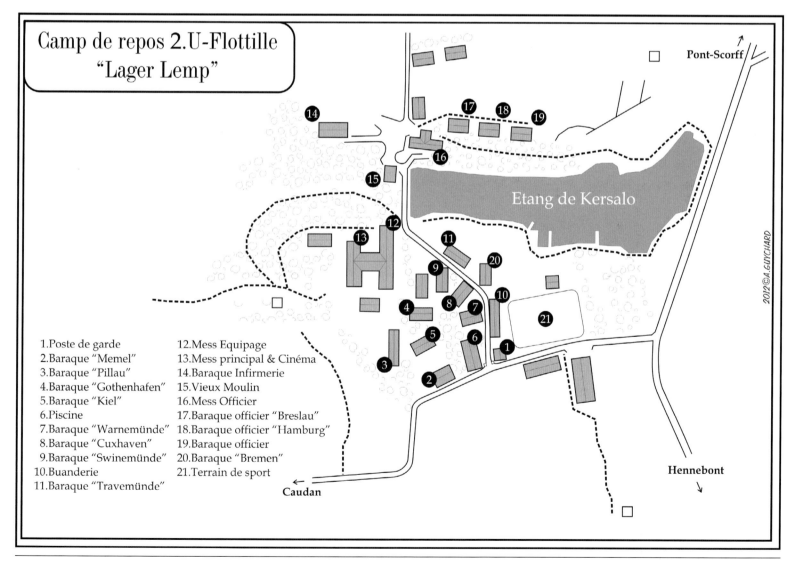

Camp de repos 2.U-Flottille "Lager Lemp"

Pont-Scorff

Etang de Kersalo

1. Poste de garde
2. Baraque "Memel"
3. Baraque "Pillau"
4. Baraque "Gothenhafen"
5. Baraque "Kiel"
6. Piscine
7. Baraque "Warnemünde"
8. Baraque "Cuxhaven"
9. Baraque "Swinemünde"
10. Buanderie
11. Baraque "Travemünde"
12. Mess Equipage
13. Mess principal & Cinéma
14. Baraque Infirmerie
15. Vieux Moulin
16. Mess Officier
17. Baraque officier "Breslau"
18. Baraque officier "Hamburg"
19. Baraque officier
20. Baraque "Bremen"
21. Terrain de sport

Caudan

Hennebont

2012©A.GUYCHARD

Plan of Lager *Lemp*. By Anthony Guychard

The officers' mess, built above an old stone mill, comprised a large cellar under a concrete slab where a reserve of good bottles of wine was probably kept. From the beginning of 1943, German women worked in the offices of the 2nd and the 10th Flotillas, or with KMW and were regularly brought to *Lager Lemp* by bus to dance with the submariners. To avoid being located by plane, the roads leading to the camp were covered with coal chips. *LB*

A pontoon was set up on Kersalo Lake to serve as a dive platform for the submariners! During the summer of 1942, the rest camp was used mostly by members of the 2nd and 10th flotillas' ground personnel, who were permanently based in the town. *LB*

Several boats were brought to the lake. *LB*

August 5, 1942: escorted by eight minesweepers and a blockade runner, the Japanese submarine I-30 approaches Lorient. *UBA*

I-30 arrives in the Scorff to berth at pontoon A4 *Vaucluse* where a crowd has gathered to welcome it. *LB*

The Japanese submarine is guided into Lorient Harbor by two German sailors, notably Heinrich Lüdmann the quartermaster of U-105, aboard a patrol boat. *UBA*

Admiral Karl Dönitz greets Shinobu Endo, commander of I-30. This photograph was published in the magazine *Kölnische Illustrierte Zeitung* on October 8, 1942. *LB*

The Japanese twin anti-aircraft machine-gun positioned on the back of I-30's conning tower will be changed in Lorient for a twin 20 mm anti-aircraft gun. On the right, the Japanese war flag. *LB*

The welcome committee from left to right: Captain Jokoi Tadao, the Japanese Naval Attaché in Berlin, Admiral Dönitz, Shinobu Endo, commander of I-30, and Admiral Otto Schultze, commander of the German Navy in France, and also former submariner in World War I. *UBA*

Watched by the workmen of *KMW Lorient*, German officers and Commander Endo on the quay in front of Péristyle Barracks. On the left is Dönitz's personal adjutant, *Kapitänleutnant* Fuhrmann; on the right is Captain Jokoi Tadao. *LB*

A toast is proposed to the celebrities at the table! *UBA*

In a large room in the Péristyle barracks, the Japanese are offered a light meal. A cameraman, at the back of the room, films the scene. *UBA*

Commander Endo makes a speech thanking the German Navy for its hospitality. Seated from left to right: *Marinestabartz* Dr. Jobst Schaeffer of the 2nd Flotilla, Admiral Schultze, Commander Endo, Dönitz, and Captain Tadao. *UBA*

The Japanese, taken by bus from Lorient, were welcomed at *Lager Lemp* by a great reception and military music. The Japanese officers are invited to Moulin de Rosmadec in Pont-Aven where they enjoy a good bottle with Dr. Hans-Ulrich Sendler, the 2nd Flotilla's doctor (on the right). *UBA*

On August 7, I-30 is towed to shelter inside the small underwater base on the Scorff where its invaluable cargo of mica and shellac will be unloaded. Its back end sticks out of the pen! *UBA*

At the base on the Scorff, Japanese submariners on I-30's foredeck chat with two *KMW* workmen. *UBA*

German laborers of *KMW Lorient* start work on I-30's hull. For security reasons, they don't have authorization to go inside the Japanese submarine. *UBA*

The German naval hospital in Lorient where the Japanese submariners will have a medical examination. Three large bunkers were built around the requisitioned French building, making it possible to keep patients safe and even carry out operations under two meters of reinforced concrete during an air raid. *AC*

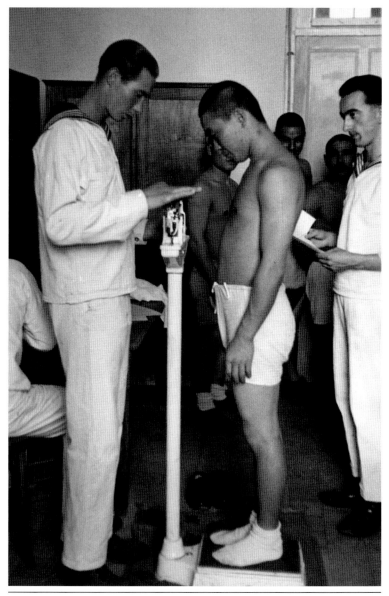

On August 7, the crew of I-30 is taken by bus to the submariners' center in Kéroman. The building in the foreground offers amusements such as a library, a billiard room, card rooms, a movie theater showing recent German films, and a bar with cheap beer. *LB*

The Japanese submariners pass their medical examination. Generally, they are much smaller than the Germans. *UBA*

Tables are laid out all around the garden where the 2nd Flotilla's orchestra plays. Although the center in Kéroman tries to do everything to satisfy the German submariners, the majority of them are men in their twenties who need livelier distractions at night. They are attracted to Lorient's red-light district and in particular to a street nicknamed *Der Strasse der Bewegung*— where strong music pouring out of gambling halls fills the street, and where girls sell their charms. At the end of their leave, when all their money is spent, the submariners are anxious to be sent out on patrols. *LB*

The guests mixed in with the German crew of U-105. Heinrich Lüdmann remembers that discussions were usually carried out in English! *UBA*

Captain Jokoi Tadao offers gifts from his country to Viktor Schütze, chief of the 2nd Flotilla. *LB*

The table with presents from Japan: a large porcelain doll with sumo wrestlers on each side, and a framed Imperial flag. Several French waitresses have been employed to serve the meal to the 110 Japanese submariners and their hosts. *UBA*

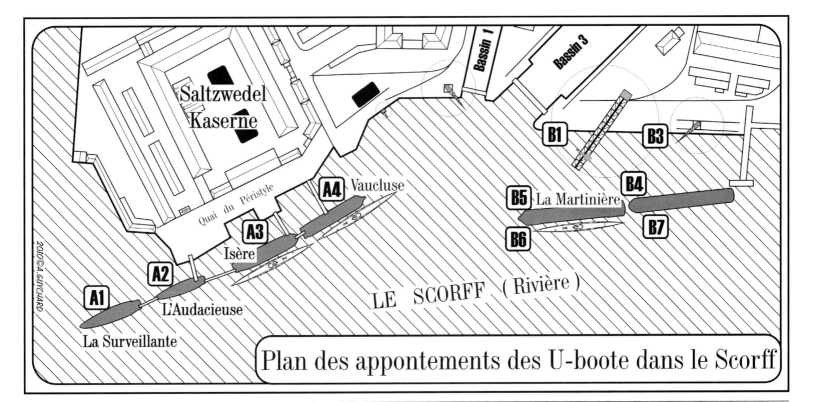

Plan of the wharfs on the Scorff. *By Anthony Guychard*

August 7 at 1637, U-161 with Commander Albrecht Achilles arrives, (2nd on the left), returning from the Caribbean where he sunk two ships and two sailing boats, notably by penetrating Puerto Limon Port in Costa Rica, as well as a third ship in a convoy on the return trip. *LB*

Watched by Japanese submariners on the *Isère's*, the traditional welcome ceremony takes place on U-161: Commander Achilles salutes Schütze, the chief of his flotilla. On the right, in the background, is the pontoon formed by the ex-*Martinière* with B5 and B6 berths. *UBA*

The day after its arrival, U-161 is unloaded. Its third victim, *Fairport*, a 6,616-ton American cargo ship in the protected AS-4 convoy, resulted in it being chased for nine hours by destroyers, which caused damage to the conning tower. *UBA*

A floating crane unloads U-161's unused torpedoes into a barge where they will be stored, as per regulations, after a mission. At left, the U-67 arrives on August 8 at 1437. *UBA*

U-67 returns from a successful patrol in the Florida sector with eight pennants, six of which are fuel tankers. In reality, only four tankers out of six were sunk, and only two were damaged. Like its previous arrival in Lorient, U-67's crew has brought out their menagerie of fluffy toys: a bear on the antenna and a small dog on the edge of the conning tower! A port pilot has come aboard from a boat in the harbor, as we can see from the presence of a bottle of champagne and bouquet of flowers. *UBA*

In front of the *Vaucluse*, an old sloop, Günter Müller-Stöckheim, commander of U-67, is congratulated by the chief of his flotilla after a successful patrol. *UBA*

Accompanied by *Vizeadmiral* Walter Matthiae, the director of *KMW Lorient*, Commander Müller-Stöckheim reviews the music and the 2nd Flotilla's Honor Company lined up in front of *Saltzwedel* Barracks. The admiral has personally come to congratulate U-67's commander because the naval shipyard is the patron of this submarine; more precisely, the torpedo service— *Torpedoressort VI* run by *Korvettenkapitän (Ing.)* Walter Holland. *UBA*

After their arrival in Lorient, half of U-67's crew is granted leave, either in Germany or in Carnac. A drink in *La Martinière Cafe* in the center of the sea resort. *UBA*

The bottles have been drunk; a submariner plays the accordion. It is said that life aboard a submarine was made more agreeable by music. Thanks to a collection of records, everyone could write down their favorite music and every Sunday the pieces chosen were played over the loudspeakers on board. The concert lasted several hours, so that those on duty in the diesel room or in the conning tower could be relieved in time to listen to the music. Apart from that, on Tuesdays and Fridays, they listened to the broadcast *Kameradschaftsdienst*. Beer was served on Saturday nights and to celebrate birthdays. *UBA*

Twelve submariners from U-67 singing in one of Carnac's streets. Two of them are in drag! The sailors were very young, usually aged between 18 and 20. *UBA*

Singing in Carnac's streets. After a dangerous two and a half month patrol, which took them to the American coast, none of the officers bother them with questions about their outfits. Some of them have bought straw hats to complete their tourist outfits! *UBA*

Studio photo taken in Lorient on August 20, 1942: Günter Müller-Stöckheim, commander of U-67, twenty-eight-years-old. Affectionately nicknamed "Alligator" by his crew, who described him as an excellent officer, he was always in a good mood and took note of his men's preoccupations. For the fifth birthday of his chief engineer's son, he asked the mechanics in the machine room to make a small mechanical toy that he had designed. *UBA*

Meanwhile, back from their trip to Paris and Berlin, I-30's crew spend the last days of their leave at Château de Trevarez in Châteauneuf-du-Faou. The submariners play at being riders and try to topple each other. *UBA*

Another game, watched by the amused crew of U-105, consists of opponents standing back-to-back and trying to remove the beret covering his adversary's face. *UBA*

At 1900, on August 19, 1942, U-172 is the first of four U-boats belonging to the *Eisbär* Wolfpack to leave Lorient in the direction of Cape Agulhas, the limit between the Atlantic and Indian oceans. In the background, on the left bank of the Scorff, is Romania Quay that was given its name for the material shipped to Romania during the First World War. *UBA*

Five minutes later, U-172 is followed by U-504, commanded by Fritz Poske. Most of the departures from Lorient were scheduled for late afternoon, so that the U-boats had a maximum of darkness during the dangerous surface crossing of the Gascony Gulf. *UBA*

The next day it is the turn of U-156, commanded by Werner Hartenstein, to leave for the Cape. On the wharf in front of the *Saltzwedel Kaserne*, he says goodbye to *Marinestabartz* Jobst Schaeffer, the 2nd Flotilla's doctor. *LB*

August 21, 1942: A last meal is organized in the *U-Bootsheim* in Kéroman for I-30's crew before they leave. On the right *Kapitänleutnant* Günther Kuhnke, chief of the 10th Flotilla is sitting under the German flag. *UBA*

The guests applaud the last number. A ground naval solider announces the rest of the program. The Japanese are due to leave the following day. *UBA*

1350, August 22: U-129 commanded by Hans Witt returns from a successful patrol in the Caribbean where eleven ships, totaling 41,570 tons, have been sunk. The *Isère*, an old sloop, is just large enough to hold everyone who wishes to welcome the submarine back, and then say farewell to I-30. In the background on the left we can see the building that was once a mechanics' college. *UBA*

Two women dressed in civilian dress come onto U-129 to offer a small bunch of flowers for the crews' buttonholes. It is exactly three months ago that these men left on patrol. *LB*

I-30 re-painted in light gray, berthed at pontoon B6 (ex *La Martinière)*, is getting ready to leave. Wooden planks have been placed alongside this pontoon-ship to camouflage it from enemy planes. On the left, U-129 has just berthed alongside the *Isère*. *UBA*

A woman offers a bouquet of flowers to Shinobu Endo, commander of I-30. Around his neck he is wearing the Merit Cross, represented by the German Eagle, a decoration awarded while he was in Berlin. *UBA*

Viktor Schütze, chief of the 2nd Flotilla, salutes the Japanese commander. Behind him, the crew is in line, along with the hydroplane's pilot, brought on board the Japanese submarine. *UBA*

The Japanese crew disperses, some of them head for the foredeck to watch the departure from Lorient. In the background on the left, we can see *la tour de la Découverte* (Discovery Tower). *UBA*

The Germans aboard *La Martinière* salute their comrades in arms who are ready to leave for a long trip. In the background to the left is the access bridge to the old landing stage for *Condé*, a former armored cruiser. *LB*

I-30 passes in front of the Péristyle casern—direction, Japan! *UBA*

It passes in front of the vast Kéroman III whose concrete roof is nearly finished. *UBA*

August 23, 1942: U-116 XB returns from the Atlantic where it damaged one ship and sunk another from the OS-33 convoy before carrying supplies to four U-boats west of Freetown. Werner von Schmidt, its commander, will be leaving U-116 to take a job on land, and will be promoted to the chief of the 8th Training Flotilla and the support group in Danzig. *UBA*

As usual, a light meal is served in the *Saltzwedel Kaserne* to the submariners returning from a patrol. Von Schmidt, the commander of U-116, chats with Günther Kuhnke, the chief of the 10th Flotilla. On the right is Wenzel, the submarine's chief engineer. *UBA*

August 23: U-154 arrives from the Caribbean; only one cargo ship and a fishing boat have been sunk. On the right is Commander Walther Kölle. This patrol will certainly be useful to the war correspondent aboard, Wolfgang Frank (on the left). His successful book *Die Wölfe und der Admiral* was published in 1953, and was translated into twelve languages (the French edition published by Arthaud in 1956 was titled, *U-Boote contre marines allies*). Enlisting in the *Reichsmarine* at the age of seventeen, Wolfgang Frank received his diploma and then studied law at university receiving a doctorate. His book *Prien greift an*, published in 1942 after his patrol the previous year aboard the U-47, during that U-boat's second to last mission, was already a great success in Germany where 120,000 copies were printed until 1944. Based in Larmor, he was the director of the *Kriegsmarine's* group of war correspondents in Lorient. *UBA*

August 24: U-160 arrives in Lorient after a two-month patrol along the Venezuelan coast, during which it sunk six ships and damaged another. On the top of the conning tower, small windows protect the lookouts during bad weather. *LB*

Late afternoon, August 24: U-159, commanded by Helmut Witte, leaves for the South Atlantic, in the direction of the Congo Delta. The crew salutes the chief of their flotilla who has come to wish them good luck! *LB*

In Lorient, Georg Lassen, commander of U-160, is awarded the Knight's Cross that he earned on August 10 while on patrol. From August 1939 to December 1940, Georg Lassen was the watch officer aboard U-29 under Otto Schuhart, with whom twelve ships were sunk including the British aircraft carrier HMS *Courageous. Charita*

Commander Georg Lassen inspects the base's honor company. *UBA*

Accompanied by Günther Kuhnke, the chief of his flotilla, and *Oberleutnant-zur-See* Helmut von Tippelskirch, his watch officer, Lassen salutes the members of his crew who are lined up on one of the Gabriel Hotel's two pavilions. He has only carried out two combat patrols as commander of U-160, along the North and South American coast. However, as they were very successful, and a lot of fuel tankers were sunk, he crossed the 100,000-ton limit necessary to obtain the Knight's Cross. *UBA*

September 1942: Seven U-boats from the 10th Flotilla Arrive as Reinforcements

Movements: Thirteen arrivals, eleven departures, number of U-boats present at the end of the month: sixteen. In September, the large-scale arrival of seven new U-boats from the 10th Flotilla as reinforcements; each had carried out its first combat patrol directly out of Kiel. For six of them, their patrol was in the Caribbean; half of them had successes, the rest returned empty-handed. No new U-boat had arrived in Lorient since June 10, 1942. An eighth submarine sent as reinforcement didn't reach its destination: U-165 of Commander Eberhard Hoffmann, out of Kiel on August 7, carried out its patrol in the waters off Canada, notably those in the Gulf of St. Lawrence at the same time as U-517, attacking the SQ-36 convoy on September 16. Damaged by an aerial attack the same day, it turned towards home; its last message signaled that it was forty-eight hours from its destination, and arrival on September 26. The next day it disappeared with the entire crew of fifty-one men during its approach to Lorient; it was sunk by depth charges from a *Wellington* bomber. During its single patrol, it had sunk three ships and damaged four others.

Observations: three U-boats were sunk by planes in Biscay Bay in July and August when they had to surface to charge their batteries. On September 3, U-705, which was sailing on the surface towards Brest, was sunk in turn, and then U-165 met the same fate west of Lorient on September 27. Others were damaged but managed to reach their base. These casualties confirmed Admiral Dönitz's fears of the renewal of Allied aerial attacks in Biscay Bay since June. He had asked for a technical solution, and it arrived in September in the form of a radar-warning receiver called *Metox*. Made by a French firm, this machine could allow U-boats to know when an enemy plane was approaching by detecting the waves put out by its radar. A test was carried out on U-128 out of Lorient from September 2-10 with five radar engineer specialists. Following this conclusive test, all U-boats leaving their French bases were equipped with *Metox* and its removable exterior wooden antenna, nicknamed "Biscay Cross." They could now hide in the deep before an aerial attack, which allowed Dönitz to lift the order of underwater navigation in Biscay Bay; this measure had made the U-boats late for their hunting grounds. So that the U-boats returning to base could benefit from the same protection, the U-boats leaving on operation, once out of the dangers of Biscay Bay, gave their machines to those returning to base; this exchange was carried out at the re-supply point in the Azores. The use of *Metox*, along with, in August in Biscay Bay, the appearance of numerous German Junkers Ju 88 C-6 aircraft from 13./KG 40 based in Nantes, forced British Coastal Command to call a halt to the aerial offensive in the sector the following month.

Off the coast of Canada, U-165, U-517 and U-518 of the 2nd and 10th Flotillas, sent at the end of August for their first patrols out of Kiel in the Gulf of St. Lawrence, managed to sink seven ships and damage two others between September 6-16. The efficient anti-submarine measures taken by the Americans meant that there were no more U-boats in operation along their coast. But in September, farther south in the Caribbean and off the coast of French Guiana, U-boats continued their attacks, principally the Type IXCs, before

Axel-Olaf Loewe, the thirty-three-year-old commander of U-505, suffered an attack of appendicitis while on patrol at the end of July 1942 in the Caribbean sector. His U-boat had to return prematurely on August 25, after only two cargo ships had been sunk at the end of June, as well as the *Roamar,* a 110-ton, three-mast Colombian schooner. His appendix was removed after his arrival in Lorient. In December, he was assigned to the U-boat corps staff. His initiative to sink the three-mast ship was not appreciated in high places: this schooner belonged to a Colombian diplomat and the action caused the country to declare itself in a "state of war" with Germany! Colombia had the German ambassador deported and then interned all German citizens in Colombia. However, U-505's disasters were far from over. *UBA*

U-BOAT	TYPE	FLOT.	COMMANDER	ARRIVAL	DEPART	NOTES
Departures						
U-43	IXA	2	Hans-Joachim Schwantke		23	Departure for the North Atlantic, Gulf of St. Lawrence, Canada.
U-67	IXC	2	Günther Müller-Stöckheim		16	Departure for the Caribbean.
U-103	IXB	2	Gustav-Adolf Janssen			Being repaired June 22 – October 21, 1942.
U-105	IXB	2	Heinrich Schuch			Being repaired June 30 – November 23, 1942.
U-106	IXB	2	Hermann Rasch		22	Departure for the North Atlantic, Newfoundland sector and Gulf of St-Laurent
U-116	XB	1	Wilhelm Grimme		22	New commander, departure for last patrol as a U-boat supply ship in the North Atlantic; probably sunk by an RAF plane 10/11/42 in Biscay Bay, no survivors, fifty-six dead. Results: one ship sunk and one damaged
U-124	IXB	2	Johann Mohr			Being repaired June 26 – November 25, 1942.
U-126	IXC	2	Ernst Bauer		19	Departure with U-161 for the South Atlantic, sector of the Gulf of Guinea and the Congo Delta.
U-128	IXC	2	Ulrich Heyse	10	2 14	Departure September 2 for the first mission testing Metox, a machine that signaled the approach of an Allied plane using its radar, with five specialists on board. New departure on combat patrol September 14, in direction of Freetown.
U-129	IXC	2	Hans-Ludwig Witt		28	Departure for the Caribbean.
U-154	IXC	2	Walther Kölle			U-boat being repaired August 23 - October 12, 1942. Change of commander, Walter Kölle named chief of the 1st Group of the Naval School in Mürwik in October 1942.
U-160	IXC	10	Georg Lassen		23	Departure for the Caribbean.
U-161	IXC	2	Albrecht Achilles		19	Departure with U-126 for South Atlantic sector, Gulf of Guinea and Congo Delta.
U-505	IXC	2	Peter Zschech			Being repaired August 25 – October 4, 1942. The new Commander, Zschech, was watch officer aboard U-124 from August 1941 to July 1942.
Arrivals						
U-256	VIIC	9	Odo Loewe	3	22	First time in Lorient; put into service 12/18/41; arrived as a matter of urgency with a restricted equipage having been very heavily damaged by destroyers and Allied planes in Biscay Bay. Departure for repairs in Brest where U-256 was turned into a *Flak-Boat* (7 models) for single mission in October–November 1943, then put back into service as before; two missions out of Brest; equipped with a Schnorchel, left Brest for the last time on September 4, 1944. Commanded by Thehmann-Willenbrock, chief of the 9th Flotilla, arrival in Bergen where U-256 was downgraded 10/23/44.
U-174	IXC	10	Ulrich Thilo	6		First time in Lorient put into service 11/26/41. Arrived from its first combat patrol out of Kiel; unsuccessful attack on the SC-94 convoy in the North Atlantic.
U-108	IXB	2	Klaus Scholtz awarded Oak Leaves to his Knight's Cross September 10, 1942.	10		Returning from a two-month patrol that took it to the north of the South American coast: three ships sunk between August 3–17. Change of commander, Klaus Scholtz named chief of the 12th Combat Flotilla in Bordeaux.
U-130	IXC	2	Ernst Kals awarded Knight's Cross on arrival.	12		Returns from a patrol of nearly two months in the mid-Atlantic, sector off Cape Verde Islands and off Freetown: seven ships sunk between July 25 and August 26.
U-509	IXC	10	Karl-Heinz Wolff	12		First time in Lorient; put into service 11/4/41. Returns from its first combat patrol, out of Kiel, in the Gulf of Mexico and east of the Caribbean where almost no traffic was spotted. No results, was jolted by a depth charge launched by the Catalina based in Guantanamo, Cuba. Change of commander, Wolff, named chief of the Naval School in Mürwik.
U-510	IXC	10	Karl Neitzel	13		First time in Lorient; put into service 11/25/41. Returns from first combat patrol out of Kiel west of the Caribbean: three ships. Escorts U-155 since August 20.
U-155	IXC	10	Adolf Piening awarded Knight's Cross on arrival.	15		Returns from a two-month patrol east of the Caribbean: ten ships sunk between July 28 and August 10. U-155 was attacked on the surface, first by a plane on August 16, and then on August 19 during which *MaschGef* Konrad Garneier fell overboard and was lost, and again on August 20; the U-boat managed to escape but could no longer dive. In spite of attempts to repair the U-boat, with help from U-510 and U-460 supply ship on September 7, it still couldn't dive but reached Lorient; crossing the Atlantic on the surface.

U-BOAT	TYPE	FLOT.	COMMANDER	ARRIVAL	DEPART	NOTES
U-508	IXC	10	Georg Staats	15		First time in Lorient; put into service 10/20/41. Arrives from its first combat patrol of nearly two months, out of Kiel, to the Antilles: two ships sunk off Cuba.
U-163	IXC	10	Kurt Engelmann	16		First time in Lorient; put into service 10/21/41. Returns without success from its first combat patrol of nearly two months out of Kiel to the Caribbean.
U-173	IXC	10	Heinz-Ehler Beucke	20		First time in Lorient; put into service 11/15/41. Arrives from its first combat patrol out of Kiel in the Caribbean, without success. Attacked four times on the surface by planes that damaged the periscopes the first time, then the torpedo launching tubes the second. Change of commander, Beucke, sanctioned for a lack of combativeness, transferred to the *BdU's* general staff.
U-66	IXC	2	Friedrich Markworth	29		Returns from a patrol of over two months east of the Caribbean: six mines dropped in Port Castries damaging two British motorboats and nine ships sunk; the Polish/American commander of an American ship was captured and brought to Lorient. September 13, a crewmember committed suicide. Following a re-supply mistake made by U-462 in the Azores, U-66 was forced, on September 25-26, to get fuel from the fuel tanker *Georg Albrecht* interned in El Ferrol, Spain, where *MaschOGef* Helmut Ehrlichmann, who was sick, was disembarked; after a stomach operation, he returned to Lorient for the next mission!
U-511	IXC	10	Friedrich Steinhoff	29		First time in Lorient; put into service 12/8/41. Beginning of June 1942: U-511 was used for experimental test firing of rockets while submerged in Peenemünde. Arrives from its first forty-five-day combat patrol out of Kiel in the Caribbean; August 28: two fuel tankers in the TAW-15 convoy sunk and a third damaged.

this sector became too dangerous and not profitable enough, after which it was almost totally evacuated in December. Apart from the Type IXs off the coast of Africa, the attacks now concentrated on the North Atlantic. In the middle of the ocean, without Allied planes to protect it, the ON-127 convoy was attacked between September 9-13; it lost seven cargo ships and a destroyer, while four other merchant ships were damaged. After this success the convoys SC-99 and ON-129, spotted by a U-boat at the limit of the North Atlantic patrol line between September 13-18, managed to escape the U-boats, which had wanted to regroup to attack them, thanks to thick fog and evasive tactics. The very bad weather in the North Atlantic also saved the SC-100 convoy, spotted on September 19 and tracked until the twenty-fifth by the two groups of U-boats on each side of the "gap" in the Atlantic. In spite of having twenty U-boats, they only sank six cargo ships in this convoy. An important change in the organization of Allied convoys took place September 17. Henceforth, the westbound convoys HX (fast) and SC (slow) would no longer leave Halifax, but would leave from New York instead, still bound for Liverpool. On September 23, the special fast convoy RB-1 out of Newfoundland, with two-funnel passenger liners, was spotted. During the attack over the next few days, the U-boats calculated that they had sunk three full troop ships; in fact they sank an empty river liner.

South of the Azores on September 12, 1942, U-156 sank the British liner *Laconia* out of Cairo bound for England; as well as the crew, there were 1,800 Italians taken prisoner after the Battle of El Alamein, British soldiers wounded in North Africa, and about eighty women and children. This torpedoing was the most deadly carried out by a U-boat during the entire Second World War with 1,658 victims, mostly Italians. When he saw hundreds of people in the water, the commander

of U-156 radioed for orders. Even though Godt, chief of operations of the *BdU* was opposed to their rescue, which might put the U-boat in danger, Dönitz ordered U-156 to take care of them while waiting for other U-boats to be sent to help, along with the two ships from the Vichy Navy *Annamite* and *Gloire* sent from Dakar. To signal the rescue operation, U-156 sent out two clear radio messages to say he was carrying survivors and had a large Red Cross flag put on the bridge; 200 were crammed into the U-boat; 400 others, aboard the ship's life boats, were towed behind. On September 15, U-506 and U-507 arrived and the survivors were distributed between the three U-boats that set off separately towards France. On September 16, an American B-24 bomber appeared and flew over U-156 at sixty meters; visibility was very good. In spite of the messages sent by a British officer, and the presence of the Red Cross flag, the plane carried out five attacks against U-156 dropping a bomb at each pass. The survivors were killed and U-156 was damaged. Following the report of the event sent by U-156's radio to the U-boat Corps Command, Dönitz ordered the abandonment of rescue operations. The cords attached to the lifeboats were cut and only the Italians were kept on board the U-boats. The other survivors were picked up on September 17 by the two French ships that arrived from Dakar. A second aerial attack was carried out against U-506 forcing it to dive with 142 survivors on board. Dönitz sent out by radio the *Laconia Order* that stipulated that henceforth U-boats were no longer to pick up survivors from the ships they sank. However, this non-assistance order did not signify in any way that survivors should be deliberately killed (during the entire war there was only one incident where a U-boat deliberately machine-gunned the survivors without the U-boat Corps Command knowing about it. The man responsible, Commander Heinz Eck of U-852, on his first

patrol, was judged by the Court of Hamburg on October 17, 1945 for having murdered the survivors of the Greek ship *"Pelus"* in the night of March 13/14, 1944. He was executed by firing squad on November 30, 1945, along with two of his officers). In spite of the *Laconia* Order, numerous U-boat commanders continued to rescue survivors. On this subject, Helmut Schmoeckel, former watch officer aboard U-504 in Lorient from November 1942 to May 1943, then commander of U-802 that stopped in the port between May and July 1944, recorded in his 1987 book, *Menschlichkeit im Seekrieg? (Humanity in the Naval War?)* 200 humanitarian actions carried out on both sides the ships they had sunk.

The British had stopped sending equipment to Russia after the PQ-17 convoy was decimated in July 1942. Later, having installed bomber-planes in North Russia, they decided to send a new Arctic convoy of forty cargo ships with sixteen destroyers, a light cruiser, and the aircraft carrier *Avenger* as escorts. PQ-18 left Scotland on September 2, 1942. It was spotted on the 8th. Luftwaffe planes sank ten ships in the convoy and the U-boats sank three, but they sustained heavy losses. Most of the convoy reached its destination. However, henceforth convoys to Russia got through almost undamaged. The Allies had definitely gained the upper hand in this sector too. During September 1942, U-boats sank 101 Allied ships for a tonnage of 454,957 tons.

Allied Reactions: still no bombardments for the fifth month running after April 17, 1942. Work on Kéroman III advanced well during this period, metallic girders already covered the two pens on the right. The Coastal Command carried out three mine-laying operations with a total of twelve devices (twenty-four mines laid) between September 8 and 24.

Three officers of the 2nd Flotilla chatting in the arsenal at the southwestern angle of Gabriel House, behind the bandstand on the *Place d'Armes*. From left to right: *Korvettenkapitän* Jobst Schaeffer the flotilla's chief doctor, *KK* police Chief Paul Behre, and Viktor Schütze, the chief of the flotilla. Among the personnel officers, for the operation of such a unit, the chief of the flotilla could also count on an aide-de-camp, a staff officer, a detail officer, the flotilla's chief engineer assisted by the second and third engineers, a deputy police chief, the chief of the honor company, and the band master. *LB*

The officers' lounge, or smoking room, inside one of Gabriel's two pavilions. It will be busy until the aerial bombardments at the beginning of 1943; the commander was a frequent visitor until his departure on mission. *LB*

To accommodate the flotilla and KMW Lorient staff, numerous huts have been set up within the arsenal, in particular here in front of Gabriel's pavilions on the *Places d'Armes*. The cleaning and up keep is done by women hired locally. *LB*

The barracks on the left with its adjacent terrace, serving as a mess for the officers of both of the Lorient flotillas, connects Gabriel House's two pavilions. It is built on an underground bunker that is used by the general staff in the event of an air raid. *LB*

Car used by the officers of KMW Lorient, whose insignia can be seen on the wing: a cogwheel symbolizing mechanics, crossed by a submarine surmounted on the letter "L" for Lorient. It is registered "WM" for Wehrmacht Marine and has a commander's pennant. *LB*

Goal! The navy regularly organizes soccer matches at the municipal sports park between the various units in Lorient. The advertisements are for clothing stores: the *St-Rémy* department store on *Place Alsace-Lorraine,* and *Au Progrès.* In the background is the building where the Todt Organization's offices. *LB*

Returning from the Freetown sector, September 1, 1942: U-130's crew holds a small ceremony on board to celebrate the Knight's Cross, awarded that same day to Commander Ernst Kals. A temporary decoration has been made in the workshop on board. A bottle of "Moët and Chandon" champagne has been opened for the occasion. *LB*

U-174's crew poses for a photographer during their first arrival in Lorient on September 6. It had left Kiel two months earlier, along with six other new U-boats belonging to the 10th Flotilla, sent as additional support. It is the only U-boat that hasn't been sent to the Antilles. It took part in several attacks on convoys in the North Atlantic, but without any results. *UBA*

From September 7-10, 1942, U-boats in the Eisbär Wolfpack, that had left Lorient between August 19 and 20, cross the equator in direction of the Cape. According to maritime tradition, a ceremony is organized on board for crossing the line, after which a nominative diploma is given to each member of the crew. U-172's hand-drawn diploma is signed by Commander Carl Emmermann on September 9. *UBA*

Ceremony held for crossing the equator aboard U-172. We can imagine, seeing the small space reserved for every crewmember on a U-boat, that a lot of ingenuity was needed to store the fancy dress somewhere! On the left: Commander Emmermann. *UBA*

In front of *Saltzwedel Kaserne* on September 10, 1942: accompanied by the chief of U-boats in the West (*FdU-West*) *Korvettenkapitän* Hans-Rudolf Rösing and Kuhnke, the chief of the 10th Flotilla, Admiral Dönitz has come to inspect the crewmembers. Late in the afternoon, he will greet U-108, whose commander has been awarded Oak Leaves to his Knight's Cross. In the background on the left are the electricity factory's two chimneys; on the far right, the small base on the Scorff. *ECPAD*

On September 10, the arrival of U-108 under Commander Klaus Scholtz, returning after a two-month mission in the Caribbean. Three boats were sunk between August 3 and 17, represented by the three pennants: 10,000 tons was an over-estimation for the 6,221-ton fuel tanker HMS *Tricula* the 8,588-ton American tanker *Louisiana,* and the 2,587-ton Norwegian cargo ship *Brenas* are correct. The three flags lower down with a silhouette of boat, correspond to firing torpedoes on July 19 for which detonations were heard, but in reality, none of the targets were hit. *UBA*

On the *Isère's* A3 pontoon, Commander Scholtz is handed flowers from German Red Cross nurses. *Charita*

The day after U-108 arrived in Lorient a ceremony takes place on the arsenal's Place d'Armes, in front of Gabriel House. Accompanied by his flotilla chief, Scholtz, who had Oak Leaves added to his Knight's Cross on September 10, 1942, inspects his crew. The officers of the two flotillas are aligned on the left. For their part, the shipyards' laborers must wait for the end of the ceremony in front of the arsenal's principal door before they can go to work. *ECPAD*

Günther Ditsch, the radio operator aboard U-108, remembers his arrival in Lorient on September 10, 1942: "We are a few hours from our destination, the port in Lorient, the 2nd Flotilla's base. Our U-boat waits under water for the escort that will guide us safely into the port. The members of the crew are in their berths, but none manage to sleep: they are already thinking about what they are going to do while on leave. The idea of having firm ground under our feet keeps us awake. I am on radio duty. From time to time we hear the detonation from depth charges far away. Is one of our boats being attacked by the English or are they randomly bombing to frighten us? But I suddenly hear the sound of propellers approaching, coming from the East. Is this already our escort? But I must be careful; the Bay of Biscay is the most dangerous sea for our submarines: the English have search and destroy patrols in service night and day. I give a report to the station chief and to the commander: 'sounds of a propeller from ninety degrees, perhaps our escort.' Towards 1130, we prepare to surface. 'Chief engineer, bring the boat to periscopic depth' announces the commander who goes to the conning tower hatch. At fourteen meters, the periscope is raised, the commander takes a look and orders, "Surface!" The hatchway is opened and he goes up into the conning tower with the watch crew. It is our escort ship, a single minesweeper. We follow at once in its wake to the Kernével Line-Louis Port where it makes a half-turn. Part of the crew goes up on the front bridge; the watch officer tells us that there are a lot of people waiting to welcome us: the U-boat corps' commander-in-chief has installed them on the Isère's pontoon where we will berth. Our comrades from the army are also there as always, today with the regimental band. The admiral boards with the flotilla chief; our commander gives an account of our submarine's mission that has brought back six victory pennants. The BdU, the flotilla chief and our commander salute all of us. From his pocket, the admiral takes several Iron Crosses and hands one to me. The watch officer receives the German Cross in Gold. Nurses offer us flowers and even kisses, in spite of the musty smell we all carry on us from being shut up in the submarine. The ceremony is over; our boat is unloaded and put under shelter in a pen. Mail is distributed and each one of us greedily reads his news from home. The lines written by our close relations or our loved ones are read over and over again. We have finally returned, after seven weeks of depth charges, storms and enormous waves. The fear of not making it back finally leaves our hearts." *UBA*

HAUS HABEKOST

KANTINE

Günther Ditsch, the radio operator aboard U-108 continues his story—photograph taken of a wing of the Peristyle barracks, named *Haus Habekost* in memory of Johannes Habekost, the commander of U-31 that disappeared on patrol on March 11, 1940. 2nd Flotilla's crews' dormitories are located on the upper floor and the canteen indicated by a sign on the left: "After (the ceremony) we all had baths that lasted a long time to remove all our filth and perspiration, and we all had hair-cuts. For us it is a real treat and we didn't hesitate to use the maximum of water. Afterward, as after every return to the home base, a feast is served. Everyone takes part, from the commander to the lowest second class. The general mood is good, even if some are already thinking of their return to the Fatherland. Tomorrow, the first group will be on leave. But today we are still a single crew. My friend Franz, and I, who are part of the second group on leave, will have to wait for the return of the first group to go on leave in our turn. While waiting, we monitor the work being done on our U-boat. In the evenings, we go to bars. Although Lorient has often been bombed by the British, one always finds a place to drink a good cognac to drown our sorrows. On Thursday, we boarded the U-boat early, but there was nothing important to do; the workmen were making rapid progress, so we went ashore again. Spare time! In the canteen, we had a quick drink and then took a bottle. Then our cook said to us, 'I still have a large block of honey that nobody wants in our group; surely the French children would be happy to put some on their bread.' It weighed approximately 10 kg, and we quickly had an idea. To this day we don't know who thought of it first, and we could never have imagined the serious consequences it would have for us. In the arsenal we found a small two-wheel cart, we took some packing paper that had contained buttered bread and put the large block of honey on it. The cook gave us a large spoon. Hans put on a white chef's hat and picked up a bell! And there we were, ready to set off to the town! I led the cart while Hans rang the bell to propose our honey. There were a lot of customers in the market place, in particular school-age children, with their mothers who stood apart and looked at us in annoyance. But when the children returned with honey they laughed and gave us small waves. We had almost given out all our honey when this happy moment came to an abrupt end. A Kübelwagen came to a halt right in front of us; two gendarmes got out and turned to face Hans and me. On the whole, they didn't look very pleased at all. Everyone disappeared; there was no one left in the market place but we two sailors with our cart, our bell and the remainder of our honey, and we didn't know what was going to happen next." *UBA*

Günther Ditsch continues his story: photo taken in front of the newspaper kiosk on Place Bison, in the background: the stained glass windows of the St-Louis Church: "The authoritative voice of a gendarme ordered us to get into the car. Direction: the police station! Hans and I were taken to the office of the oldest person in charge: a major. A sergeant handed him his report concerning our 'fault': damage towards the prestige of the German army. Then the gray-haired major said in a typically military voice: 'I will submit a report against you for destruction of army material and fraternization with the enemy!' We were then informed of the great value of this block of honey and the major started talking about a military tribunal … we hoped he would calm down, but he didn't. It seemed that he found this a matter of the highest importance! We were put in cell where time crawled by; we didn't know how much time we spent there because they had taken our watches away. Through the bars we could see it growing dark but no one brought us anything to eat. Suddenly, through the door we heard voices, I thought I recognized the voice of our commander and I said to Hans: 'I believe that the Old Man is here; if he can get us out of this, I will never eat honey again.' Then the lock turned, a gendarme stood in front us and shouted: 'outside to the major, you know the way!' When we reached his office, we immediately stiffened in impeccable and strict attention. In front of us stood our commander, then the major and, behind him, our watch officer who couldn't hide his grin when he saw us. Suddenly our commander spoke: 'Have you been bitten by wild apes, or is there another explication for your behavior? But we will talk about it later, I can assure you!' He turned to the watch officer and said: 'IWO, take charge of these two hapless thieves.' As the major obviously wanted to know what was going to happen to us, our commander saluted him and said: 'Dear comrade, they are my men and I will find a punishment to match the crime, so that relations between the army and the navy remains good.' Then, with a smile before closing the door he added: 'I'd really like to invite you to take part in our next mission!' Back at the base, we were nevertheless given a lesson about morals like good parents give to their children, as well as two normal guard duty turns and two guard duty turns from midnight to four in the morning. There was no more question of extended leave, which had nothing to do with our 'honey run.' Our boat was nearly ready and we wouldn't have time to go far. We were taken to Carnac to spend the rest of our leave there." *LB*

With 200,000 tons of Allied ships declared sunk, Commander Scholtz joined the circle of the rare commanders decorated with the Knight's Cross with Oak Leaves. At age thirty-four, he will leave for Bordeaux to becomec of the new 12th Combat Flotilla on October 15. Actually, he sank twenty-five ships, one an armed merchant ship, for a total of 144,435 tons.

On September 12, 1942, U-130 has just berthed alongside the *Isere*. Schütze, the chief of the 2nd Flotilla, and Hans-Rudolf Rösing, the commander of U-boats in the West, and who was in Lorient for two days, have come to welcome the crew. *UBA*

On the bridge of his U-boat, Ernst Kals the commander of U-130 receives the Knight's Cross; he is congratulated by Rösing. The U-boat is back from a patrol of almost two months in the middle of the Atlantic, in the sector of the Cape Verde Islands and opposite Freetown, where seven ships were sunk between July 25 and August 26 for a total of 51,528 tons. Following his report of tonnage sunk, his decoration was awarded on September 1. *UBA*

On the *Isere's* bridge, Commander Kals shakes hands with his flotilla chief. One more patrol at sea and he will take his place at the head of the 2nd Flotilla! *UBA*

On September 12, the 19,695-ton British steamer
Laconia, used to transport troops, was torpedoed by
U-156, northeast of the small British Ascension Island,
below the equator. On board were 2,789 people: 1,800
Italian prisoners captured in Libya, a crew of 463, 286
passengers mainly repatriated wounded British soldiers,
160 Polish soldiers serving as prison guards, and finally
eighty civilians, mainly women and children, and British
families of civil servants stationed in North Africa. They
embarked in Cairo on August 12, these passengers were
to go to England after stopovers in Aden, Mombasa,
Durban, then Cape Town, which the ship left on
September 1. *DR*

Rudolf Sharp, the captain of the *Laconia*, had already
survived a terrible shipwreck two years before. At the
time he was the captain of a steamer of the same type,
the *Lancastria*, which sank in twenty minutes off St.
Nazaire on June 17, 1940. A bomb dropped by a
Luftwaffe plane fell into one of its chimneys taking the
lives of at least 3,000 British soldiers who were to be
repatriated to England at the end of the campaign in
France. For the *Laconia*, he will decide to remain on
board after the ship is hit. *DR*

After torpedoing the steamer, U-156 surfaced to find
hundreds of shipwrecked people in the water, some
calling for help in Italian. The commander decided to take
them on the bridge, and announced the position of the
shipwreck on all the radio waves, specifying that no one
should attack the ships taking part in the rescue. *UBA*

On the bridge of U-156: British civilians, who will be later
taken aboard the French ship *Glory* sent from Dakar.
After the surfaced U-boat was attacked by an American
B-24, in spite of being loaded with survivors, and with
large Red Cross flags on the bridge, the U-boats received
orders to no longer stop and rescue shipwrecked
survivors. *UBA*

Awards ceremony for U-509 crewmembers in the *Hundius Kaserne's* courtyard on September 13, 1942. Günther Kuhnke, the chief of the 10th Flotilla, shakes hands with the newly decorated officers who have just received the Iron Cross 2nd Class. The two sailors in the foreground are veterans of the U-boat corps during the First World War, as the decoration on their chests attests: the submarine is surmounted by a crown instead of an eagle. *UBA*

Watched by U-509's commander, decorations are awarded. *Korvettenkapitän* Karl-Heinz Wolf, who will celebrate his thirty-third birthday in October, had been in the *Luftwaffe* during the Spanish Civil War, as his decorations show. He joined the *Kriegsmarine* in March 1941 to carry out only one mission as the commander of U-509, before taking up various stations on land. *UBA*

On September 14, 1942, U-128 leaves on a combat patrol near Freetown. Schütze, the chief of the 2nd Flotilla, makes an encouraging speech to the crew. In the background, on the left: work is carried out filling up the *Pointe de Malheur*, on the right: the light cruiser *Strasbourg* being used as DCA post that will be stationed in front of Kéroman III at the beginning of 1942. *LB*

Several members of the *Todt Organization* (from the *Todt Organization* Command School based in Pont-Callec chateau), U-128's patron unit, are assembled on the back bridge of U-510 that arrived the day before, come to welcome the crew of their "adopted" submarine. *UBA*

On U-128's conning tower, the insignia of a white horse surrounded by a motto refers to this sponsorship: the words come from a song by the *Todt Organization. UBA*

0900 on September 15, 1942: the arrival of U-155 returning from a patrol of more than two months east of the Caribbean. Between its painted insignias on each side of the conning tower, is the insignia of the 10th Flotilla to which it belongs. The crew wears the sand-colored tropical uniform. *UBA*

Günter Kuhnke, chief of the 10th Flotilla, has come to welcome U-155's crew on their return from a patrol of more than two months. Between the end of July and the beginning of August, two cargo ships were sunk off the Antilles by the combined action of a torpedo and shells from their 105 mm gun. This type of attack on the surface will become increasingly rare in the future with the increase in Allied air presence. *LB*

In front of the A2 pontoon *Audacieuse* Adolf-Cornelius Piening, commander of U-155, is welcomed by his flotilla chief. A former minesweeper, Piening followed his officer training on U-48 during its last patrol from May to June 1941. He had commanded U-155 since August 23, 1941. *UBA*

The same day, three hours later, U-508 arrives, returning from its first combat patrol of nearly two months. Leaving Kiel, it sailed out to the Antilles where two ships were sunk close to Cuba. To go to berth at the A3 pontoon *Isere*, it passes U-155 that boasts ten victory pennants on its periscope representing the ten ships it sank between July 28 and August 10. *UBA*

The commander of U-155 knows he will receive the Knight's Cross on his arrival in Lorient. The decoration was awarded to him on August 13 following his latest successes. The following day, September 16, he will also celebrate his thirty-second birthday! *UBA*

U-155's ten pennants for a total of 43,518 tons sunk. Identifiable: 7,049 for the British cargo ship *Empire Arnold,* sunk on August 4; 6,096 for the American cargo ship *Cranford,* torpedoed on July 30; 6,088 for the British cargo ship *McNaughton Clan,* sunk on August 1; and 2,445 for the Norwegian cargo ship *Bill,* torpedoed on July 29. *UBA*

To celebrate their return from patrol, their commander's decoration and his thirty-second birthday, a party is organized for U-155's crew in *Saltzwedel Kaserne*. They were very lucky to return after three air raids on the other side of the Atlantic rendered their U-boat incapable of diving! *UBA*

On September 16, 1942, U-67 is on the point of setting out to sea once more, destination: the Caribbean. Two members of the crew have kept their straw hats bought during their stay at Carnac. *Bootsmaat* Jörg Haring remembers the first experiment with the *Metox* radar detector newly installed on board: "After having left our escort on September 17 at 0409, we dived and spent the day advancing submerged. At 2300 we surfaced, but had to dive each time the detector sounded the alarm. In fact, we seldom stayed more than five to fifteen minutes on the surface. The following day we went up to air out the U-boat. We were there for barely half an hour when the alarm went off. A plane appeared flying out of the sun, at too close a distance to have time to dive! We fired at it but it dropped seven bombs, three of which exploded very close to us. Inside everything fell all over the place, it took us half an hour to pick everything up, and another hour before it was all stored in its correct place." *UBA*

In the foreground: back of the minesweeper M153 responsible for escorting U-boats out to sea, with its two paravanes to detonate magnetic mines. On left, the demagnetization station, where each U-boat passed before leaving on patrol in order to avoid detonating magnetic mines. In spite of the thousands of mines set by Allied aircraft in front of Lorient, only two submarines struck one on arrival at Lorient, and not on their departure. In the background: the Péristyle barracks. *LB*

September 19: Albrecht Achilles, the commander of U-161, is on the point of leaving on patrol. He was awarded the Iron Cross 1st Class on April 5, 1942, three days after returning from his second combat mission as commander of U-161. *UBA*

Kuhnke, the chief of the 10th Flotilla, has come to salute the crew of U-161 that will be leaving, followed fifteen minutes later by U-126. Both will head towards the South Atlantic, the Gulf of Guinea and the delta of the Congo sector. *LB*

U-66 arrives on September 29, 1942, returning from a patrol of more than two months to the east of the Caribbean where nine ships were sunk. On board is the commander of the one of these ships, an American of Polish origin who will be taken to the Merchant Navy prison camp *Milag (Marine Internment LAGer) North*. The order, dating back to the beginning of 1942, to capture the commanders of ships sunk, was intended to weaken Allied personnel. The music is provided by the army while the 6th Battery of the *Marine Flak 704*, a navy anti-aircraft unit based in the north of Lorient at Kerviniac, has come to serve as an honor company. It is the patron unit of this U-boat since it has been under Friedrich Markworth's command. *UBA*

Three months before its arrival in Lorient at the end of September 1942, U-511 carried out rocket launching tests in the Baltic Sea while submerged. They were carried out by Dr. Erich Steinhoff, engineer at the rocket launching test base in Peenemünde. He was the brother of Friedrich Steinhoff, the commander of U-511! The tests were a success; the racks installed on the submarine's back bridge launched six 30 cm Würzkörper *42 Spreng*-type rockets from a depth of twelve meters! The only problem was that at that time these rockets were not advanced enough to hit a target at sea; however, they could be used to bombard land targets like refineries. This project was shelved shortly afterwards. The idea was brought out again at the end of 1944, on paper only, for launching V2s from Type-XXI U-boats! *UBA*

In September 1942, the roof framework of metal beams already covers two pens at Kéroman III. On the right-hand side, which will be numbered later 13-14, a timber coffering has been positioned ready to receive the concrete. *UBA*

A concreted embankment prevents water from flooding the Kéroman III pens. It will be dynamited at the end of October 1942. *UBA*

The metal beams being used as framework are aligned side by side above the future 15-16 pen. *UBA*

Last interior preparations before exploding the embankment in October. On the top in the background: the metal framework of the pen's pediment. *UBA*

October 1942: U-171, the First U-boat Sunk by a Mine Off Lorient

Movements: Eleven arrivals, twelve departures, number of U-boats present at the end of the month: fifteen. Also saw the arrival of eight new submarines from the 10th Flotilla as reinforcements in Lorient, with numerous successes for seven of them. As in the preceding month, an expected U-boat didn't arrive. This was U-171, sunk by a mine on October 9. This U-boat from the 10th Flotilla, out of Kiel on June 17 for its first combat patrol, had spent nearly four months at sea in the Gulf of Mexico where it had sunk three ships. After crossing the Atlantic, U-171's lookouts sighted the Brittany coast on October 9 at 1147. Towards midday, the lookouts saw what they thought was a British submarine in the distance. Their U-boat used zigzag evasive tactics to avoid being hit by a torpedo. They then returned to their planned route towards the rendezvous point where their escort was waiting to guide them to Lorient. But only minutes later the air-raid alarm sounded! Because of the slight depth of the sea in this sector, diving wasn't an option. The men hurried to the anti-aircraft guns, but to their surprise, they were German planes including a Junkers Ju 52/MS based in Vannes, especially equipped with a fourteen meter diameter ring on its fuselage, intended for exploding the magnetic mines dropped in the sea by Allied aviation, at a distance of 100 meters. This plane flew over the U-boat that continued on its way. The crewmembers were already thinking about what they were going to do once ashore. The commander allowed several crewmembers to come onto the bridge to get some

fresh air. The fore oblique hatch, for loading torpedoes aboard the submarine, was opened to air-out the interior. The U-boat encountered a patrol boat at about 1300, with which it exchanged a first message in Morse for a bearings check. At 1330, when it arrived at the *Lucie 2* rendezvous, fifty miles southwest of Lorient, its escort wasn't there. A blockade runner could be seen, but it was anchored off Groix Island to repair the electrical installation of its anti-magnetic mines equipment (this was the *Sperrbrecher 4 Oakland*). At 1340, Günther Pfeffer, the commander of U-171, had a message sent to it in Morse using the signal lamp asking if it was his escort. Two minutes later the *Sperrbrecher* sent a message in Morse to the *Sperrbrecher 134 Falke* which approached and was affected to escort duty: "From CDT to CDT: the U-boat is at Lucie 2 and is waiting for you." Then at 1345 it sent the following message to the submarine: "From CDT to CDT: The blockade runner escort is on its way." At the same time they sent this message, the signals men on the ship's bridge saw an explosion coming from the direction of the U-boat, sending up a vast spray of water. Five minutes earlier, Commander Pfeffer had decided to turn 280° to port. The U-boat hit a mine with the front of the hull level with the junior NCO's quarters, between the control room and the diesel compartment. At first, the commander thought he could maintain the U-boat and immediately gave the order to stop all engines. But when the order wasn't received and the diesels continued turning, he gave the orders: "All men

abandon ship!" Then, as the U-boat began to sink, "All men over the side!" Miming a rotating movement with his hands, he gave the order to the two men that he could see through the torpedo-loading hatch, to make sure it was closed tightly! The U-boat sank; those in the conning tower or on the bridge were sucked under by the backwash but managed to swim to the surface. The others were taken to the seabed.

Those in the machine rooms situated in the rear were almost immediately suffocated because the diesel engines that continued turning pumped out all the air for their combustion and their breathing apparatus' were underwater. At a depth of about forty meters, six crewmembers in the control room whose hatchways had been closed in time were still alive and sixteen others isolated in the front compartment, including Watch Officer *Oberfähnrich* Kurt Lau. He recalls: "I was in the officers' quarters when the explosion occurred, and as the U-boat was sinking front first I headed in that direction. After we hit the bottom, where we all hung onto whatever we could, we were thrown forwards by the shock and found ourselves in the dark. After the emergency lights came on we all put on our breathing apparatus so that we didn't inhale the chlorine emissions. We pulled ourselves together and discussed means of getting out. Of course, we'd all taken survival courses during our training. We had to get out two by two through a torpedo tube with our breathing apparatus and swim to the surface. But first we had to find the tool that unblocked the outside

OCTOBER 1942

U-BOAT	TYPE	FLOT.	COMMANDER	ARRIVAL	DEPART	NOTES
Departures						
U-66	IXC	2	Friedrich Markworth			Maintenance September 29 – November 9, 1942.
U-103	IXB	2	Gustav-Adolf Janssen		21	Being repaired in Lorient for four months since June 22; departure for the Freetown sector with a new commander.
U-105	IXB	2	Jürgen Nissen			New commander; being repaired June 30 – November 23.
U-108	IXB	2	Ralf-Reimar Wolfram		25	New commander; departure for Freetown.
U-124	IXB	2	Johann Mohr			Being repaired June 26 – November 25 1942.
U-130	IXC	2	Ernst Kals		29	Departure for the mid-Atlantic.
U-154	IXC	2	Heinrich Schuch		12	New commander was former commander of U-105 blocked in Lorient for several months, departure for the north coast of South America.
U-155	IXC	10	Adolf Piening			In maintenance September 15 – November 7, 1942.
U-163	IXC	10	Kurt Engelmann		17	Departure for the Antilles.
U-173	IXC	10	Hans-Adolf Schweichel			New commander, former watch officer aboard U-126. In maintenance September 20 – November 1, 1942.
U-174	IXC	10	Ulrich Thilo	8	7 / 8	Departure for Brazilian coast.
U-505	IXC	2	Peter Zschech		4	Departure for the north coast of South America.
U-508	IXC	10	Georg Staats		17	Departure for the Antilles.
U-509	IXC	10	Werner Witte		15	New commander, former Watch Officer aboard the U-109. Departure for the Freetown sector.
U-510	IXC	10	Karl Neitzel		14	Departure for Freetown.
U-511	IXC	10	Friedrich Steinhoff		24	Departure for the Mid-Atlantic.

U-BOAT	TYPE	FLOT.	COMMANDER	ARRIVAL	DEPART	NOTES
Arrivals						
U-176	IXC	10	Reiner Dierksen	2		First time in Lorient; put into service 12/15/41. Returns from its first combat patrol, out of Kiel, in the North Atlantic: attacked the SC-94 and ONS-122 convoys. It sunk six ships (35,643 tons), five from the two convoys.
U-109	IXB	2	Heinrich Bleichrodt Awarded Oak Leaves to his Knight's Cross on September 23.	6		Returns from Cape Verde and the Gulf of Guinea sectors, five ships sunk for a total of 35,601 tons. The British commander of the fuel tanker *Vimera* taken prisoner and brought to Lorient; and the radioman from the cargo ship *Tuscan Star* and the captain of the cargo ship *Peterton*.
U-164	IXC	10	Otto Fechner	7		First time in Lorient; put into service 11/28/41. Returns from its first combat patrol, out of Kiel in the Caribbean: two ships sunk. Forced to leave the sector on September 13 after an aerial attack damaged its fuel tanks. Because of its long first patrol, (nearly three months) the crew receives the U-boat Combat Badge from Kuhnke. The crew had suffered from skin diseases caused by the heat in the Caribbean, treated by the radioman while the commander was treated for slight wounds. A doctor would be onboard for the next patrol.
U-507	IXC	2	Harro Schacht	12		Arrives from a patrol of nearly three months off the Brazilian coast: seven ships (18,132 tons) sunk in August: six Brazilian that resulted in this country entering the war on August 22. The U-boat crossed the Atlantic to Freetown where it took part in the *Laconia* rescue operation.
U-515	IXC	10	Werner Henke	14		1st time in Lorient; put into service 2/21/42. Returns from its first combat mission south of the Antilles, with 8 ships sunk (42,114 tons) and 2 damaged.
U-118	XB	10	Werner Czygan	16		First time in Lorient; put into service 12/6/41. After U-116 lost at sea on October 11, this is the second Type XB U-boat minesweeper to arrive in Lorient. For its first patrol it was used as a supply ship off the Azores.
U-517	IXC	10	Paul Hartwig	19		First time in Lorient; put into service 3/2/42. Returns from its first combat patrol, out of Kiel, to Canada where it penetrated the Gulf of St. Lawrence. It torpedoed the *Chatham*, first American troop transport ship sunk since the beginning of the war: eleven victims out of 562 passengers, eight more ships sunk: one corvette escorting a convoy. Total tonnage sunk 31,231 tons (for 44,000 declared).
U-513	IXC	10	Rolf Rüggeberg	22		First time in Lorient; put into service 1/10/42. Returns from its first patrol during which it sunk two anchored ships in Conception Bay, Newfoundland, before being attacked by coastal batteries. Damaged a third ship on the way home.
UD-3	Holl.	10	Hermann Rigele	22		First time in Lorient; put into service 6/8/41. Former Dutch submarine scuttled in May 1940, captured by the Germans and repaired. Mission unsuccessful. The commander was born in Sarajevo during the Austro-Hungary monarchy.
U-175	IXC	10	Heinrich Bruns	27		First time in Lorient; put into service 12/5/41. Arrives from its first combat patrol, north of the South American coast: nine ships sunk for 33,426 tons.

partition of the tube, which a security system normally prevents. The emergency lights suddenly turned off and we only had two torches; water reached to our knees. We couldn't unblock the torpedo tubes outside partition that had obviously buckled when we hit the seabed. We had to abandon this escape route and the water continued rising. We decided to get out through the bridge's slanting hatch used for loading torpedoes, but it opened outwards. We would have to flood the compartment so that the pressure would be equal inside and out. After half an hour, when the water reached up to our necks, Hauptgefreiter Karl Sauter opened the hatch and the water poured in, filling the last small air space. One by one, we went through the hatch towards the light."

Matrosenhauptgefreiter Fritz Müller recalls: "I was in the front compartment, in my hammock when the explosion happened. We all wondered if was a bomb or a torpedo, but none of us thought it could be a mine. As the torpedo-loading hatch was open, my friend Paul Ziska climbed the ladder onto the bridge. I was just behind him on top of the ladder, I saw him running towards the conning tower, where the commander was making signs to close the hatch. Suddenly, the U-boat began to sink and a wave washed over my face. Immediately, I closed the hatch tightly, helped by Maat Scholz who was just below me on the ladder. The U-boat descended dangerously and water poured in from about everywhere. I headed for the senior NCOs' quarters where I saw that the kitchen and officers' quarters were empty, and the partition leading to the control room was closed. As the senior NCO's quarters were filling up with water, I returned to the front compartment and we closed the door. The water was rising rapidly and we sat on the bunks with our legs dangling in the water... We didn't know how deep we were and the depth gauge was broken. None of us panicked, we stayed calm by thinking of our loved ones back home, and how we would be back with them in a few days. We talked about how to escape from here. The following plan was adopted: we would get out through a torpedo launching tube. Meanwhile, we had all put on our breathing apparatus, even the officer-candidate who'd left his in his quarters. I dived under the bunks and found him a spare one. Unfortunately, *Torpedo-Hauptgefreiter* Karl Sauter, an old seadog who had sailed with Lemp, discovered that his Tauchretter wasn't working properly. Then he tried to open the hatch, but without success in spite of all his efforts as the pressure difference was too great. While we were all sitting in silence on the bunks, the telephone rang! It was really creepy. A quick swim and the receiver was lifted; an incredible and good surprise: it was a diesel machinist who was calling to say that six men were stuck in the control room! They were going to try to blow the ballasts. That would have been great, but our hopes were quickly dashed; the only result was that the submarine settled a little more on its right side. To be able to open the hatch, we tried to open the outside partition of a torpedo-launching tube to let in water so that the interior and exterior pressure would be the same, but that didn't work. All of a sudden, our friend Charlie Sauter, who was watching the pressure, cried out 'Nil!' and he managed to open the torpedo-loading hatch. Water poured in and knocked us off the bunks. It completely filled the compartment and we escaped one after the other and swam towards the surface. Fifteen of us managed to get out, one didn't make it." The six men blocked in the control room managed to get out through the conning tower hatch, but one of them died half an hour after reaching the surface. Outside rescue operations were organized with three ships that were nearby when the submarine exploded: the *Sperrbrecher 4* and *134* and the patrol boat *VP-1421.* The motorboat from the *Sperrbrecher 4* with the in it was the first arrive on the scene at 14:30; Commander Pfeffer and six men were pulled out of the water. They were taken to the *Sperrbrecher 134* close-by. The motorboat turned back and pulled seven new escapees on board. The other survivors were picked up by motorboats from *Sperrbrecher 134* and by the patrol boat. In the officers' mess in the *Sperrbrecher 134*, the survivors were given hot drinks, dry clothes and blankets. They recounted their adventures; apparently, the plane that had flown over them had seen the mine and had sent a warning radio message. There were twenty-seven survivors out of forty-nine crewmembers. These were certainly those in the rear, apart from diesel mechanic Emil Heber; at the moment of the explosion, he just managed to jump into the control room before the hatch was closed. Two men were missing from the control room and five from the front. At 1600, the patrol boat placed a buoy marking the place where U-171 had sunk. In Lorient, a reception had been planned but under the circumstances it was cancelled. The *Sperrbrecher* docked in an old coal-port where a bus and an ambulance were waiting on the quay. Before boarding, the survivors heard the ship's crew receive the order to turn their heads to the right when their dead comrade *MaschGefreiter* Erwin Klein was carried past. The survivors were immediately taken to the Maritime Hospital in Lorient. Admiral Dönitz came to see them a few days later and promised them that after a long leave in the Navy hostel situated in Krummhübel, they would be given a new U-boat. Following this loss, measures taken by the U-boat Corps Command meant that, henceforth, U-boats would no longer cross the fifty meter depth line without being escorted by a minesweeper. The new rendezvous point, "Laterne," was moved from off Groix Island to deeper water than those of "Lucie 2."

Observations: The results of the Type IX U-boats were still very satisfying off Trinidad and the coast of Venezuela, where twenty-five cargo ships had been sunk between October 1 and November 7, for the loss of only one U-boat. However, they were very disappointing in the Gulf of Saint Lawrence sector where between four and six U-boats patrolled in October, and off Freetown where six to eight U-boats patrolled during the first three weeks of the month. This sector was more or less abandoned until April 1943, when the situation in the North Atlantic had considerably deteriorated. However, there was a success against the SL-125 convoy chased between the Azores and the Canaries by the eight U-boats heading for Freetown in the middle of October, and which sank twelve ships for 80,000 tons. During the last week of October, U-126 and U-161, which had been sent farther south below the equator to the mouth of the Congo, didn't produce the desired results. Even further away, the *Eisbär* Wolfpack, out of Lorient at the end of August, was engaged from October 7. In three days, U-68, U-159 and U-172 carried out a surprise attack off Cape Town where thirteen cargo ships were sunk. On October

17, the fourth in the pack, U-504, sank the first Allied ship in the Indian Ocean. These U-boats more or less joined up with the Japanese submarines that went on to patrol around Madagascar in June and July! In a single month, they sank twenty-three ships for a total of 155,335 tons, which is rather high. Nearly out of fuel, they were re-supplied on the way home by U-461, and reached Lorient in December. They were relieved in the Indian Ocean by the first four operational Type IXD-2 U-boats: U-177, U-178, U-179 and U-181. U-179, which left a month before the others, was sunk off Cape Town on October 8. Their results up to mid-December, was twenty-seven ships sunk; they then returned to their base in Bordeaux.

During August to October 1942, the results obtained by the Type IX U-boats in distant seas were very high, accounting for three-quarters of Allied ships lost during this period. The wolfpack attacks in the mid-Atlantic by the Type VIIs, even though they had more U-boats at their disposal, were only responsible for a quarter of the total tonnage destroyed. Throughout the war, the 194 different Type IXs built destroyed 40% of Allied tonnage sunk by U-boats: three times more than the Type VIIs.

At the beginning of October, two large lines of Type VII U-boats waited on each side of the "gap" in the Atlantic. One stretched vertically west of the Atlantic, 300 miles from Newfoundland to spot the SC and HX convoys out of New York for Liverpool, the other in the east 700 miles from Liverpool, where the ON convoys left for New York. The slow SC-104 convoy was spotted on October 12; from then until October 15 it lost eight ships. The next day, the ON-137 convoy was spotted and chased by twenty-seven U-boats. It was saved by the atrocious weather conditions. On October 22, it was the ON-139 convoy's turn to avoid the worst thanks to its great speed that stopped the U-boats coming together to attack. Operations continued from October 24-28 against the fast HX-212 convoy that lost six ships. The best result was against the SC-107 convoy. Attacked straight after its passage off Newfoundland on October 30, it continued until the convoy reached the safety of aerial cover on November 5. It lost fifteen cargo ships totaling 88,000 tons, while only two U-boats were sunk during the operation. Several factors explain the success against the

convoys since August: the number of available U-boats; the permanent presence of re-supply, which meant that the attack U-boats could stay in the zone for longer periods; decoding Allied radio messages by the German *B-Dienst* service; and the fuel restrictions on the Allies side which forced the convoys to stay more-or-less on the most direct route. Also, the U-boats, which had been equipped with the *Metox* radar detector since mid-September, discovered a very practical use for the apparatus: it didn't just protect them from aerial attacks, it also helped them to detect Canadian escort ships which still used their old metric radar, and this put them on the convoys' trail. As the Canadians escorted a third of the convoys in the North Atlantic, mostly the slow SC-type, these became the victims of U-boat attacks until the end of the year. During October 1942, German U-boats sank 105 Allied ships for a total of 566,939 tons.

In the Mediterranean, on October 30, U-559 was forced to surface after being damaged by 288 depth charges launched from five destroyers above it. Quickly, a special boarding party on the British destroyer *Petard* assembled to capture the Enigma coding equipment and the U-boat's secret codebook. The mission was very risky; two British sailors sank with the U-boat trying to bring out the Enigma four-rotor coding machine. The discovery of these documents allowed the British Decoding Center in Bletchley Park to start working more efficiently: on December 13, 1942, a first U-boat radio message was decoded, which hadn't happened since February, when the German U-boats had been equipped with an Enigma four-rotor. After Christmas, most of the U-boat radio messages were decoded. In February, on their side, the German *B-Dienst* service continued to use the Naval Cipher 3 decoding system used by the Allied Navies in the Atlantic. This code was also used for all messages concerning convoys. On October 22, 1942, U-412 was the first U-boat to be sunk at night north of England by a Wellington equipped with a *Theigh-Light* searchlight."

The French-German "*Relève*" system, created in July 1942, which planned on sending 150,000 French specialized workers to Germany in exchange for the repatriation of 50,000 prisoners, wasn't a success. On September 4, 1942, the French government passed a new law: "The use and

On October 2, 1942, U-176 commanded by Reiner Dierksen arrives in Lorient after a very successful first patrol in the North Atlantic, with six boats sunk, mainly from the SC-94 and ONS-122 convoys. *UBA*

guidance of the workforce" subjecting them to do any work the government considered necessary. On the Atlantic, under this law, the Todt Organization was able to requisition the essential laborers available. After taking a census of the working population, the Germans ordered 600 workers at the arsenal in Lorient to go to Germany and work in the shipyards. The arsenal's engineer Jacques Stosskopf, who came from Alsace, named deputy director of the arsenal on September 23, managed to convince the Germans only to send 200 by arguing that most of the men were already working for the Kriegsmarine in Lorient. He signed most of the contracts of the "volunteers" so that the workers would benefit from advantages from Germany. Finally, 191 French shipyard workers left Lorient by train on October 24, 1942, to work in the Deschimag-Seebeck shipyard in Wesermünde. On October 31, a second train took another forty-four workers from Lorient to Germany. Several thousand Lorient workers (6,000 on October 24 according to a report by the *Gendarmerie*) converged at the railroad station to vigorously protest against these forced deportations. The French engineer, considered responsible, was loudly booed. However, thanks to his negotiations, only 235 workers were sent to Germany instead of the 600 asked for. Moreover, since the beginning of the Occupation, he had been informing, through the *Deuxième Bureau* of the Vichy-French Navy, the Allies about everything the Germans were doing in Lorient: construction of U-boat bases, U-boat movements etc. But obviously, this important mission was carried out in the greatest secrecy! With the German

Occupation of the Free Zone on November 11, 1942, engineer Jacques Stosskopf could no longer pass information via the *Deuxième Bureau*. At the beginning of 1943, he was able to contact Joël Lemoigne of the *Alliance Réseau*; after that, his information was transmitted to London by the *réseau* radio operators based in Brest. In May 1943, the deputy-director of the arsenal in Lorient officially became a member of the *Alliance Réseau* as an intelligence officer. Four other departures for Germany of total of eighty-two workers in private companies in the district took place in November 1942.

Allied reactions: after a six-month lull, Lorient was once again the target of Allied bomber raids on October 21, 1942. It was the first American bombardment by day, with fifteen B-17s out of the ninety planned, due to bad weather conditions. As the raid was taking place in daylight hours, the bombers should have been escorted by twenty-four American P-38 fighters and 107 Spitfires! But as they weren't able to accomplish their mission either, the bombers were attacked by German Focke-Wulf Fw 190 fighters and two B-17s didn't return to base. The bombs that fell in the Kéroman sector destroyed the *Crépelle*, *Lepage* and *Siemens-France* workshops, where forty-six workers of different nationalities were killed and 138 wounded. The bombs also fell on a part of the town center, killing ninety-four civilians. The Coastal Command carried out seven mine-laying operations with a total of twenty-eight Wellingtons each with two mines; one of these sank U-171.

Born in Constantinople, Turkey, Peter Zschech, a young *Oberleutnant-zur-See*, here on the balcony of the villa "*Les Flots*" in Larmor, was given the command of U-505 on September 6, 1942, one month before his twenty-fourth birthday. Although U-505's crew were saddened that their first commander, Axel-Olaf Loewe, who they regarded as a father figure, was transferred to a land position, they welcomed Zschech rather well as he had a good reputation. For a year he had been the watch officer on U-124. But they also had a new watch officer, *Oberleutnant* Thilo Bode, Zschech's friend with whom he had done his officer training in 1936. A divide immediately cropped up between these new officers: on one side, those in favor of absolute authority as a means of command, and the veteran crew of the other. One of Zschech's first initiatives was to organize an infantry-training program for the crew on leave. U-505 was due to leave Lorient on October 4 in the direction of the Antilles. *UBA*

With five pennants on its periscope, U-109, under Commander Heinrich Bleichrodt, arrives in Lorient on October 6, 1942 and berths alongside the A3 pontoon *Isere* opposite *Saltzwedel Kaserne*—as is the general practice for great receptions. Several officers come to salute the crew, and address the commander by his nickname: "Hey there, Ajax, so you've managed to bring this old relic back to the right port again!" Behind the aligned crew is a rather old man without a hat; he is one of the three prisoners brought back to Lorient after his ship was torpedoed, almost certainly the British captain of the tanker *Vimera*, Norman Ross Caird. Viktor Schütze, the chief of the 2nd Flotilla, welcomes the crew; at his side is Commander Bleichrodt who is hardly recognizable after having lost a considerable amount of weight during his patrol. He has also suffered a lot since the end of August after injuring his leg during a rapid descent from the conning tower when the submarine dove after the sudden appearance of an aircraft. Contrary to his habit of wearing a garrison cap, he is wearing a white cap and has only shaved his cheeks, which, according to his crew, makes him look like an officer of the Tsar! In his memoirs, Wolfgang Hirschfeld, U-109's former radio operator, recalls that the aligned crew was much more interested in the legs of the girls opposite the *Isere's* bridge, than in the welcoming speech! *UBA*

After its arrival, U-109's crew is invited to the traditional reception in a room in the barracks. They pass between the two large concrete personnel shelters built in the middle of the courtyard. Two members of the party were invited to the reception; they probably belonged to the German ex-serviceman association, *Kyffhäuserbundes*, the U-boat's patron unit. *UBA*

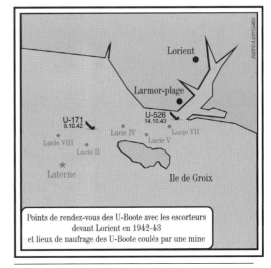

In the barrack's reception hall, the flotilla chief addresses U-109's crew who have been given beer. Several of them probably thought that they were going to join their comrades from U-165 for a joint party. Indeed, on September 26, six days after U-109 had been refueled by U-460 to the north of the Cape Verde Islands, and was heading in direction of Lorient, *Leutnant-zur-See* Helmut Bruns recommended by radio to the 2nd Flotilla, that *BtsMaat* Berthold Seidel, who had carried out fourteen combat patrols in eighty weeks at sea, and had taken part in the destruction of sixty-one ships, be decorated with the German Cross in Gold. The same day, they received a radio message from U-165, telling them that their U-boat was only forty-eight hours from Lorient, where a party had been organized to celebrate the Iron Cross 1st Class that had been awarded to Eberhard Hoffmann, their commander. A joint party had been agreed on, however, U-165 was sunk by a Wellington bomber the following day and U-109's crew only found out after they reached Lorient. As for the decoration recommended at sea, it was awarded to Seidel, but on November 10. During its last patrol, U-109's commander, Bleichrodt, sunk five ships for a total of 35,601 tons, which pushed him over the symbolic 200,000-ton mark. He was automatically awarded the Oak Leaves to his Knight's Cross. He was the 125th Wehrmacht officer to receive this distinction. *UBA*

Chart of the rendezvous points between U-boats and their escorts in 1942-43, and places where the wrecks of U-boats sunk by mines were to be found. *Drawn by Anthony Guychard*

The day after their arrival in Lorient, Wolfgang Hirschfeld (on the left) and Ferdinand Hagen (on the right), U-109's two radio operators, went to Kernevel to take part in the radio operators' debriefing. Afterwards, they visited the rooms where the *Enigma* coding machines were housed and asked after U-165's crew. The transmissions officer told them that U-165 had given no signals since its message indicating it was forty-eight hours from Lorient. It was registered on a list alongside eighteen other U-boats of the 2nd Flotilla reported missing since July. The two radiomen were shocked by this number; this type of information was obviously not given out to crewmembers. After his medical examination at the maritime hospital, Hirschfeld was declared temporarily ill due to a skin disease. When it cleared up at the beginning of December, U-109 had just left on patrol a few days before. Hirschfeld was transferred to the coding room in Kernével.

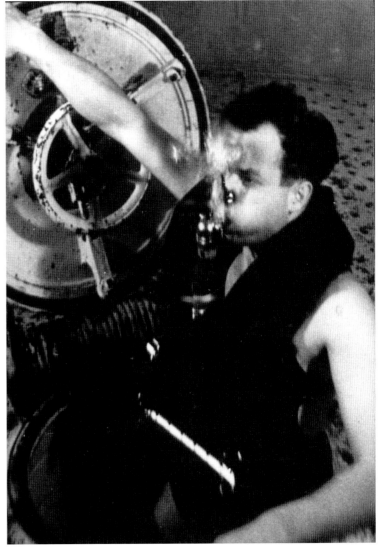

U-171 hit a mine near Lorient and sank on October 9, 1942. Thanks to their breathing sets (*Tauchretter*), twenty crewmembers were able to escape from the stricken ship, which was on the seabed at forty meters. *LB*

Burial of several crewmembers of U-171 in the cemetery in Kerentrech, in the presence of Kuhnke, the chief of the 10th Flotilla. Of a total of forty-nine submariners, twenty-two died. During its training period in the Baltic Sea, the U-boat had remained rather a long time in Stettin where the commander's wife was invited on board. Submariner Lehmann, a former crewmember aboard U-100 under Schepke, saw this as an ill omen: "When a woman boards a U-boat, it will not return from a mission!" He predicted this to his comrades who had laughed at the time, but the survivors recalled his words once they reached Lorient. *LB*

Dönitz came to Lorient to try to comfort the survivors of U-171. Opposite him is Commander Günther Pfeffer, and Chief Engineer Otto Dingeldein. After having listened to the account of each surviving crewmember, the admiral promised that they would not be separated. He assured them that after two weeks leave at home and another two weeks in the ski resort at Krummhübel, they would integrate U-170's crew together. Engineer Dingeldein would continue his career in the *Bundesmarine* after the war with the rank of *Flottillenadmiral*. *UBA*

On October 12, 1942, Commander Harro Schacht's U-507 returns from a long tour of more than three months along the coast of Brazil where seven ships, totaling 18,132 tons, were sunk in August, including six Brazilian ships that caused the country's entry into the war on August 22. The U-boat then crossed the Atlantic towards Freetown where it took part in the *Laconia* shipwreck rescue operation. *ECPAD*

U-154 leaves the base on the Scorff on October 12, in the direction of the Antilles. Its new insignia, which replaced the cow spitting projectiles out of its orifices, is a star that was once on U-105 that the men called "*Die Stern von Rio*"— "The Star of Rio"—in reference to a famous film at the time. *UBA*

U-154 moves away in reverse. Its commander and crew are from U-105 that arrived in Lorient badly damaged on June 30. Repairs would take several months. *UBA*

Through the conning tower's hatchway, nine of the ten pennants brought back by U-515. One can see, starting from the bottom, 2,412 for the Norwegian cargo ship *Lindvangen,* sunk on September 23, and 4,838 for the British cargo ship *Reedpool*; after torpedoing this ship, its surviving crewmembers, covered with oil, were taken on board, fed and given clean clothes. The fourth pennant, with the figure 4,801, is for the Norwegian steamer *Sörholt. UBA*

On October 14, 1942, U-515 arrives in Lorient after a successful first patrol to the south of the Antilles where eight ships were sunk representing 42,114 tons, and two others damaged. Members of the crew are aligned on the front bridge for the welcoming ceremony. *LB*

The first group from U-515 on leave is taken to Lorient station in a truck. *LB*

The group from U-515 on leave wait in front of Lorient station for the special train reserved for submariners that will take them to Germany. Behind them are the hotels St. Christophe and Terminus on the right-hand side, where the *Kriegsmarine* had a brothel. *LB*

Those that are staying behind to help the *KMW* workers repair their U-boat have come to say goodbye! *LB*

The crewmembers on leave have boarded the train nicknamed "*BdU-Zug;*" the train is leaving, the last goodbyes. *LB*

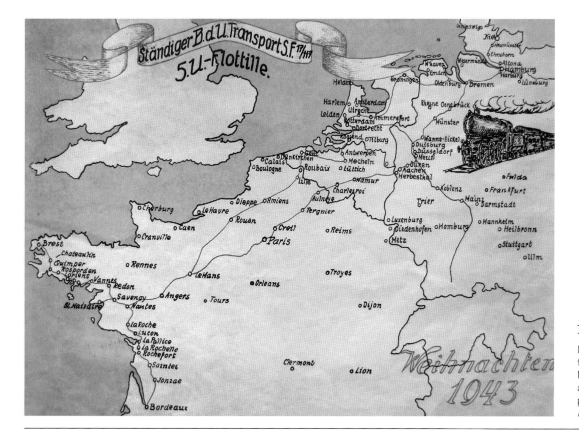

The submariners' special train's itinerary: Departure from Brest-Lorient to Savenay where the train from St. Nazaire arrives, then on to Nantes where the Bordeaux-La Rochelle train arrives, then east where it will pass by the large ports of Brème, Hamburg and Kiel. *M. Jean-Philippe Lamotte*

October 16: U-118 arrives after its first patrol as a supply boat in the Azores. On U-118's bridge Kuhnke, the chief of the 10th Flotilla, salutes the crew; behind him is Commandant Werner Czygan. This is the second of the XB-type minelayer submarine to arrive in Lorient. *UBA*

After a month's patrol at sea, U-118's crew enjoy a Kiel beer. Their fifty-five comrades from the XB-type U-116, the first to arrive in Lorient, left the port a month earlier and were all lost at sea on October 11. *UBA*

For the commander of U-517, Paul Hartwig, former watch officer aboard U-125 in 1941, the port at Lorient wasn't new. His crew arrived for the first time with seven other submarines of the 10th Flotilla sent as reinforcements that month. Twenty-seven-years-old, his first patrol as commander was a success, with nine ships sunk including one corvette escorting a convoy. If the reception was prestigious at the time of his arrival in the Scorff on October 19, 1942, with an orchestra and a speech given by Kuhnke, the flotilla's chief, the departure on November 17 was so discreet that the submarine's radio was turned on to make up for the lack of music! U-517 was seriously damaged during an air attack four days later when it had just dived; as they were taking on water, the commander gave the order to surface. As two destroyers and other aircraft were approaching, the crew received the order to gather on the bridge while smoke poured out of the submarine. A torpedo man was sent to activate the three charges that would scuttle the U-boat, but he didn't come back up. The three charges exploded and the sailor was killed. The crew sang the national anthem "*Deutschland über Alles*" in his honor, then gave three cheers before jumping into the water. The survivors were picked up by one of the two destroyers. As is the custom, once aboard, the commander was immediately separated from his crew; however, he was allowed to send them a message saying that he regretted being unable to shake their hands for their remarkable courage and not to forget his security instructions … don't talk. *UBA*

Aerial photo of the Kéroman peninsula taken by the United States Army Air Force on October 21, 1942, just before the air raid by fifteen B-17 bombers. The concreted roofs of KI and KII appear very clearly, as well as the base of KIII still under construction, where one can see the pens' sidewalls. *NA*

Two bombs dropped from a B-17 in the direction of the target. Low clouds appeared that prevented eighty-five other planes from dropping their bombs. *NA*

These exploded directly on the Kéroman submarine base! U-124's logbook noted that two bombs fell near the U-boat; two members of crew were wounded, and work that was almost completed would have to be prolonged another month because of damage caused by shrapnel. Other bombs dropped the same day weren't recorded as accurately. *NA*

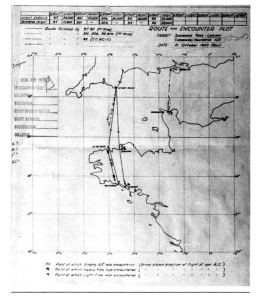

The round trip itinerary of the American bombers on October 21, 1942: south of England towards Batz Island, change of course in direction of Quimperlé, then towards Lorient where the German heavy anti-aircraft defense takes action, return by Lannion. *NA*

The first bombs hit the bridges beside KI and KII. We can clearly see that the covering work on KIII is only 50% complete. Only the workshops of the last pens are already protected. *NA*

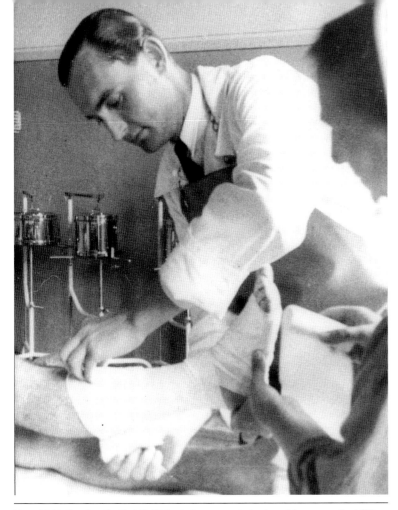

Hans-Ulrich Sendler, the 2nd Flotilla's doctor, suggests treatment for a casualty. *UBA*

Gustav-Adolf Jansen, the new commander of U-103, came to Lorient several times in 1940-41, when he was then third officer aboard U-65. This time he has come as a commander; he takes charge of a U-boat that, after four months of work, is as good as new, and leaves for Freetown. Twenty-seven-years-old, he belongs to the third generation of commanders since the beginning of the war. The first were already commanders during the pre-war period, and had come to Lorient during the second half of 1940; the second had become commanders in 1941 after having been the first generations' watch officers. *UBA*

On October 29, 1942, U-130 leaves the small base on the Scorff in the direction of the center of the Atlantic. It will be the last patrol at sea for Commander Ernst Kals before becoming the new chief of the 2nd Flotilla. *Benoit Senne*

Rolf Rüggeberg, the commander of U-513 arrives for the first time in Lorient on October 22, 1942, with four pennants on the periscope of his U-boat adding up to 29,000 tons. In reality, he sank two cargo ships for 12,789 tons, and damaged a third of 7,174 tons. On Sunday October 25, he was decorated with both the Iron Cross 2nd Class and the Iron Cross 1st Class: the 1st Class is only awarded to a soldier having already obtained the 2nd Class! Kuhnke, the flotilla chief, also awarded the Iron Cross 2nd Class to all the U-boat's officers and eight other crewmembers. *Bernd Siepert*

The *Todt Organization* blows up the concreted embankment that kept water out of the KIII pens. The concrete work on the roof will continue until January 1943. *UBA*

November 1942: U-boats Faced by Allied Landings in North Africa

NOVEMBER 1942

U-BOAT	TYPE	FLOT.	COMMANDER	ARRIVAL	DEPART	NOTES
Departures						
UD-3	Holl.	10	Hermann Rigele		3	Departure for the Cape Verde Islands.
U-66	IXC	2	Friedrich Markworth	11	9	Departure for the West Atlantic, was attacked during the evening of the tenth southwest of Lorient by a plane equipped with a projector; returns for repairs, escorted from *Kern* point by three trawlers and two Ju-88 planes. Part of the crew went to the Anti-aircraft Artillery School in Mimizan.
U-105	IXB	2	Jürgen Nissen		23	Departure for the Antilles.
U-109	IXB	2	Heinrich Bleichrodt		28	Departure for the Antilles.
U-118	XB	12	Werner Czygan		12	Change of Flotilla on 11/1/42; U-118 joins the 12th Flotilla created in Bordeaux in October with XB, IXD-2 and XIV type U-boats, which are welcomed to the port in January 1943. Departure for a supply mission off the Azores.
U-124	IXB	2	Johann Mohr		25	After five months being repaired, since June 26, 1942, departure for the Antilles.
U-155	IXC	10	Adolf Piening		7	Departure for the Atlantic, on the eighth sent to the west of Gibraltar following the Allied Landing in North Africa.
U-164	IXC	10	Otto Fechner		29	Departure for its second and last patrol, off the Brazilian coast; sunk on 1/6/43 by depth charges launched from a plane; the U-boat was broken in two! The two survivors were swimming when the plane arrived and found the conning tower's hatch closed, they were projected into the water by the explosion; the plane dropped them a dinghy with which they reached the coast. Fifty-four dead including the commander. Results: three ships sunk.
U-173	IXC	10	Hans-Adolf Schweichel		1	Departure for its second and last patrol, in the mid-Atlantic; sent to the Moroccan coast after the Allied landings in North Africa. Sunk on 11/16/42 by destroyers, no survivors; fifty-seven dead. Results: one ship sunk, three damaged.
U-175	IXC	10	Heinrich Bruns			In maintenance October 17 – December 1, 1942.
U-176	IXC	10	Reiner Dierksen		9	Departure for the coast of Brazil.
U-507	IXC	2	Harro Schacht	26	24 28	Departure for its fourth and last patrol, off Brazil; sunk 1/13/43 by depth charges dropped from a plane, no survivors, fifty-five dead. On board: the Allied captains from two of the three ships sunk during the mission. Results: nineteen ships sunk.
U-513	IXC	10	Rolf Rüggeberg		21	Departure for the Azores.
U-515	IXC	10	Werner Henke		7	Departure for the mid-Atlantic then to the west of Gibraltar after the Allied landing.
U-517	IXC	10	Paul Hartwig		17	Departure for its second and last patrol, in the Atlantic; scuttled 11/21/42 after the attack by a British plane northwest of Cape Finisterre (northwest of Spain), three dead, fifty-two prisoners including the commander. Results: eight ships and one corvette sunk, one damaged.
Arrivals						
U-69	VIIC	7	Ulrich Gräf	5		New commander since March 1942, this VIIC type operates out of St. Nazaire since July 1941. Returns from mining operations along the American coast and then the Gulf of St-Laurent, Canada where two ships were sunk.
U-602	VIIC	7	Philipp Schüler	6		First time in Lorient; put into service 12/29/41. This Type VIIC of the 7th Flotilla arrives from its first combat patrol against convoys in the North Atlantic, without success. Schüler has already been to Lorient three times in 1941 as the commander of U-141, a Type IID.
U-203	VIIC	1	Hermann Kottmann	6		New commander since September 1942. The U-boat normally based in Brest returns from attacking the SL-125 convoy in the Azores sector where it sank two ships for 12,309 tons.
U-125	IXC	2	Ulrich Folkers	6		Returns from a three-and-a-half-month patrol in the Freetown–Monrovia sector: six ships were sunk totaling 25,415 tons.
U-506	IXC	10	Erich Würdemann	7		Returns from a three-and-a-half-month patrol off Freetown; with U-156 and U-507 it participated in the Laconia rescue operation. Sank five ships for 28,023 tons.
U-575	VIIC	7	Günther Heydemann	8		First time in Lorient; put into service 6/19/41. The U-boat normally based in St. Nazaire returns from attacking convoys in the North Atlantic with only one success.
U-514	IXC	10	Hans-Jürgen Auffermann	9		First time in Lorient; put into service 1/24/42. Arrives from its first three-month combat patrol in the Antilles and off the coast of South America: five ships were sunk for 17,354 tons and a sixth damaged.

U-BOAT	TYPE	FLOT.	COMMANDER	ARRIVAL	DEPART	NOTES
UD-5	Holl.	10	Bruno Mahn	12		First time in Lorient; put into service 11/1/41; former Dutch submarine under construction and captured in May 1940, operational since August 1942; arrives from its first combat patrol off Freetown: one ship sunk. Change of commander, Mahn named in April 1943 Chief of U-boat Fortifications in Hamburg.
U-436	VIIC	6	Günter Seibicke	12		First time in Lorient; put into service 9/27/41. Arrives from Kiel, it had already carried out several combat patrols off Norway. Returns from attacking convoys in the North Atlantic: three ships sunk and two fuel tankers damaged.
U-516	IXC	10	Gerhard Wiebe	14		First time in Lorient; put into service 3/10/42. Arrives from its first combat patrol of three months in the Caribbean: five ships sunk for 29,357 tons and one damaged.
U-260	VIIC	6	Hubertus Purkhold	15		First time in Lorient; put into service 3/14/42. Arrives from its first combat patrol out of Kiel, chasing convoys in the North Atlantic, without success.
U-156	IXC	2	Werner Hartenstein	16		Returns from a three-month patrol off Ascension Island below the equator, with three pennants (one represents the Laconia).
U-107	IXB	2	Harald Gelhaus	18		Returns from a three-month patrol off Freetown with three ships sunk for 23,508 tons. On October 7, met U-333 off Freetown; its commander and two officers were wounded and four crewmembers killed during an attack by the British corvette Crocus. Commander-in-training Lorenz Kasch who was on U-107 was transferred to U-333 to take it to La Pallice.
U-662	VIIC	7	Wolfgang Hermann	18		First time in Lorient; put into service 4/9/42. Arrives from its first patrol out of Kiel, in the North Atlantic and around the Azores, without success.
U-117	XB	11	Hans-Werner Neumann	22		First time in Lorient; put into service 10/25/41; third Type XB in Lorient. Arrives from its first combat patrol placing mines off Reykjavik, Iceland, and then supplying U-boats in the Azores.
U-108	IXB	2	Ralf-Reimar Wolfram	26		Returns from the coast of North Africa without success against the Allied fleet; damaged during an aerial attack on November 18 off the coast of Morocco.
U-509	IXC	10	Werner Witte	26		Returns from Canaries sector where the SL-125 convoy had been heavily attacked, then west of Gibraltar following the Allied landings; returns with six pennants. In reality only four ships were sunk and three others damaged. The U-boat was damaged by a mine off Casablanca.
U-511	IXC	10	Friedrich Steinhoff	20	15	Returns from the sector off Gibraltar but without success faced with the Allied landings.

Movements: Nineteen arrivals, fifteen departures, number of U-boats present at the end of the month: nineteen. On November 15, U-66 is the first U-boat to actually be repaired in Kéroman III; this base for thirteen U-boats was totally operational in February 1943. In the arsenal, and in KI and KII, the work on the U-boats seemed to continue normally in spite of the air attack on October 21. Out of fifteen U-boats present in Lorient at the beginning of November, fourteen left on patrols during the month; only U-175 was still in port, and would be leaving on December 1, after six weeks' maintenance. A total of six Type VIIC U-boats from the 6th and 7th Flotillas, normally based in St. Nazaire, arrived in Lorient during the month. About twenty U-boats were repaired in this port by the beginning of November, which corresponded to the number of protected spaces offered by the base. As the bombers of the 8th US Army Air Force carried out five massive air raids on St. Nazaire in November, the general staff preferred to send U-boats returning from patrols to Lorient because their home bases were not safe; especially as the shipyards in Lorient were not being used to their full capacity, with only a dozen Type IX U-boats to look after.

Observations: the Allied landings on November 8, 1942 in Algiers, Oran, and Casablanca in North Africa, which needed the gathering and deployment of over 800 ships, was a total surprise to the Germans. They did not believe that the Allies could gather ships, men and equipment so fast, nor that they would risk landing on a coast defended by numerous French coastal batteries that they believed would remain faithful to the Vichy government. The worst battles took place during two days in Casablanca where the battleship *Jean-Bart* was berthed. Around 1,000 men were lost amongst the French in this port, and 347 in Oran. As the German Navy was heavily outnumbered, only the U-boats could have tried to oppose them. In spite of several warnings given by intelligence officers, the German general staff thought it totally improbable that there would be an Allied landing in North Africa. The few messages sent by real spies announcing the landings were lost under piles of false messages, sent by double agents working for the British Intelligence Service. The German general staff thought there might be some risk of a small-scale landing in Dakar, Senegal, on the west coast of Africa. The group of U-boats sent to the Freetown sector at the end of October, to replace the previous group, was considered sufficiently close to intervene in Dakar if necessary. Therefore, no U-boat operating in the Atlantic was sent to Gibraltar, where most of the Allied ships were obliged to pass, until the beginning of the landing in North Africa. The Allied convoys no longer had to worry about U-boats that had totally abandoned the sector: six U-boats were sent to the Mediterranean in September, and the eight sailing towards Freetown had passed Gibraltar fifteen days earlier. Messages from agents based in Gibraltar signaled the passage of numerous ships towards the Mediterranean on November 4, but the general staff thought they were reinforcement convoys heading for Malta. However, in consequence, a supplementary group of seven U-boats was sent to the Mediterranean to beef up the number to thirty-five boats in this sector; between November 7-11, they passed without any problem as British escort forces were busy with the landings. When the German general staff learned of the landings in North Africa on November 8 at 0630, it immediately sent the fifteen U-boats in the sector between the Cape Verde Islands and England to Gibraltar. U-572 arrived first off the coast of Morocco on November 9, but it couldn't penetrate the Allies' anti-submarine defenses. When the others arrived on November 11, the Allies had already set up airstrips so their planes could intervene off-shore, and had deployed destroyers equipped with radar in a circle around the ports on the west coast of Morocco, Casablanca, and Fedala. Only U-173 managed to sink a transport ship out of Fedala, and damage a fuel tanker and destroyer on November 11. It was also able to damage a second transport off Casablanca before being sunk by destroyers. On November 12, U-130, commanded by Kals, sank three troopships also out of Fedala, in less than five minutes! Such successes were rare off Gibraltar for the fifteen or so U-boats that converged in this sector on November 12. U-515, commanded by Henke, sank a 10,850-ton destroyer/supply ship and damaged a destroyer. On November 14, U-413 sank the 20,107-ton troop/transport ship *Warwick Castle*. Finally, during the night of November 14/15, U-155, commanded by Piening, sank the aircraft carrier HMS *Avenger* escort ship, and a troop transport, and damaged a second troop transport. But the Allies' anti-U-boat defenses were strong, as between November 15-18, two U-boats were sunk, and four others were forced to return to base after being damaged. This forced the U-boat Corps Command general staff to order the U-boats to move farther west, and away from the Allied patrols. They were reinforced by U-boats from the west of Ireland that had enough fuel to join them, but to no avail. During the night of November 19/20, two Allied convoys were attacked, but only one of them lost two ships. At the same time, ten U-boats reported being attacked by planes or destroyers. On November 21, the U-boats were moved farther west; five days later they were positioned off the Azores. Direct consequence of the landings: the Allies could now ensure complete aerial protection of convoys going from Gibraltar to Freetown. In France, the German army invaded the French Free Zone on November 11. Under orders from Admiral de Laborde, the French scuttled their fleet in Toulon on the twenty-seventh just before the Germans arrived.

Meanwhile, the U-boat Corps Command remarked that escort ships for the convoys in the North Atlantic had been reduced. This was because 160 warships had been requisitioned to ensure protection during the landings in North Africa! The U-boats patrolling the North Atlantic, therefore, had little difficulty penetrating the convoys, which was notably the case for the ONS-144 convoy that lost five ships and one corvette between November 15-21. The HX-217 convoy, attacked between November 29 and December 4, lost three cargo ships. For the first time since the beginning of 1942, the tonnage sunk by U-boats in November overtook the 700,000-ton objective fixed by Admiral Dönitz at the beginning of the year, with 123 ships sunk for 768,732 tons. As was the case each month, other commercial ships were damaged by torpedoes launched by U-boats but were able to reach port and be repaired. A total of nineteen ships were damaged in November 1942. The last time this number of ships was sunk was during May-June 1942; but as their average tonnage was inferior, the 700,000-ton objective hadn't been reached.

Allied reactions: The 8th US Army Air Force carried out two daytime raids on Lorient on November 18 and 22, with respectively thirteen and eleven bombers escorted by Spitfires. The port was less damaged than St. Nazaire, which was attacked five times by bombers at least twice as numerous. Covering the last three unprotected pens in Kéroman III was finished the following month. British Coastal Command carried out twelve mine-laying operations with about six Wellingtons each time, each carrying two mines. In Liverpool, on November 19, 1942, Admiral Max Horton, former submariner during the First World War, replaced Admiral Percy Noble as commander-in-chief, Western Approaches. Ironically, with Dönitz as his opponent, two former submariners of the First World War were confronting each other in the Battle of the Atlantic.

Born in Bremen in 1915, Hans-Adolf Schweichel was twenty-seven-years-old when he left Lorient as commander of U-173 on November 1, 1942, for his last patrol. Fifteen days later, he and his crew of fifty-six men were lost at sea while trying to counter the Allied landings in North Africa; their U-boat was hit by depth charges dropped from destroyers. Before that, he succeeded, along with Kals on U-130, in penetrating Port Fedala, Morocco, and launching several torpedoes on ships at anchor. These two commanders were together in 1939 as young officers on the light cruiser *Leipzig*. *UBA*

On November 5, 1942, the 6th Battery, 704th Battalion of the *Flakmarine* based in the north of Lorient at Kerviniac welcomes the crew of U-66; this battalion is the unit's patron. U-66's former commander, Richard Zapp, appointed chief of the 3rd U-Flotilla at La Rochelle, is present for the occasion. *AC*

A wooden U-boat memento in honor of U-66. "In memory of the sponsored submarine" is indicated, as is the date "Christmas 1942." *AC*

During the festive get-together, the men of the anti-aircraft battery invite the U-66 crew to go horse riding. *Anthony Guychard*

On November 6, 1942, U-602, a Type VIIC U-boat belonging to the 7th Flotilla, returns from its first combat patrol against the North Atlantic convoys, but without success. Thirty-one-year-old *Kapitänleutnant* Philipp Schüler, commander of U-602, had already been to Lorient twice in 1940 as Commander Schepke's watch officer aboard U-100, and three times in 1941 as commander aboard U-141, a Type IID coastal U-boat. *UBA*

On November 7, at 1710, U-506 returns from a three-and-a-half-month mission off Freetown. Along with U-156 and U-507, it participated in the rescue of survivors from the *Laconia*. *UBA*

U-506, under commander Erich Würdemann, returns with five pennants representing 28,023 tons of shipping sunk. On the conning tower (note the damaged protection shield) is the U-boat's insignia—the "Water Carrier of Hamburg" whose shipyards, *Deutsche Werft*, built this U-boat—and the 10th Flotilla's insignia. *UBA*

Like U-156, U-506 was attacked by a plane even though it had 198 survivors from *Laconia* on board. It dived to avoid being hit, and surfaced thirty minutes later. The shipwrecked men were then transferred to the French ship *Annamite*. *UBA*

On November 9, 1942, crewmembers of U-176 say goodbye to their friends on the bridge of the former transport sloop *Vaucluse*, renamed A4 pontoon. Several *KMW Lorient* workmen also came to watch the departure of their comrades. The same day in Saint-Nazaire, the first American bombardment in full daylight took place killing 186 people, mainly young apprentices in the shipyards. This attack came to be called the "bombardment of the apprentices." *UBA*

Alfred Eick and Hans Hey, watch officers aboard U-176, check their lists for a last time to make sure that nothing was forgotten before departing on a long patrol along the coast of Brazil. On the conning tower we see the U-boat's insignia; a knight's hand holding a collection of weapons. *UBA*

On the U-boat's fore-bridge, Alfred Eick, U-176's watch officer, gives the last instructions to the crew before their departure at 1630. Eick, born in 1916, would eventually take over command of U-510 on May 22, 1943. *UBA*

At the same time, on November 9, in the wake of a minesweeper, U-514 arrives for the first time in Lorient. It had carried out its first three-month combat patrol in the Antilles, and along the coast of South America, during which time five boats were sunk for 17,354 tons, and a sixth was damaged. *LB*

A welcome ceremony with German beer is organized for the crew of U-514 in the Péristyle barracks. *LB*

At 1700, U-514, with periscope lowered, moves towards the Kéroman I slipway to be put into a dry pen. *LB*

Mail, held in Lorient for the last three months by the 10th Flotilla's administrative service, has been distributed to each crewmember. *LB*

In the St. Joseph Chapel at the center of Péristyle barracks (which had been transformed into a pre-war period museum), a work and maintenance plan is organized for U-514. The U-boat's chief engineer is present, as well as the chief machinists. The ground staff is represented by the 10th Flotilla's engineers as well as *KMW Lorient* engineers. *LB*

The day after his arrival, Hans-Jürgen Auffermann, commander of U-514, submits his patrol report to the commander of the U-boat corps, Admiral Dönitz. *LB*

On the same day, Dönitz awards the German Cross in Gold to *Boostsmaat* Berthold Seidel of U-109. *UBA*

Once they've washed and shaved, U-514's crewmembers dress in their blues for the medal awards ceremony that will take place in *Hundius Kaserne's* courtyard. *LB*

Kapitänleutnant Kuhnke, chief of the 10th Flotilla, pins an Iron Cross 1st Class onto the shirt of one of U-514's crewmembers. *LB*

He then awards several Iron Cross 2nd Class medals. *LB*

The last preparations in front of the mirror before celebrating their arrival in Lorient, healthy and safe after three months at sea, and their recent decorations. *LB*

A party with the *U-Bootsheim* of Kéroman! The submariner in the foreground on the left has kept his recent Iron Cross 2nd Class pinned to his chest (after this soldiers only wore a ribbon). *LB*

On November 12, 1942, UD-5 arrives in Lorient. It is a former Dutch submarine seized by the Germans in May 1940, and made operational in August 1942. *UBA*

UD-5 arrives from its first combat patrol off Freetown with one ship sunk. Its insignia represents a Dutch woman with clogs. This submarine will not make another combat patrol, but will be sent back to Germany as a submarine training boat. We can see its commander, Bruno Mahn, above the insignia. Forty-four-years-old, Mahn is a First World War veteran where he commanded UB-21! He will be replaced in Lorient by his watch officer and will take command of the 8th Flotilla in Germany. *UBA*

Just after UD-5, which has the particular "bathtub" shape, U-436 arrives. It is a Type VIIC belonging to the 6th Flotilla based in Saint-Nazaire. Because of the massive aerial bombardment in Saint-Nazaire on November 9, whose underwater base is already filled with twenty U-boats in maintenance, a total of six U-boats of the 6th and 7th Flotillas where diverted to Lorient in November to have their maintenance performed there. U-436, which already carried out several combat missions in Norway, returns from attacking convoys in the North Atlantic with three ships sunk and two damaged. *UBA*

U-118, a Type XB minelayer, moored in B5 position (the ex-*Martinière*) is ready to leave. The wooden projections affixed along this pontoon ship to camouflage it from the air, seem to have suffered from the latest bombardments. *UBA*

On the bridge of U-118, the containers normally intended to carry mines before anchoring them at sea, will not be filled with mines this time, but probably with fuel or food. The U-boat's next mission will be to supply U-boats to the southwest of the Azores; it will leave on November 12, 1942. A crewmember recalls: "This mission was very calm at that time. The crew spent its time, when there was nothing to supply, swimming, getting a tan on the bridge and fishing! Like most supply boats, in addition to food and fuel, we carried books and magazines as well as cartons of cigarettes! We had the impression at that time that there were only U-boats in that part of the Atlantic! On December 7, however, we thought our last hour had come. After each supply-run, we had to dive to balance the submarine. This time, debris had blocked something; U-118 dived at 55° to 190m! The commander ordered the chief engineer to blow the ballasts and we shot up like a cork! The following day, at the same time as celebrating our U-boat's first birthday, we also celebrated our escape from the deep. We toasted each other with beer and the cook prepared a special meal with a cake." *UBA*

Aerial photo of Kéroman taken by the Americans on November 18, 1942, just before a bombardment by thirteen B-24 bombers. KIII base's roof is nearly finished: out of seven pens, only three roofs are incomplete. *NA*

The bombardment is rather precise. Zone A, where the KIII bloc is under construction, seems to have been badly hit. *NA*

After the bombardment on November 18, the German Navy and the *Todt Organization* bury their dead in the German military section beside the Lorient Cemetery. *LB*

Accompanied by music supplied by the army, the coffins are lowered into the graves. On the left, a sailor, on the right, a member of the *Todt Organization*. A detachment of the Navy fires a salvo to honor the dead. *LB*

Oberleutnant-zur-See Richard von Harpe, a former minesweeper officer, finished his U-boat training in October 1942. He arrived in Lorient in November to take his place as watch officer aboard U-108, which would be leaving on patrol on November 26. While waiting to board, he went to a last party in Lorient that took place at Hans-Ulrich Sendler's place; he was the 2nd Flotilla's doctor and was nicknamed Dr. Bobby.

On November 22, 1942, in the middle of the Atlantic, U-505 transfers its wounded watch officer onto the "milk cow" U-462. Twelve days earlier, in the Antilles to the east of Trinity, U-505, commanded by Peter Zschech, had been attacked on the surface by a Lockheed Hudson based on the island, which caused a lot of damage after dropping four bombs. One of these exploded directly on the 37mm rear gun that was destroyed. The plane that attacked U-505 dropped its bombs from so close that it was caught up in the explosion on the bridge – it crashed with four members of its crew. One of U-505's machinists collected aluminum debris from the plane that he found on the bridge. During the return trip, he used these pieces to make lots of tiny axe insignias that the crewmembers would later wear on their garrison caps as a talisman. Unable to dive, U-505 nevertheless managed to cross the Atlantic on the surface and reached Lorient on December 12, where it stayed for over six months for repairs. According to one of the flotilla's engineers, U-505 was the most badly damaged U-boat to gain Lorient under its own steam! *UBA*

On November 21, 1942, U-513 commanded by Rolf Ruggeberg, left Lorient for the Atlantic. A lucky charm—a teddy bear— sits on the edge of the conning tower, above the submarine's insignia, a Norwegian viking ship. The three MG34 machine guns installed in the conning tower show that enemy aerial presence during the crossing of the Gascony Gulf was omnipresent. Seven days later, the diesel motors were having problems; a supply of new injectors was delivered at sea by U-68. After several days work, one diesel motor was repaired and the U-boat was able to return to Lorient the following month. The cause of the problem was discovered in the shipyard: the aluminum paint used in the oil reservoirs was of bad quality, had detached itself, and had broken the diesel motors' pumps and valves. In mid-January 1943, the crew of U-513 was confronted by aerial attacks; three incendiary bombs even fell on their U-boat! Removing one, a crewmember was wounded and hospitalized; he was replaced by a submariner from UD-3 that had arrived on January 7. During trials at sea, the day before the programmed departure on January 16, the diesel motors had the same problems with paint mixing in with the motor oil and the U-boat had to return to the base on the Scorff. Extremely annoyed, the commander didn't want to wait for a tug to tow them back. The submarine was swept off-course by the current and hit one of Guesdon Bridge's pilings, which damaged the dive rudders! On arrival, seven crewmembers were sent to Rennes to get spare parts, while the submarine was put into dry dock, the dive rudders replaced, and the oil reservoirs emptied and repainted. The new departure date was fixed for Thursday, February 18, but the seven crewmembers sent to Rennes, and expected that morning, didn't arrive until the afternoon, which delayed the departure. With no departures taking place on Fridays, U-513 didn't leave on patrol until Saturday, February 20! *UBA*

On November 22, 1942, U-117, a Type XB minelayer, arrived in Lorient for the first time. It was the third and last submarine of this type to come to this port. For its first combat patrol, mines were placed opposite Reykjavik, Iceland before it carried supplies to U-boats in the Azores. Contrarily to U-118 that had left several days earlier, its mine containers weren't situated in the middle of the fore-bridge, but on each side of the U-boat. Among the people who welcomed it to Lorient was Dr. Heinz Schrenk, who had disembarked from the U-203 on November 6. He recalls: "On Sunday, November 22, U-117 arrived and I saw it for the first time. It's the new U-boat where I am to be affected. I went to greet the commandant and his officers who gave me a warm welcome, and I was immediately integrated into the crew. We will be seven officers aboard! Commander Neumann, who joined the navy in 1924, is an old-school commander. The watch officer has extensively travelled the world and always has a good story to tell. We also have two engineers on board and two junior officers. While the U-117 was in the Lorient shipyards for maintenance, we met up regularly in the Kéroman submariners' mess where, from officers to simple sailors, everything is done to divert us: a canteen, games rooms with cards and billiards, reading rooms, theatre, a cinema showing a different film every night, swimming pool and a bar. In the evenings, we can dance with German girls in a large common room. I remember one particular party where the drink flowed and everyone talked about their time in Danzig and Kiel, but there were no girls to dance with that evening. Max Hauptmann, a sailor affected to the base, decided to call the chief of the female army auxiliaries' hostel (his surname Hauptmann means 'captain' in German). He phoned and said: 'This is Hauptmann Max, I would like to invite the auxiliaries to a dance.' Thinking she was talking to a real captain, the chief immediately agreed to let the girls out. When they arrived, our explanation made them all laugh!" On August 6, 1943, this German doctor, after participating in two supply missions aboard U-117 was transferred to U-66 to treat the commander who had been wounded. A junior officer joined him to take command of the U-boat and take it back to Lorient. The two U-boats were attacked the next day by planes; U-66 escaped but U-117 sank with sixty-two crewmembers aboard. *UBA*

The insignia of U-507 that left Lorient on November 24 for its fourth and last patrol in the direction of Brazil. On January 13, 1943, it was bombed by a plane and sank with all fifty-five crewmembers aboard. *LB*

U-124, commanded by Johann Mohr, left on November 25 for the Antilles, after five months of repair work in Lorient. This U-boat, launched in 1940, had already carried out ten combat patrols. A lot of officers from the *Todt Organization* were present for the departure ceremony. *UBA*

On November 26, the crew of U-108, who had just returned from an unsuccessful mission against the Allied landing fleet along the North African coast, greets the crew of U-509, which was also unsuccessful in this sector, but which had good results around the Canary Islands against the SL-125 convoy. *UBA*

U-509 managed to sink four ships in the SL-125 convoy, and damaged three others. As was often the case in convoy attacks at night, they weren't able to clearly identify their targets, which explains the estimated tonnage on their pennants. On the front of the conning tower, a tarpaulin hides the radar antennas, but its wolf's head insignia and flotilla insignia are clearly visible. *UBA*

Werner Witte, commander of U-509 is congratulated for his patrol. *UBA*

During the welcome party in the Péristyle barracks, Witte chats with Kuhnke, his flotilla chief. *UBA*

Friedrich Steinhoff, commander of U-511, whose submarine returned to Lorient on November 28 after an unsuccessful patrol against the Allied landing fleet along the North African coast. *UBA*

December 1942: A Second Wave of Departures to Cape Town, *the* Seehund *Wolfpack*

Movements: Twenty-one arrivals, seventeen departures, number of U-boats present at the end of the month: twenty-three. The arrival of five U-boats from the 2nd Flotilla as reinforcements, returning from their first patrols, once again increased the number of U-boats present in Lorient to twenty-three by the end of the month, the largest number since the summer of 1940. The length of time spent in the shipyards differed, between six weeks for a normal service, and two months if repairs were necessary. The Type VIIs, normally based in St. Nazaire, and that had been rerouted to Lorient the month before as their base was full and menaced by aerial attacks, left on patrol in December after normal servicing. Three commanders were awarded the Knight's Cross upon their arrival in Lorient; a fourth received the award three days later. This was the first time that such a number of decorations were awarded in Lorient since September 1940! As was often the case, several of the commanders receiving this distinction took posts on land afterward. *Korvettenkapitän* Ernst Kals, former commander of U-130 that arrived on December 30, 1942, was named chief of the 2nd Flotilla in Lorient on January 2, 1943. His predecessor, Viktor Schütze, was sent to Gotenhafen in Germany as commander of Flotilla Training. U-130 and U-155 were among the rare U-boats to obtain high results against Allied landing forces in North Africa. U-183 was the first Type IXC/40 to come to Lorient; this was a slightly improved version of the Type IXC. A

total of eighty-seven models of this new type were put into service by German shipyards. It had a top surface speed of nineteen knots (the IXC had a top speed of 18.3 knots), and its range was increased by 400 miles, which brought its surface autonomy up to 13,850 miles.

Observations: Between December 14-23, U-506, U-509 and U-516 left Lorient for Cape Town where they formed a new wolfpack named *Seehund* in this far-flung sector. They were later joined by U-160 that had left Lorient on January 6, 1943, and by U-182, a long-range Type IX D-2, commanded by Nicolai Clausen, arriving directly from Horten, Norway, which it left on December 9, 1942. These five U-boats arrived south of the Cape Verde Islands in mid-January and continued south. They crossed the equator and were supplied by the "milk cow" U-459 at the end of January 1943, 600 miles south of St. Helena. The following month they were in attack position off Cape Town. The wolfpack before them had caused a lot of damage in this sector in October 1942, with twenty-three ships sunk.

In the North Atlantic, on the night of December 8/9, during a wolfpack attack, a collision while diving caused the loss of a U-boat out of Brest, U-254 commanded by Gilardone. The damage caused by the collision meant that the U-boat could no longer dive and it was later sunk on the surface by an Allied plane. Following this accident, it was decided to limit wolfpack attacks to a

maximum of fifteen U-boats around a convoy at any one time. In December, two convoy attacks took place in the mid-Atlantic but bad weather conditions stopped the U-boats from working as an efficient pack. The ONS-152 convoy only lost one ship. Convoy ON-153, attacked on December 21, lost three ships and an escort ship. Two groups of U-boats then attacked the ONS-154 convoy that lost thirteen ships totaling 67,000 tons. The oldest Allied escort destroyers were replaced by new *River*-type frigates, equipped with 10 cm radar, and *Hedgehog* multiple depth-charge launchers that exploded on contact.

Because of the implementation of convoys off Trinidad, and the coast of French Guiana, the results in the Cape Town sector were disappointing and only two U-boats patrolled there in mid-December. However, several U-boats still had some success in these remote areas; off the west coast of South Africa and to Cape Town, where twenty ships were sunk, or off the coast of Brazil where seven merchant ships were destroyed. The U-boat Corps Command decided to send a new group of Type VII U-boats there in January 1943, along with their own U-boat-supplier. Because of the feeble results obtained from convoy attacks, December 1942 marked a decrease of more than half of the tonnage sunk by U-boats in relation to the preceding month, with sixty-three ships sunk representing 316,508 tons.

U-BOAT	TYPE	FLOT.	COMMANDER	ARRIVAL	DEPART	NOTES
Departures						
UD-5	Holl.	10	Klaus-Dietrich König		21	New commander who had been watch officer aboard UD-5. Departure for Germany and turned into a ship school; sent to Bergen (Norway) the 5/9/45; put back into service in the Dutch Navy. Results: one ship sunk.
U-66	IXC	2	Friedrich Markworth			In maintenance November 11, 1942 – January 6, 1943, after being damaged during an aerial attack on November 10.
U-69	VIIC	7	Ulrich Gräf			In maintenance November 5, 1942 – January 2, 1943.
U-107	IXB	2	Harald Gelhaus			In maintenance November 18, 1942 – January 30, 1943.
U-108	IXB	2	Ralf-Reimar Wolfram			In maintenance November 26, 1942 – January 20, 1943, after being damaged during an aerial attack off Morocco on November 18.
U-117	XB	12	Hans-Werner Neumann	24	23 24	Change of flotilla on 12/1. Returns after a problem with the radar detector discovered four hours after leaving Lorient; departure the next day for a re-supplying operation north of the Azores.
U-125	IXC	2	Ulrich Folkers		9	Departure for the Caribbean.
U-156	IXC	2	Werner Hartenstein			In maintenance November 16, 1942 – January 16, 1943, after being damaged during an aerial attack on September 16.
U-175	IXC	10	Heinrich Bruns		1	Departure for the African coast.
U-203	VIIC	1	Hermann Kottmann		6	Departure to the North Atlantic, returns to Brest; 4/25/43 forced to surface after a two-hour depth charge attack, sunk by gunfire; commander and thirty-eight men taken prisoner, eleven dead. Results: twenty-two ships sunk and four damaged.
U-260	VIIC	6	Hubertus Purkhold		14	Departure for the North Atlantic.
U-436	VIIC	6	Günter Seibicke		17	Departure for the North Atlantic, returns to St. Nazaire then eighth and last patrol; sunk the 5/26/43 by depth charges launched by British ships, no survivors, forty-seven dead. Results: four ships sunk and two damaged.
U-506	IXC	10	Erich Würdemann		14	Departure for Cape Town sector with U-160, U-182, U-509 and U-516 to form the *Seehund* Wolfpack.
U-509	IXC	10	Werner Witte		23	Departure for Cape Town sector, *Seehund* Wolfpack
U-511	IXC	10	Fritz Schneewind		31	New commander, Schneewind, was watch officer aboard U-506 from September 1941 to November 1942.
U-514	IXC	10	Hans-Jürgen Auffermann		9	Departure for the Caribbean.
U-516	IXC	10	Gerhard Wiebe		23	Departure for Cape Town sector, *Seehund* Wolfpack.
U-575	VIIC	7	Günther Heydemann	15	13 17	First departure cancelled because of water in the periscope during test diving. Departure for the North Atlantic; numerous patrols out of St. Nazaire; sunk by aerial attack 3/13/44, eighteen dead, commander and thirty-five men taken prisoner. Results: eight ships and one corvette sunk, one damaged.
U-602	VIIC	7	Philipp Schüler		1	Departure for the Mediterranean; passage through Gibraltar during the night of December 7-8, sank for unknown reason on 4/23/43, no survivors, forty-eight dead. Results: one destroyer sunk, one ship damaged.
U-662	VIIC	7	Wolfgang Hermann		19	Departure; did several patrols out of its base in St. Nazaire. Sunk by a Catalina off the coast of Brazil on 7/21/43. Forty-six dead, three survivors including the commander taken prisoner seventeen days later. The commander was repatriated to Germany in March 1944 because of serious wounds. Results: three ships sunk and one damaged.
Arrivals						
U-522	IXC	2	Herbert Schneider awarded the Knight's Cross during his next patrol on January 16, 1943.	2	31	First time in Lorient; put into service 6/11/42; arrives in Lorient with eleven pennants for its first patrol when it attacked convoys in the North Atlantic; in reality, only four ships were sunk and one damaged. Departure for its second and last patrol in the mid-Atlantic; sunk 2/23/43 by depth charges launched from a ship, no survivors, fifty-one dead. Results: seven ships sunk, three damaged
U-68	IXC	2	Karl-Friedrich Merten awarded Oak Leaves to his Knight's Cross on November 16.	6		First U-boat from the *Eisbär* Wolfpack to return from Cape Town with a result of nine ships sunk for 56,329 tons conforming to exact numbers. Change of commander, Karl-Friedrich Merten named chief of the 24th Training Flotilla in the Baltic Sea.

U-BOAT	TYPE	FLOT.	COMMANDER	ARRIVAL	DEPART	NOTES
U-521	IXC	2	Klaus Bargsten	8		First time in Lorient; put into service 6/3/42. Arrives from its first combat patrol in the Canadian waters and then attacking the SC-107 and ONS-144 convoys, with two ships sunk for 12,351 tons, although the commander's report notes that three other ships representing 16,000 tons had been sunk; Klaus Bargsten was watch officer under Kretschmer aboard U-99 from June to December 1940, and commander of U-563 from March 1941 to March 1942.
U-43	IXA	2	Hans-Joachim Schwantke	9		Returns from a two-and-a-half-month patrol deep in the Gulf of St. Lawrence, Canada, where the ship traffic had stopped. Damaged one fuel tanker spotted on the way home and declared damaging two others.
U-160	IXC	10	Georg Lassen	9		Returns from a two-and-a-half-month patrol in the Caribbean off Trinidad, with eight pennants for eight ships sunk representing 44,865 tons, and one ship damaged.
U-504	IXC	2	Fritz Poske Knight's Cross awarded on his arrival.	11		Second U-boat returning from Cape Town sector, with six ships sunk for 36,156 tons, including on October 17 the first ship sunk by a U-boat in the Indian Ocean. Change of commander, Fritz Poske named chief of the *1. U.L.D. (Unterseebootschule)*, the U-boat School in Pillau.
U-505	IXC	2	Peter Zschech	12		Sank a 7,173-ton cargo ship at the beginning of the patrol in the mid-Atlantic. Arrives in Lorient after a heavy aerial attack, stayed six-and-a-half months in repairs until July 3, 1943. An officer on watch had been badly wounded as well as another crewmember.
U-510	IXC	10	Karl Neitzel	12		Returns from a two-month patrol west of Freetown and off the African coast trying to counter the Allied landings. Only one 5,681-ton cargo ship had been damaged at the beginning of the patrol, the U-boat had been damaged during an aerial attack on November 24.
U-118	XB	10	Werner Czygan	13		Returns from re-supplying seven U-boats in the Azores sector.
U-518	IXC	2	Friedrich Wissmann	15		First time in Lorient; put into service 4/25/42; returns from its first special patrol: disembarking an Abwehr agent in Canada (who was caught the next day). Returns with six pennants; in fact two ships were torpedoed in Conception Bay and on the way home, two others were sunk, and two only damaged.
U-513	IXC	10	Rolf Rüggeberg	18		Returns without success after a month-long patrol. Had to return prematurely because of technical problems that the shipyard in Lorient explained: the aluminum paint used in the fuel tanks had detached itself and mixed with the fuel, which broke the diesel motor's pumps and valves.
U-67	IXC	2	Günther Müller-Stöckheim awarded Knight's Cross in Paris.	21		Returns from patrol of nearly three months in the Caribbean, with four ships sunk for 20,467 tons and two damaged. Part of the crew leave for the Anti-aircraft Artillery School in Mimizan.
U-183	IXC-40	2	Heinrich Schäfer	23		First time in Lorient; put into service 4/1/42; first Type IX C-40 in Lorient. Arrives from its first combat patrol off the Canadian coast: one ship of 6,089 tons was sunk.
U-106	IXB	2	Hermann Rasch awarded Knight's Cross on December 29.	26		Returns from a three-month mission in the Gulf of St. Lawrence where one ship of 2,140 tons was sunk, then in the Azores sector, without success.
U-172	IXC	10	Carl Emmermann awarded Knight's Cross in Paris.	27		Third U-boat to return from a patrol of four months off the Cape: eight ships sunk for 60,048 tons. A very successful mission!
U-519	IXC	2	Günter Eppen	29		First time in Lorient; put into service 5/7/42. Arrives from its first combat patrol, out of Kiel, off the African coast to try to counter the Allied landings, without success.
U-103	IXB	2	Gustav-Adolf Janssen	29		Returns from a patrol off the African coast: two ships were sunk, and a third damaged.
U-155	IXC	10	Adolf Piening	30		Returns from attacking Allied ships covering the landings in North Africa, sank the 13,785-ton escort aircraft carrier HMS *Avenger*, the 11,279-ton British troop ship *Ettrick*, an 8,456-ton Dutch cargo ship, and damaged another ship transporting materiel.
U-130	IXC	2	Ernst Kals	30		Managed to penetrate Fedala Port, Morocco, on November 12 and sink three troop ships in the harbor representing 34,407 tons. Change of command, Kals named chief of the 2nd Flotilla on January 2, 1943.

Allied reactions: The 8th US Army Air Force only carried out one attack on Lorient on December 30, 1942, but with large numbers of aircraft: forty B-17 bombers, escorted by nine Spitfire squadrons from Fighter Command, and one squadron of Typhoons. Eighty tons of bombs were dropped over the submarine bases in Kéroman. Around the bunkers that remained intact, numerous wooden huts used by the Todt Organization's sub-contractors were destroyed. Several bombers were damaged during the raid and three were lost. British fighters claimed the destruction of nine German Fw 190s. Meanwhile, four mine-laying operations were carried out by fourteen planes.

On December 1, 1942, U-602, commanded by Philipp Schüler, left Lorient for the last time, heading for the Mediterranean. After a call at La Spezia, and later Toulon, it sank for an unspecified reason with its crew of forty-eight on April 23, 1943. *UBA*

U-522 arrives in Lorient for the first time on December 2, with eleven pennants for its first patrol attacking convoys in the North Atlantic. Actually, it only sank four ships and damaged another. In the background on the right: the ex-*Martinière* which has the numbers B5 and B6 painted on its' sides, indicating the berthing places for submarines. *UBA*

U-522's crew come ashore after a patrol that lasted nearly two months. The submarine's emblem, painted on the conning tower, represents a diver astride a broom. The crewmembers also have a miniature of this insignia on their garrison caps. *UBA*

Herbert Schneider, the commander of U-522, shakes hands with *General Ritter* von Epp. Behind the general is Viktor Schütze, chief of the 2nd Flotilla and in the center is *Kapitänleutnant (Ing.)* Ewald Engler, U-522's chief engineer. On his sleeve, above his rank stripes, he has the engineer corps' insignia—a cogwheel—instead of the star that was worn by the navigation crew. *UBA*

This photo of Herbert Schneider is edited from a studio photo taken in Lorient in December 1942. In reality, he was awarded the Knight's Cross on January 16, 1943, while he was in the Azores sector, following a radio report of his combat successes. However, he never returned from this mission to receive the medal; U-522 sank with all hands on February 23, after being hit by depth charges from a British sloop. *UBA*

On December 6, U-68 is the first *Eisbär* Wolfpack U-boat to return from the Cape with a realistic total of nine ships sunk for 56,329 tons. Its commander, Karl-Friedrich Merten, is surrounded by Schütze, chief of the 2nd Flotilla (on his left), Kuhnke, chief of the 10th Flotilla (behind him on the right) and Engler, the 2nd Flotilla's chief engineer (on his right). *UBA*

On December 6, Lorient's ground personnel wish good luck to Hermann Kottmann, nicknamed "Zirkus (Circus) Kottmann," commander of U-203. His U-boat, normally based in Brest, left Lorient for the last time for the North Atlantic. *UBA*

Commander Karl-Friedrich Merten, of U-68, was the 147th German soldier to be decorated with the Oak Leaves to the Knight's Cross, awarded on November 16. He later took up a post on land as chief of a training flotilla in the Baltic Sea. Like a lot of commanders, Merten often took pity on the crew of the ships he sank; the survivors from the British cargo ship *City of Cairo*, sunk on November 6, 1942, remembered that he called out: "Goodnight! Sorry for sinking you!" *UBA*

As well as the coat-of-arms of Essen, its patron town, a new insignia adorns the bottom of U-203's conning tower—the Olympic rings. This was to remind everyone that Kottmann, the new commander, graduated in 1936 the same year as the Olympic Games in Berlin. After its stay in Lorient, this U-boat will continue its patrols from its home port of Brest. *Bernd Siepert*

On December 9, U-125 commanded by Ulrich-Johann Folkers, is ready to leave for the Caribbean. On the Scorff, the *Kriegsmarine* officers invite an army officer and a Luftwaffe officer to visit the U-boat. On the right, at the end of the railroad bridge, are pens 5 and 7. A few months later, U-125 met a terrible end. On May 6, 1943, at 0300 in the North Atlantic, it was rammed by the destroyer HMS *Oribi*, an escort of the ONS-5 convoy. Although badly damaged, it managed to escape and sent a radio message to the *BdU* asking for nearby U-boats to pick up crewmembers because it had to scuttle the boat. Four submarines searched in vain until the morning of May 7. Actually, it was spotted on the surface by corvette HMS *Snowflake* that had turned on its spotlight, and found the damaged U-boat on the surface. The ship tried to ram it but the U-boat evaded and the crew leapt from the boat that was then scuttled by explosives. Another corvette, the HMS *Sunflower* arrived on the scene, but its radio request to the escort captain aboard the HMS *Tay* to pick up the survivors received the reply: "Not approved to pick up survivors." The two corvettes left the area, abandoning U-125's fifty-four crewmembers who were never found. *UBA*

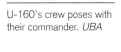

U-160's crew poses with their commander. *UBA*

On December 9, U-160 returns from a two-and-a-half-month patrol in the Caribbean off Trinidad. Commander Georg Lassen is shown wearing the Knight's Cross, awarded in Lorient during his last visit in August. *UBA*

December 9: in the foreground the eight pennants representing 44,865 tons of ships sunk by U-160. In the background, U-43 arrives from the Gulf of St. Lawrence, Canada, with three pennants. *LB*

On the A3 pontoon, Georg Lassen, commander of U-160, chats with Hans-Joachim Schwantke, commander of U-43. *UBA*

December 10, 1942, in Lorient: the day after his arrival, Rudolf Schreiber, the U-160's radioman wrote: "Half of the crew was immediately on leave, the rest waited for their turn. I took the train in Lorient and travelled during the night via Paris, and arrived in the Sarre region of Germany early in the morning. Then the train had to stop in a tunnel because of an air raid. I got off at Marburg to see my pen pal who wrote to me regularly. She was a nurse working in a hospital. I spent the night alone in a hotel and we met up the next day for a long walk. It was our fate: we fell in love. I took a train to Königsberg where my mother, my sister and her son lived. I was proud to show off the medals I'd been awarded in Lorient: the submariners' decoration and the Iron Cross 2nd Class. On my way back I stopped off at Marburg. That was how all my future leaves were spent. We spent Christmas with the family, and the New Year with the flotilla, which was much more fun. When I came back to Lorient our U-boat was ready; the workmen in the shipyards work very well. In a few days we were ready to leave on patrol." *Schreiber/UBA*

On his third patrol, Georg Lassen, commander of U-160, declared sinking nine ships for 54,868 tons. Kuhnke, the flotilla's chief awards the Iron Cross 2nd Class to ten crewmembers. *UBA*

Once the Iron Cross 2nd Class are awarded, four crewmembers, who have already been decorated with this medal, are awarded the Iron Cross 1st Class, notably *Obersteuermann* Gerhard Zirpel. *UBA*

Im Namen des Führers
und Obersten Befehlshabers
der Wehrmacht

verleihe ich

dem

Funkobergefreiten

Rudolf Schneider

das

Eiserne Kreuz 2.Klasse

Befehlsstelle ,den 12. Dezember 1942

Admiral und
Befehlshaber der Unterseeboote
(Dienstgrad und Dienststellung)

Document for the Iron Cross 2nd Class, awarded to Rudolf Schreiber of U-160 in Lorient, on December 12, 1942. *Schreiber/UBA*

On December 11, 1942: U-504 is the second U-boat to return from the Cape with six ships sunk for a total of 36,156 tons (on October 17, the first ship sunk by a U-boat in the Indian Ocean). *UBA*

Fritz Poske, commander of U-504, receives the Knight's Cross when in arrives in Lorient, which was awarded to him on November 6, 1942. Having had a large experience as a captain aboard surface ships since joining the German Navy in 1923, he was one of the few U-boat commanders who had been given the command of a submarine without having been a watch officer beforehand, nor having attended an officers training course. *Charita*

December 15, 1942: U-518 approaches Lorient; on the left is Paul Weidlich, the chief engineer and *Oberleutnant-zur-See* Gerhard Seehausen, the watch officer. The two horizontal rows of dipoles arranged in a half-circle on the front of the conning tower are the *FuMo 29* radar antennas. *UBA*

Once berthed on the Scorff, U-518's crew poses around their commander, Friedrich Wissman. *UBA*

U-518's six pennants when it arrived in Lorient on December 15; at the top, the 10,172-ton American petrol tanker *Caddo*, torpedoed on November 23. Only three other ships were really sunk, and two more were damaged. *UBA*

A small reception in the Péristyle barracks during which U-518's crew open their mail that has been held at the flotilla base during their three month patrol. *UBA*

Unfired torpedoes are unloaded from U-518 through the rear hatchway. *UBA*

Unloading a torpedo through the fore-bridge hatchway. *UBA*

Document for the Knight's Cross awarded to Werner Henke. Even though his two missions didn't push over the 100,000-ton mark, the decoration was awarded for his combativeness in a particularly difficult zone. *UBA*

On December 17, 1942, a homemade "large model" Knight's Cross is awarded to Commander Werner Henke, of U-515, to tide him over until the real one is awarded in Lorient on January 6, 1943. He sank several ships off Gibraltar: the 10,850-ton supply ship HMS *Hecla* on November 12, 1942, and the 18,713-ton troop ship *Ceramic* on December 6. *LB*

On the same day, Commander Hans-Ludwig Witt of U-129 also received a "small model" homemade Knight's Cross, made from an Iron Cross, 2nd Class. *Charita*

On December 23, 1942, Gerhard Wiebe, commander of U-516, in a gray leather uniform, leaves for the Cape sector to join the *Seehund* Wolfpack. Müller-Stöckheim, commander of U-67, comes to the outside of the small base on the Scorff to see him off. *UBA*

Admiral Matthaie, chief of the war shipyard in Lorient, is part of a committee on the quay of the base on the Scorff come to see U-516 off. *UBA*

On December 19, 1942, U-662 left Lorient for the last time. During the interrogation of the survivors, after it had been sunk in July 1943, the Americans noted that the morale among the crewmembers wasn't high; this seems to have been caused by Commander Wolfgang Hermann, judged as being too prudent. He was replaced in February 1943. The survivors said that they had often talked on board about the possibility of Germany losing the war and that they would probably be sunk quite soon. *UBA*

U-516 leaves the base on the Scorff with a small Christmas tree in the antenna! *UBA*

December 24, 1942: In his personal cabin, Gerhard Wiebe, commander of U-516, celebrates Christmas with Dr, Ernst Frenzel, the U-boat's doctor. *UBA*

In the *U-Boots-Heim* at Kéroman, Speer chats with the two flotilla chiefs; in the background: Commander Hermann Rasch of U-106. *UBA*

On December 26, 1942, Albert Speer, Minister of Armaments and War Production, arrives in Lorient. With Schültze, the chief of the 2nd Flotilla, he welcomes U-106 returning from a patrol. *Charita*

After their three-month mission, U-106's crew is invited to a Christmas dinner in the *U-Boots-Heim*; Speer is also present. *UBA*

Opposite Speer is Hermann Rasch, commander of U-106, who will be awarded the Knight's Cross three days later. *UBA*

On December 27, 1942, U-172 arrives in Lorient. It is the third submarine to return after a rather successful four-month patrol off the Cape, sinking eight ships for a total of 60,048 tons. Commander Emmermann salutes the welcome committee. The silhouette of the American cargo ship *Alaskan* has been painted on the gun barrel; this ship was torpedoed and finally sunk by artillery fire on November 28. This was to be the last time U-172 used its gun to sink a ship, because of omnipresent enemy aircraft. There was only one survivor from the British cargo ship *Benlomond*, sunk by the U-boat five days earlier: the Second Stewart Poon Lim, of Chinese origin, who was alone aboard a lifeboat for 133 days before being picked up ten miles from the Brazilian coast! *UBA*

Commander Emmerman was awarded the Knight's Cross a month earlier while he was on mission, following his radio report of tonnage sunk. He was decorated in Paris by Dönitz in person, along with Commander Müller-Stockheim who had arrived a week earlier. He gives a speech to his crewmembers, some of who have been awarded the Iron Cross. *UBA*

On December 29, 1942, U-130 arrives. This U-boat managed to penetrate Fedala Port, Morocco, on November 12, and sank three American troop transport ships in the harbor, representing 34,407 tons. Its commander, Ernst Kals, became the chief of the 2nd Flotilla on January 2, 1943. *UBA*

Commander Hermann Rasch of U-106, with his Knight's Cross, awarded on December 29, 1942. *Charita*

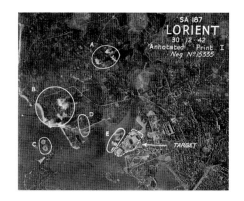

On December 30, 1942, the 8th US Army Air Force carried out an air raid on Kéroman with forty B-17s that dropped eighty tons of bombs in the direction of the U-boat bases. *NA*

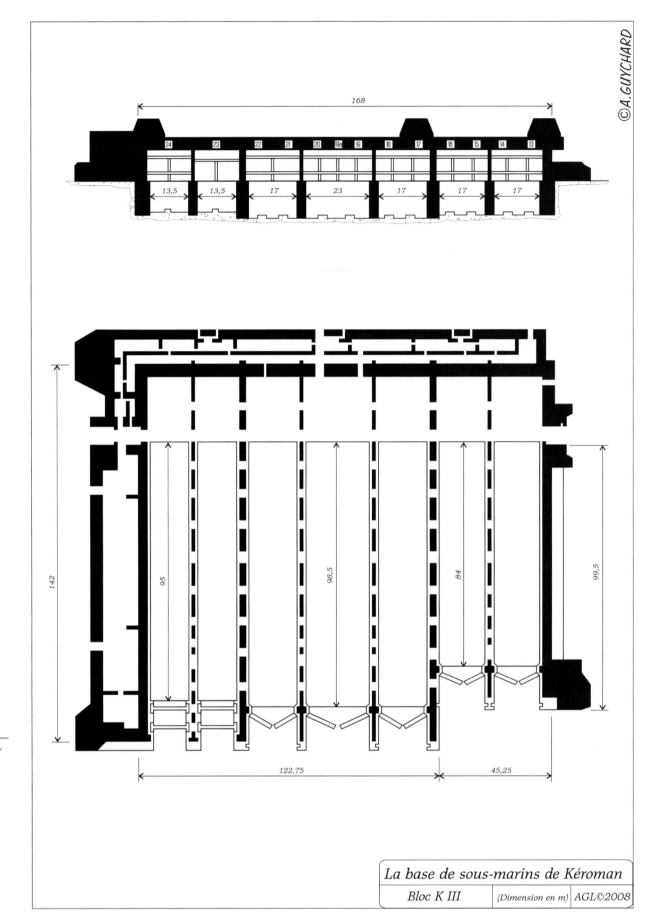

168

| 24 | 23 | 22 | 21 | 20 | 19b | 19 | 18 | 17 | 16 | 15 | 14 | 13 |

13,5 13,5 17 23 17 17 17

142

95 98,5 84 99,5

122,75 45,25

Plan of Kéroman III. *Drawing by Anthony Guychard.*

©A.GUYCHARD

La base de sous-marins de Kéroman

Bloc K III | *(Dimension en m)* | AGL©2008

Summing up the Battle of the Atlantic in 1942

During 1942, the Allies lost 1,664 ships totaling nearly 7.8-million tons, which almost represented the accumulated tonnage lost in 1940 and 1941. The U-boat's role, which until the end of the preceding year had been responsible for half of the ships lost, increased considerably during 1942 with 1,154 ships sunk for 5,873,393 tons. However, the U-boat Corps Command was not to know that during the same year, the American shipyards alone had built eight million tons thanks to Liberty Ships that were mass-produced. It couldn't have imagined either that after Christmas the Allies would be able to decode the German submarine radio messages. Also, eighty-six German U-boats were sunk during the year, most of them during the second half of the year. Admiral Dönitz found this a bad omen for the coming year. However, he had nearly 300 U-boats at his disposal, of which two-thirds were operational; a substantial asset.

FIRST HALF OF 1943:
A TURNAROUND IN
THE BATTLE OF THE ATLANTIC

January 1943: Massive Air Raids on Lorient

Movements: Thirteen arrivals, fourteen departures, number of U-boats present at the end of the month: twenty-two. The results of numerous U-boats, returning from three or four month-long patrols in remote seas, were still very encouraging. Five commanders were awarded the Knight's Cross on their arrival or a few days later—a record in Lorient! U-159 returned with eleven ships sunk for 63,740 tons, which represented the fourth most successful mission of the war. In January 1943, the base shipyards began equipping the U-boats with a supplementary rear platform for two, new double-barrel anti-aircraft guns and a 3.7 cm gun; most of the U-boats were equipped by April. Adding this equipment meant a lot of extra work for *Ressort III* in charge of the shipyards, and increased their stay in the ports by about seventy-five days. While work was carried out, part of the crew were sent on a five-day anti-aircraft weapons courses at the *Flak* school in Mimizan on the Basque coast; they took the train in Lorient direction Bordeaux where they changed trains for Mimizan. Each session comprised three classes of eight to ten submariners from different bases on Biscay Bay. Day one: description, assembly and dismantling *2cm Flak 30* and *Flak 38* anti-aircraft guns. Day two: in the morning, firing three twenty round chargers at a glider towed by a plane at 200 to 400 meters, and at a distance of 1,000 to 1,500 meters, and the cleaning of the gun; in the afternoon, firing twenty rounds of illumination shells from left to right. Day three: theory in the morning; in the afternoon, firing fifty rounds at a glider simulating a curve and an attack, and then cleaning the gun. Day four: in the morning firing sixty rounds at a glider simulating side, frontal and rear attacks; in the afternoon firing eighty rounds in the same conditions. Day five: learning the MG15 in the morning; in the afternoon firing 150 rounds at a glider at a distance of 1,500 meters. In the twilight of the evening, firing twenty rounds at a glider equipped with a searchlight, and then twenty rounds at a glider lit up by a spotlight on land. In the event of an aerial attack, the lookout officer in the conning tower had to decide whether to dive or confront the plane. If the plane was spotted at more than 3,000 meters, he would give the order to crash dive; if the plane was spotted nearer than this, it meant a surprise attack and the crew had to use the anti-aircraft guns on it.

Observations: Of the 209 operational U-boats at the beginning of 1943, twenty-four were in the Mediterranean, and twenty-one in the North Sea, which left 164 for the Atlantic. In spite of the three wolfpacks stretched out on each side of the North Atlantic, few convoys were spotted during the month. The atrocious weather conditions didn't help the U-boats in their hunt. But above all, since Christmas 1942, their radio messages were once again being decoded by the British. This permitted the Allies to completely reroute their convoys that had been following the same sealanes for over six months. As the U-boat Corps Command general staff didn't want to believe in the possibility of their messages being decoded, an in-depth security investigation was carried out on the officers in the concerned departments. Obviously, this yielded negative results, which caused Dönitz to say jokingly to his faithful chief of the general staff *Konteradmiral* Godt: "Now it can only be either you or me!" On January 19, the German U-boat wolfpacks moved towards Greenland, farther in the north, but without any significant success. Farther south, between the Azores and the Canaries, the *Delphin* Wolfpack was a little luckier when it unexpectedly stumbled on the TM-1 convoy of fuel tankers out of the Caribbean for Gibraltar, with only a light escort. Between January 3 and 11, the *Delphin* Wolfpack claimed fifteen fuel tankers sunk (for a convoy that only had nine tankers in all!). In reality, seven tankers were sunk, as sometimes up to five torpedoes were necessary to sink one of these huge ships! This attack deprived the Allied armies in North Africa of 100,000 tons of fuel. In mid-January, a second group of five U-boats, the *Rochen* Wolfpack, was formed between the Canaries and the coast of Morocco. During the month of January, six

U-BOAT	TYPE	FLOT.	COMMANDER	ARRIVAL	DEPART	NOTES
Departures						
UD-3	Holl.	10	Hermann Rigele		10	Departure for the last time, turned into ship school in Germany; relegated 10/13/43 after being damaged in a bombardment on Kiel; scuttled the 5/3/45.
U-67	IXC	2	Günther Müller-Stöckheim			In maintenance December 21, 1942 – March 3, 1943.
U-68	IXC	2	Albert Lauzemis		3	Departure for the Caribbean.
U-103	IXB	2	Gustav-Adolf Janssen		7	Departure for west of Gibraltar, with five other U-boats, in the fear of an Allied landing in Portugal.
U-106	IXB	2	Hermann Rasch		17	Departure for the Azores sector.
U-126	IXC	2	Ernst Bauer			In maintenance January 7 – March 20, 1943. Change of commander, Ernst Bauer becomes an instruction officer then chief of the 27th Training Flotilla in the Baltic Sea.
U-128	IXC	2	Hermann Steinert			New commander. In maintenance January 15 – April 6, 1943.
U-129	IXC	2	Hans-Ludwig Witt			In maintenance January 6 – March 11, 1943.
U-130	IXC	2	Siegfried Keller		28	Departure for its sixth and last patrol, in the Azores; sunk 3/13/43 by depth charges launched by a destroyer, no survivors, fifty-three dead. Results: twenty-five ships sunk and one damaged.
U-154	IXC	2	Oskar Kusch			In maintenance January 7 – March 20, 1943. New commander, Kusch was watch officer on U-103.
U-155	IXC	10	Adolf Piening		8	Departure for Florida and the Gulf of Mexico.
U-159	IXC	10	Helmut Witte			In maintenance January 5 – March 4, 1943.
U-161	IXC	2	Albrecht Achilles			In maintenance January 9 – March 13, 1943.
U-163	IXC	10	Kurt Engelmann			In maintenance January 6 – March 10, 1943.
U-172	IXC	10	Carl Emmermann		21	Departure for the Azores sector.
U-174	IXC	10	Ulrich Thilo			In maintenance January 9 – March 18, 1943. Change of commander. Ulrich Thilo name unit chief at the Flotilla School for torpedomen.
U-185	IXC-40	10	August Maus		8	Departure for its second patrol in the Antilles, returns to Bordeaux; then its third and last patrol off the coast of Brazil; part of the crew from the damaged and then scuttled U-604 were taken on board; but U-185 was sunk 8/24/43 by depth charges launched by planes, twenty-nine dead, thirty-six survivors including some from U-604.
U-505	IXC	2	Peter Zschech			Being repaired for over six months from December 12, 1942, to July 1, 1943.
U-508	IXC	10	Georg Staats		22	Departure for the Azores.
U-513	IXC	10	Rolf Rüggeberg		20	Departure for the Azores.
U-515	IXC	10	Werner Henke		21	Departure for the Azores.
U-524	IXC	10	Walter Freiherr von Steinaecker			In maintenance January 9 – March 3, 1943.
Arrivals						
U-123	IXB	2	Horst von Schroeter	6		Returns from the Azores and the North Atlantic where it took part in a wolfpack attack on convoys, with one ship of 3,385 tons sunk, and another damaged. New commander affected in Kiel: Horst von Schroeter knew this U-boat very well as he was its former watch officer.
U-117	XB	12	Hans-Werner Neumann	7		Returns from a re-supplying operation for ten U-boats in the Azores sector.
U-514	IXC	10	Hans-Jürgen Auffermann	12		Returns from a mission in the Caribbean, and then in the Azores with the *Delphin* Wolfpack, with one ship of 7,177 tons sunk and one damaged.
U-124	IXB	2	Johann Mohr awarded Oak Leaves to his Knight's Cross on January 13.	13		Returns from a patrol of nearly three months off the Antilles and the Gulf of Guinea with five ships sunk for 28,282 tons. Admiral Dönitz will do everything he can to convince its commander, the most decorated in the Flotilla, to take a post on land, but Mohr only wants to leave on another patrol.
U-105	IXB	2	Jürgen Nissen	14		Returns from a patrol of nearly three months in the Caribbean, with four ships sunk for 19,844 tons.

U-BOAT	TYPE	FLOT.	COMMANDER	ARRIVAL	DEPART	NOTES
U-176	IXC	10	Reiner Dierksen	18		Returns from a three-month patrol in the mid-Atlantic, between the Cape Verde Islands and the coast of Brazil, with three ships sunk for 13,432 tons, including the Dutch cargo ship *Polydorus* chased for fifty hours; a record for the longest chase!
U-125	IXC	2	Ulrich Folkers	19		Returns empty-handed from a patrol of more than two months west of the Canaries and the Azores as a part of the *Delphin* Wolfpack.
U-108	IXB	2	Ralf-Reimar Wolfram	24		Returns without success from the *Delphin* Wolfpack west of the Canaries, damaged during an aerial attack by a Catalina that dropped four depth charges on February 10.
U-175	IXC	10	Heinrich Bruns	24		Returns from a patrol of nearly three months off Freetown and the Ivory Coast where one ship of 7,177 tons was sunk.

Type IX U-boats hunted in the remote sectors of the Caribbean and along the coast of Brazil, but the results were disappointing, except for U-124, commanded by Johann Mohr, which sank four American cargo ships for a total of 23,590 tons on January 9. During the month of January 1943, the U-boats only sank forty-five ships for a total of 215,496 tons, a third less than the preceding month, which had already been low. Among these losses, only ten ships in convoys were sunk! On January 30, Karl Dönitz was promoted to the rank of *Grossadmiral* and also became the commander-in-chief of the Kriegsmarine, replacing Erich Raeder. He also remained commander-in-chief of the U-boat corps. This nomination allowed him to insist that the U-boat corps, in which he had always believed, was the only real threat against the Allied fleet. The Allies also thought along the same lines. Therefore, during the conference at Casablanca where Roosevelt, Churchill, and De Gaulle met between January 14-24, top priority was given to the Battle of the Atlantic. The elimination of the German U-boat threat was the first step before any idea of a landing in France could be considered.

Lorient, January 6: An extra passenger was taken discreetly aboard U-66, which was ready to depart. It was a special mission: the U-boat was to take French agent Jean-Marie Lallart, recruited by the Abwehr and trained in sabotage techniques, to the north coast of Mauritania. He was to disembark at Cap Blanc, just below the Moroccan border. Mauritania was controlled by the *Forces Françaises Libres*. U-66 reached its destination on January 20 and found a small bay at 1600. It stopped at a depth of twenty meters waiting for nightfall. At 2043, it surfaced; the coast was only 1.5 miles away. A dinghy was put in the water with the spy and two crewmembers, *Bootsmaat* Wagner, and *Matr.Ob.Gef.* Daschkey. It was a moonlit night. In the conning tower, the lookouts watched their progress to the beach; the mission seemed to be going well. But as soon as the three men went ashore, the lookouts could no longer see them. They then saw the French agent climbing over the dune and coming back to the beach ten minutes later. Meanwhile, conditions in the water had changed; a swell had risen up and large waves seemed be keeping the two submariners from leaving the beach. At 0700 the next morning, January 21, without any sign of life on the beach, Commander Markworth decided to dive to periscope depth, but there was nothing to see. At 1100, the U-boat surfaced, but still there was no sign, nor at 1649 or later at 2030, except for a plane the second time it surfaced, forcing it to crash dive. On January 22, at 0012, U-66 resurfaced and sailed along the coast until 0813 in the morning. A last attempt to search on the surface from 1343 to 1347, produced no results, there was no trace of the three men. U-66 headed out to sea, where, on January 30, they received a radio message saying that the three men had been taken prisoner by the *Forces Françaises Libres*. In fact, after a two-and-a-half-day march across the desert, Lallart gave himself up at a French police station. From there he was transferred to Dakar where the assistant of the Chief Executive Officer of Security in French West Africa interrogated him. He recalls: "One day a Frenchman was delivered to us; we were told that he'd been dropped off in Mauritania by a German U-boat. According to him, he was waiting for orders. Finally, he told us that he'd been a volunteer for this mission, but that all he had really wanted to do was to find a way to get out of France and reach sub-Saharan Africa. He gave us details about his mission, which was vague and poorly prepared, and we thought we were dealing with a joker. We kept him for a while, then he was put under house arrest and we gave him work in a large Import-Export company in FWA." The "amateur" spy was entrusted to the British for a month because they wanted to learn more about Abwehr methods. His file as a German agent, preserved in the archives under the reference KV 2/1462, allows us to reconstitute this poorly prepared mission: "Lallart was a Frenchman recruited by the Abwehr to act as a sabotage agent in French West Africa. Landed by small boat from a U-boat in French West Africa, Lallart and the two submariners (who were meant to return to the U-boat) immediately abandoned their mission, and undertook instead a 'Boys' Own Paper' style march across the desert to Port Etienne (in present day Mauritania) in order to surrender to the French authorities. This file chiefly concerns Lallart's subsequent interrogation by the British, who were interested in the Abwehr's training and tactics. It contains reports of his arrest, and a French interrogation report with British assessment. The French subsequently handed Lallart over to the British for one month's questioning, and he was interrogated at Camp 020 before being returned to French North Africa in May 1943. Lallart, a former sculptor, produced line-drawing caricatures of his contacts, which are on file, as well as sketch maps of central Munster, Berlin, Paris and Olfen and a cut-away diagram of the U-boat that dropped him in West Africa, U-66. The file includes descriptions of his two-and-a-half-day trek across the desert. Lallart's mission is not known—his claim was that he was to receive his sealed orders from an Arab reception party, so he never knew himself."

Allied reactions: Since February 1941, a total of thirty pens had been built in Lorient for the U-boats, sheltering them from Allied bombs (*Dom Bunker* 1, KI 5, KII 7, Scorff 4 and KIII 13). These gigantic building sites, while being vulnerable, weren't especially targeted by Allied bombing raids. This wasn't the case for the 6th U-boat base, which should have been built in Marseille, France. Targeted during a massive raid on December 2, 1943, building was totally interrupted. However, in England on January 14, 1943, following the huge number of ships sunk in the Atlantic by the German submarines, the British War Cabinet sent a clear directive to Air Marshal Harris, chief of Bomber Command: "A decision has been accordingly taken to submit the following bases to a maximum of night attacks under your command, with the aim of effectively devastating all the territory where the U-boats are to be found, their maintenance facilities and their services: energy, water, lights, communications and other resources that their operations depend upon." The first base on the list was Lorient. The same evening, during the night of January 14/15, 1943, the 317th air raid sounded in the town. The RAF sent 128 bombers, ninety-nine of which carried out the mission by dropping 73.6-tons of explosive bombs and above all 83,548 incendiary bombs. The German commander of Lorient Port made a report about the damage sustained by this massive attack: "Minesweeper M 83 in basin 1 damaged by a large bomb putting two boilers out of use; blockade runner 134 galley damaged by incendiary bombs; platform A4 Vaucluse sunk, five equipment transport barges sunk; tugs Saint-Herblain, Ingrid and Helga damaged; finally U-118 slightly damaged. Buildings: former aviation hall in Lanester used by Ressort V—port constructions destroyed; several Port Company guard posts destroyed or damaged; numerous garages belonging to the 4/14 MKA—Navy Transport Company destroyed; one truck burnt and others damaged; buildings used by Transport Unit NSKK destroyed; the hut used by the general staff of the 10th U-Flotilla badly damaged; a large part of the buildings in *Saltzwedel Kaserne* used for the 2nd U-Flotilla unusable. In the *Flamenlager* barrack used by the Todt Organization eleven huts either partially or completely destroyed by fire; a room used by the leisure organization KdF—Kraft durch Freude (Strength through Joy) destroyed by an explosive bomb; in Seydlitz barracks a stone building destroyed by an explosive bomb and two huts burnt. Human losses: for the navy two dead and sixteen wounded; for the army three dead and four wounded, for the air force one wounded; for the TO fifteen dead (thirteen foreign) and thirteen wounded." In the town center, 120 houses were destroyed. As for the U-boats, only U-108, due to leave on January 15, was damaged; its departure was delayed by five days, after foodstuffs and equipment arrived by truck from Brest. The British returned during the evening of January 15. Out

of the 154 planes planned, 132 carried out the mission, dropping 140.4-tons of bombs and 87,163 incendiary bombs; 400 fires started in the town and 800 buildings were hit. Homeless civilians were evacuated. On January 20, the Director of the *Kriegsmarinewerft Lorient* posted a notice intended for the French workers in *KMW* ordering them to restart work without delay. The notice went on to say that they would be warned in advance in the event of an air raid and that they could use the German shelters; a bonus representing two weeks' pay would be awarded. Finally, the *KMW* would see to their accommodation, their food, and their transport to the shipyards. The Americans took the relay in broad daylight operations on January 23 when thirty-six B-17s dropped ninety tons of bombs. Lorient's suffering was far from over. On the night of January 23/24, out of 100 bombers sent by the RAF, forty-seven

dropped their bombs on the town bringing the number of houses uninhabitable to 1,300. Two-thirds of the population had fled the town. Once again, in the night of January 26/27, out of 168 planes planned, a total of 136 dropped eighty tons of bombs and 56,687 incendiary bombs. During this attack, Hennebont, at a distance of seven miles, was also badly hit. January ended with a sixth massive bombardment by the British on the night of 29/30, during which 130 bombers were sent to drop 50.7-tons of bombs. In addition to the firefighting corps, two French services did their best during the bombardments: the 3rd Company of *marins-pompiers* commanded by Crew Officer Lusseaux in charge of protecting the arsenal, and the Maritime Health Service. Minelaying operations in the harbor continued with thirty-three planes each dropping two mines.

U-159 arrives in Lorient on January 5, 1943, returning from a four and a half-month patrol off the Cape, the last of the *Eisbär* Wolfpacks. Its commander, Helmut Witte, was awarded the Knight's Cross on October 22, 1942, following his successes in this sector. With eleven boats sunk for 63,740 tons, his patrol reached a fourth place rank of most successful patrols. On November 13, 1942, he voluntarily disobeyed the order to deprive the Allies of qualified personnel by capturing the captain of the ship he had just sunk: This was Captain Constantin Flink of the American six-masted ship *Star of Scotland*, sunk by gunfire. The captain boarded the U-boat and talked with Witte; he explained that without him, the only navigator aboard the lifeboat, the survivors would die because they were 1,200 miles from the coast. Commander Witte explained that his orders were to take him prisoner, but that he would let him leave provided that he promised never to fight against Germany again; a sextant was handed over and the two men promised to write to each other after the war. When their captain returned to the lifeboat, the survivors gave out three cheers. Three weeks later, the radio operator of U-159 intercepted a message saying that the boat had arrived on the African coast. After the war, the two men became firm friends until the end of their lives. *UBA*

U-126's fifth combat patrol lasted for nearly three and a half months. After their arrival in Lorient on January 7, crewmembers Fritz Eidling and Ewald Weiss went to a photographer in Lorient to be immortalized with their beards – the pride of all submariners! *UBA*

Born in March 1917, Commander Walter *Freiherr* von Steinaecker of U-524, was twenty-five-years-old when he arrived in Lorient on January 9, 1943. He had already been to the port several times in 1941-42 as the watch officer aboard U-502. Two and a half months later, he and all his crew were lost at sea, their U-boat sunk southwest of Madeira by a B-24. *UBA*

In February 1942, Air Marshal Sir Arthur T. Harris was named commander-in-chief of Bomber Command. In mid-January 1943, he took over from the 8th US Army Air Force the massive bombing campaign on the U-boat bases along the French Atlantic coastline that had started the previous October. Nicknamed "Bomber Harris" by the press, and often "Butcher Harris" by the Royal Air Force, he got the maximum use out of the enormous destructive capacities of the heavy four-engined Stirling, Halifax, and Lancaster bombers. *IWM*

During the night of January 14-15, 1943, a total of ninety-nine British bombers dropped 73.6 tons of bombs, including many incendiary devices, on Lorient, mainly on the town center. The arsenal's French workshops were hardly touched; here the M buildings situated between docks 3 (in the foreground) and 1 (in the background). Theodor Bahr, who was a fireman with the *Compagnie de Defence Passive* at KMW Lorient, recalls: "During the first fifteen days of January, the French workers at the naval shipyard told us that they had heard on the radio that the British saying that by the end of the month the arsenal and the town of Lorient would be reduced to ashes. We didn't really believe this, but what followed showed that they were right. At 2300 on the evening of January 14, there was an air raid alert! We got our fire-fighting gear ready; only a few minutes after the alert the sky was light up by flares. The real bombardment began ten minutes later; it was of an intensity that we had never seen before. Bunches of exploding and incendiary bombs were dropped without stopping, and a large part of the town was quickly on fire. The bombardment lasted ninety minutes but in our sector the arsenal was barely touched. During the next day, the French firemen managed to put out the fires in the town, but the following night a new bombardment began. Ten minutes after the alert, my group and I got the order to take our fire hoses to the maritime hospital. We soon saw that several incendiary bombs had penetrated the roof and it took us an hour to put out the fire. When we got back to our sector we were immediately sent out to the wood depot – it took us eight days to put the fires out there! We didn't stop working until mid-February, when apart from the submarine bases, the entire town center had been destroyed."

The second bombardment took place the following evening. This time the Péristyle barracks building were on fire all night long. *LB*

On the morning of January 16, the silhouettes of the two bunkers built in the middle of the barracks can be seen standing among the ruins of the old barracks that was completely destroyed in the fire. Returning from a four and a half-month patrol off Freetown, U-128 arrived in Lorient on January 15 at 1100. It was welcomed by about fifty girls from the *Todt Organization* in Paris, specially sent by their patron unit! It then berthed at a pontoon on the Scorff to be unloaded as usual; most of the crewmembers were then taken by bus to *Lager Lemp*. It was there that they were warned by some French girls they knew of a possible air raid that evening. They therefore decided to reinforce the crew on guard duty aboard the U-boat to seven. Effectively, in the evening of the fifteenth, a new air raid began and the pontoon where U-128 was berthed caught fire! The seven men on guard duty maneuvered their U-boat to the middle of the Scorff. U-128 was moved to a shelter in Kéroman the following morning. Its crew wandered around the arsenal looking at the damage: they saw that the officers' quarters in the *Préfecture Maritime* had been devastated by the explosion of fifty mines stored in a depot near the *Place d'Armes*, and that the cafes and brothels outside the arsenal had been destroyed. What stressed them the most was that all of the promotion orders that had just arrived in Lorient had disappeared. *UBA*

The buildings outside the arsenal, like the kitchen, were destroyed by explosive and incendiary bombs. As for the U-boats, only U-108 was slightly damaged, which didn't stop it from leaving on patrol on January 20! A truck had to be sent to Brest to pick up food supplies before its departure! *UBA*

In a few hours, the barracks looked like a barren landscape. The U-boat personnel's air raid shelters were intact. U-109's former radioman, Wolfgang Hirschfield, was inside during the two air raids. He had been placed a month earlier in the coding rooms between the Prefecture and Kernével. He recalls: "During the first attack, when the explosives bombs landed around us, inside the bunker everything moved as if we were aboard a ship, but it held. The second night, when the bombardment had just finished, Hans Freidrich, officer of the 2nd Flotilla's general staff, called me on the phone and told me to go and remove all of the French hand grenades in the arsenal. I pointed out that I could hear bombs going off outside, but he assured me that there wasn't any danger, and that the bombers had left. I took two men with me and we left the bunker. It was as light as day, fire was billowing out of the barracks' windows. All of a sudden I realized that I needed more men for the job so we returned to the bunker for reinforcements. As soon as the armoured door closed behind us an enormous explosion rocked the bunker! The phone rang again; it was the officer of the general staff again. Trying to control my fear, I said that he had told me that everything was supposed to have calmed down and that a giant explosion had just occurred. He explained that the planes really had left, and the explosion was caused by the mines stocked on the sea front. We went back outside but we had to cover our faces with scarves to be able to breathe because of all the smoke. Finally, the fifteen of us reached the store building, about to catch on fire from the building next to it and we carried out all the French grenades that were then evacuated by truck. After two raids, the barracks are uninhabitable so we were transferred to a rest camp near Pont-Scorff." *UBA*

The *rue du Lycée* leading to the small arsenal door. A small group from U-505, which arrived in Lorient on December 12, 1942, were having a party in a café in Lorient when the alert sounded in the evening of January 14; stuffed dummies had been put in their beds in the barracks. Half drunk, the sailors didn't hurry to find a shelter, thinking that after all it would be less dangerous than a patrol aboard their submarine. They wandered around the streets. and it was only when they saw a 37 mm anti-aircraft gun on a rooftop opposite firing ceaselessly, that they realized enemy planes were very close! All of a sudden the first bombs fell nearby and they were surprised by the violence of the explosions! They decided to go to a shelter for 300-400 people on the middle of a square, but when they went down the steps to the shelter they found the metal door firmly shut. Suddenly, the bombs got closer, a series of four or five exploded near the shelter's entry! The submariners curled up in a ball, and for several minutes they couldn't see anything because of the smoke and dust caused by the explosions. When the series of bombs had finished, they decided to take shelter in the building where the DCA was set up. They started to run, passing several dazed people who wandered the streets, blood coming out of their noses and ears. They had just gone inside the building when a bomb made a direct hit on the roof! They managed to reach the roof where they found a 37 mm anti-aircraft gun; they rescued the only survivor, who was gravely wounded, the others had disappeared in the explosion. Going back down the stairs they saw a huge unexploded bomb – was it a timebomb meant to hinder rescue? They decided not to hang around to find out and carried their wounded comrade to a first aid post. As soon as the end of danger alarm sounded, they were amazed to see hundreds of panic-stricken people pouring out into the streets. The police tried to maintain a certain order. They made it back to the *Saltzwedel Kaserne* buildings, which hadn't been touched by this first massive air raid, and that they really believed had targeted the town center. The next day, on January 15, security measures having been reinforced, they were unable to stay out late; they were in bed when the air raid alert sounded. This time they were ordered to go directly to the bunkers built in the center of the barracks. When they came out the next morning it was to find a landscape that looked as if the world had ended – all of the buildings around them had burnt to the ground. The same day they were taken to *Lager Lemp* by bus. *LB*

Quai des Ancres: the main shopping stores' building requisitioned by *Ressort IIIF* of the naval constructions at *KMW Lorient,* no longer has a roof or windowpanes. *UBA*

The submariners can no longer sleep on the upper floors of the former apprentice mechanics' barracks, which was re-baptized *Haus Habekost*. We can see the pre-war built exterior toilets on the left of the porch; the canteen, situated in the left wing has also been destroyed. The crews of the 2nd Flotilla will use the two bunkers still standing, where they are taken to *Lager Lemp* two or three days before departure, to help with loading their U-boat. The crews of the 10th Flotilla will do the same—driven from *Lager Rostin* to the *Hundius Kaserne,* which was less badly damaged by the bombing. *UBA*

After the second bombardment on the night of January 15-16, civilians leave Lorient where life has become impossible. On bikes, carts, in cars or on the bus, they flee the town with the few belongings they have managed to rescue from the flames. *LB*

Safe from attacks in the concreted bases, U-boats continue to be repaired and cared for so that they can leave once more on patrols. During the first half of 1943, departure and arrival ceremonies are held in the pens in the small base on the Scorff or at Kéroman III, sheltered from bombs. On January 16, 1943, the friends of U-510 have come to wave off their comrades who are leaving on patrol. *Ulf-Normann Neitzel*

Last words of encouragement to the crew of U-510 commanded by Karl Neitzel. A tug is ready to help the U-boat maneuver out of the small base on the Scorff. *Ulf-Normann Neitzel*

A diver checks that the propellers aren't tangled up in the ropes. That is what happened to U-164 on November 28, 1942; its propellers got tangled up in the camouflage netting while it was outside on the Scorff. To get it off, the U-boat had to be put back into dry dock in Kéroman, which delayed its departure by twenty-four hours. *Ulf-Normann Neitzel*

Helped by the tugs from *KMW Lorient*, U-510 leaves its shelter. For a while it will be in the Cape Verde sector before crossing the Atlantic to hunt along the South American coast. *Ulf-Normann Neitzel*

Marines who have stayed behind salute their comrades aboard U-510. In the background is the arsenal, whose buildings have suffered bomb damage. *Anthony Guychard*

Ulrich Heyse, the commander of U-128, arrives in Lorient on January 15. On January 21, while still in Lorient, he is decorated with the Knight's Cross. He will be taking a land job. He was very popular among his crew, never hesitating to sit with them in the submarine, or taking out his pocketknife and peeling potatoes while chatting about many subjects. On land he often went out for a beer with his men. Coming from the merchant navy, he had a very correct attitude towards the survivors of the ships he had torpedoed, telling them that he was sorry and handing out food, cigarettes and even rum. *Charita*

The *Lager Lemp* rest camp became fully operational in mid-January 1943 and was immediately camouflaged. To avoid being located from the air, even the roads leading to it had camouflage netting. The lake was also camouflaged to hide it from enemy planes. *UBA*

Covered with netting, the huts are unrecognizable. The submariners say that not long after their arrival French travelling salesmen set up around the main entrance to sell alcohol, clothes, and even books with risqué photos in them. More discreetly, the young women from Lorient continued to sell their charms to the marines. *UBA*

After all his patrols as commander of U-130, which won him the Knight's Cross, *Korvettenkapitän* Ernst Kals was named chief of the 2nd Flotilla on January 2, 1943. *UBA*

The 2nd Flotilla's general staff posed with their new chief on the steps of the hut that serves as the officers' mess at *Lager Lemp*. *UBA*

Zones hit during the bombardment of January 23, 1943 in Lorient's town center. Thirty-six American B-17s dropped ninety tons of bombs. *NA*

In *Lager Rostin*: on the left Hermann Laufs, chief engineer of the 10th Flotilla; next to him is Günter Kuhnke, the chief of the flotilla. *UBA*

Zones destroyed by successive bombardments between January 14-24. It's clearly the town center that was targeted during these raids and not the Kéroman sector situated on the left of the aerial photo. *NA*

Aerial photo taken just after the American bombardment on January 23 in the *Hundius Kaserne* sector, relatively spared by the raids until then, contrary to the civilian quarter situated just below it. The huts serving as quarters and mess for the 10th Flotilla haven't been touched. *NA*

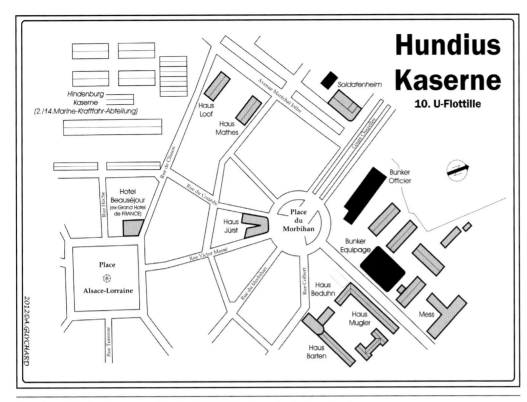

Hundius Kaserne
10. U-Flottille

Plan of the *Hundius Kaserne* used by the 10th Flotilla. *Drawn by Anthony Guychard.*

The large, two-story bunker for the officers of the 10th Flotilla situated on *Cours Chazelles*. Two ventilation outlets are protected by reinforced chimneys in the shape of cupolas. *LB*

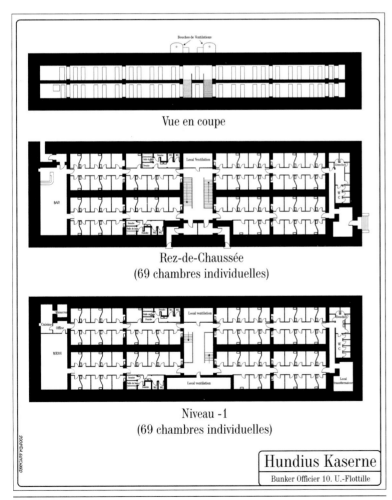

Plan of the large bunker for the officers that is nearly 2,000 square meters (57x18m per floor), and has 138 individual bedrooms, a bar, a mess, a kitchen and six sanitary complexes, including four baths! Inside, the walls are entirely paneled. *Drawn by Anthony Guychard.*

A requisitioned building called *Haus Jürst*, part of the *Hundius Kaserne* but on the other side of the *Place de Morbihan*, was unable to resist the bombardment on January 23. It had been named in memory of Commander Harald Jürst of U-104 who was lost at sea on November 20, 1940. After the war, this building became the Café de Paris. *LB*

The large bunker used by the crews of the 10th Flotilla. The ventilation oulets on the roof are concreted. *UBA*

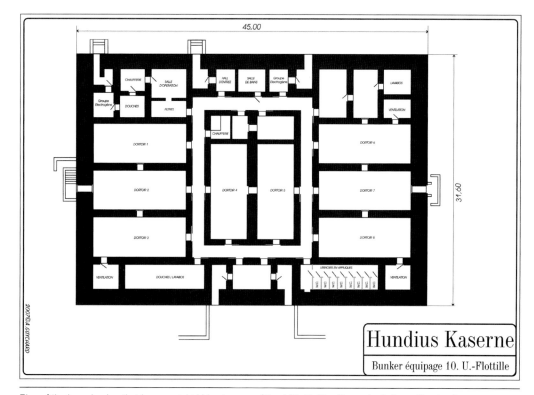

Hundius Kaserne

Bunker équipage 10. U.-Flottille

Plan of the large bunker that houses eight U-boat crews of the 10th Flotilla. *Drawn by Anthony Guychard.*

This aerial photo, taken on January 26, 1943, shows the zones hit in the Péristyle barracks and arsenal sectors. *NA*

February 1943: Departures to the Azores Sector for the Second Month Running

Movements: Nine arrivals, eleven departures, number of U-boats present at the end of the month: twenty. For the second month running, seven U-boats left Lorient for the Azores sector. They regrouped there in two wolfpacks, most of them Type IXs, to intercept Allied convoys sailing between North America and Gibraltar, and between England and Africa. The Type VIIs from other bases in Biscay Bay were sent to the North Atlantic. While new U-boats had regularly arrived each month as reinforcements in Lorient since September 1942, none arrived in February 1943. Three experienced commanders left their U-boats to take up land posts. The last base of Kéroman III was now completely operational. Its back workshops housed the electrical service, while shipbuilding services were installed in KI, and

machine services in KII. The still important numbers of German U-boats present in Lorient, and the systematic changes made to the Type IVs' conning towers, to receive the new anti-aircraft gun, meant that these U-boats were immobilized in the shipyards for at least two months.

Observations: Beginning of February 1943: a first convoy, HX 224, heading east was attacked by five U-boats. It lost three ships before being protected by planes out of Iceland. But a survivor of one of the ships sunk, picked up by U-632, imprudently talked about a large, slow convoy that would be following after his. The general staff sent twenty U-boats in the direction of the SC-118 convoy comprising sixty-one slow cargo ships. For four days and nights, a fierce battle took place, during which

eleven ships and three U-boats were sunk. But the attacks were difficult, if not impossible, for most of the U-boats; U-402 sank seven ships out of the eleven. On February 20, the ON-166 convoy heading west was spotted entering the "gap" in the Atlantic. In four days of battle, fourteen ships and three U-boats were sunk. The German U-boats' results increased throughout February with seventy ships sunk representing 359,276 tons, and eighteen others damaged. The proportion of cargo ships in convoy to be sunk was clearly higher. Several victims also came from the *Rochen* and *Robbe* Wolfpacks, operating off the Moroccan coast, thanks to supply ships, but Allied naval and air escort so close to the coast was very strong. It was the same for a convoy to Gibraltar attacked off the Portuguese and Spanish coasts on February 12/14; the only two losses were

U-BOAT	TYPE	FLOT.	COMMANDER	ARRIVAL	DEPART	NOTES
Departures						
UD-3	Holl.	10	Hermann Rigele		10	Departure for the last time, turned into ship school in Germany; relegated 10/13/43 after being damaged in a bombardment on Kiel; scuttled the 5/3/45.
U-67	IXC	2	Günther Müller-Stöckheim			In maintenance December 21, 1942 – March 3, 1943.
U-68	IXC	2	Albert Lauzemis		3	Departure for the Caribbean.
U-103	IXB	2	Gustav-Adolf Janssen		7	Departure for west of Gibraltar, with five other of U-boats, in the fear of an Allied landing in Portugal.
U-106	IXB	2	Hermann Rasch		17	Departure for the Azores sector.
U-126	IXC	2	Ernst Bauer			In maintenance January 7 – March 20, 1943. Change of commander, Ernst Bauer becomes an instruction officer then chief of the 27th Training Flotilla in the Baltic Sea.
U-128	IXC	2	Hermann Steinert			New commander. In maintenance January 15 – April 6, 1943.
U-129	IXC	2	Hans-Ludwig Witt			In maintenance January 6 – March 11, 1943.
U-130	IXC	2	Siegfried Keller		28	Departure for its sixth and last patrol, in the Azores; sunk 3/13/43 by depth charges launched by a destroyer, no survivors, fifty-three dead. Results: twenty-five ships sunk and one damaged.
U-154	IXC	2	Oskar Kusch			In maintenance January 7 – March 20, 1943. New commander, Kusch was watch officer on U-103.
U-155	IXC	10	Adolf Piening		8	Departure for Florida and the Gulf of Mexico.
U-159	IXC	10	Helmut Witte			In maintenance January 5 – March 4, 1943.
U-161	IXC	2	Albrecht Achilles			In maintenance January 9 – March 13, 1943.
U-163	IXC	10	Kurt Engelmann			In maintenance January 6 – March 10, 1943.
U-172	IXC	10	Carl Emmermann		21	Departure for the Azores sector.
U-174	IXC	10	Ulrich Thilo			In maintenance January 9 – March 18, 1943. Change of commander. Ulrich Thilo name unit chief at the Flotilla School for torpedomen.
U-185	IXC-40	10	August Maus		8	Departure for its second patrol in the Antilles, returns to Bordeaux; then its third and last patrol off the coast of Brazil; part of the crew from the damaged and then scuttled U-604 were taken on board ; but U-185 was sunk 8/24/43 by depth charges launched by planes, twenty-nine dead, thirty-six survivors including some from U-604.
U-505	IXC	2	Peter Zschech			Being repaired for over six months from December 12, 1942 to July 1, 1943.
U-508	IXC	10	Georg Staats		22	Departure for the Azores.
U-513	IXC	10	Rolf Rüggeberg		20	Departure for the Azores.
U-515	IXC	10	Werner Henke		21	Departure for the Azores.
U-524	IXC	10	Walter Freiherr von Steinaecker			In maintenance January 9 - March 3, 1943.
Arrivals						
U-123	IXB	2	Horst von Schroeter	6		Returns from the Azores and the North Atlantic where it took part in a wolfpack attack on convoys, with one ship of 3,385 tons sunk, and another damaged. New commander affected in Kiel: Horst von Schroeter knew this U-boat very well as he was its former watch officer.
U-117	XB	12	Hans-Werner Neumann	7		Returns from a re-supplying operation for ten U-boats in the Azores sector.
U-514	IXC	10	Hans-Jürgen Auffermann	12		Returns from a mission in the Caribbean, and then in the Azores with the *Delphin* Wolfpack, with one ship of 7,177 tons sunk and one damaged.
U-124	IXB	2	Johann Mohr awarded Oak Leaves to his Knight's Cross on January 13.	13		Returns from a patrol of nearly three months off the Antilles, and the Gulf of Guinea with five ships sunk for 28,282 tons. Admiral Dönitz will do everything he can to convince its commander, the most decorated in the Flotilla, to take a post on land, but Mohr only wants to leave on another patrol.

U-BOAT	TYPE	FLOT.	COMMANDER	ARRIVAL	DEPART	NOTES
U-105	IXB	2	Jürgen Nissen	14		Returns from a patrol of nearly three months in the Caribbean, with four ships sunk for 19,844 tons.
U-176	IXC	10	Reiner Dierksen	18		Returns from a three-month patrol in the mid-Atlantic, between the Cape Verde Islands and the coast of Brazil, with three ships sunk for 13,432 tons, including the Dutch cargo ship *Polydorus* chased for fifty hours; a record for the longest chase!
U-125	IXC	2	Ulrich Folkers	19		Returns empty-handed from a patrol of more than two months west of the Canaries, and the Azores as a part of the *Delphin* Wolfpack.
U-108	IXB	2	Ralf-Reimar Wolfram	24		Returns without success from the *Delphin* Wolfpack west of the Canaries, damaged during an aerial attack by a Catalina that dropped four depth charges on February 10.
U-175	IXC	10	Heinrich Bruns	24		Returns from a patrol of nearly three months off Freetown, and the Ivory Coast where one ship of 7,177 tons was sunk.

German. The two wolfpacks in this sector were moved away from the coast to south of the Azores. It was here that U-522 spotted the UC-1 convoy, made up of fuel tankers heading west. In spite of the ten escorts, three fuel tankers were sunk and two others damaged, for the loss of one U-boat.

In February, taking advantage of the recent arrival in England of two American B-24 Liberator squadrons, equipped with 10 cm radar, Coastal Command launched a new aerial offensive against the U-boats in Biscay Bay. The first, that lasted from June to October 1942, had been confounded by the use of *Metox* radar detectors and the appearance of German escort planes. But *Metox* was useless against the Allies' new centimetric radar that could detect a U-boat up to sixteen miles, instead of the previous eight! The nomination of Air Vice-Marshal Sir John C. Slessor as chief of Coastal Command on February 5, also boosted the morale of the pilots who chased U-boats. For the escort ships equipped with the centimetric radar, the distance of detection of a submarine on the surface went from three to six miles. Their *Asdic* systems, that detected submerged U-boats, was also improved. Henceforth, they were effective up to two miles and the echoes appeared on a plotting chart, which made determining their positions a lot easier.

Allied reactions: In February 1943, the RAF Bomber Command carried out four raids on Lorient with destructive devices superior to those in previous attacks. The first raid, during the night of 4/5, was carried out by 120 planes out of 128 planned; 90.6 tons of bombs and 63,376 incendiary bombs were dropped on the port and the town. However, the worst was yet to come. During the night of February 7/8, 296 British bombers out of the 352 planned, dropped 254.1 tons of bombs! Nearly all of the civilians, who had been evacuating the town since mid-January, had left the area. Out of 46,000 recorded in the census in 1939, only about 500 people still lived among the ruins. A report from the *Service Interministériel de Protection contre les Evénements de Guerre* (SIPEG) of the French government noted that a new bombardment method had been inaugurated on Lorient: "The Allies no longer restrict themselves to the destruction of more-or-less limited targets, but to the destruction of the entire town. This is achieved by the use of an enormous quantity of incendiary bombs that complete what the explosive bombs have started. This method shows that the attacks are more aimed at the systematic destruction of the town than at the German military buildings." The already high number of bombers in use was increased for the next raid during the night February 13/14, carried out by the RAF with 422 planes out of the 476

planned; the bombs dropped exceeded 500 tons (524.3 tons) with some 26,168 incendiary bombs, meaning that 5,000 were 7.5 times heavier than those used before. Three days later, it began again with 360 British bombers dropping 461.9 tons of bombs, and above all, 230,916 incendiary bombs. To reassure the personnel working in the bases, *Generaladmiral* Marschall, superior commander of the Navy in the West, made the following statement in his agenda of February 16, 1943: "During the last few weeks, the navy arsenal in Lorient, commanded by Rear Admiral Matthiae, has faced a considerable number of heavy air attacks. The British have not reached their goal, that is, to put the U-boat bases out of action. Even if enormous damage has been caused to the town and the buildings in the old arsenal, repairing and cleaning the submarines' hulls has continued without interruption. Through their energy, their relentlessness, their sheer will not to be beaten, the command and the troops in Lorient have managed to protect and repair the largest part, by far, of the machines and equipment. I express here my gratitude to the arsenal commander, his section leaders and to the entire personnel." Now that the town of Lorient had been destroyed, Allied bombers turned to the ports of St. Nazaire and Brest. Coastal Command carried out seven mine-laying operations with a total of twenty-six planes.

On February 5, 1943, the British Air Vice-Marshal Sir John C. Slessor was named commander-in-chief of the Coastal Command. This former World War I pilot soon got down to the job of ensuring that the Allied planes, principally those that had a very large scope, became responsible for the destruction of more than half of the U-boats. *IWM*

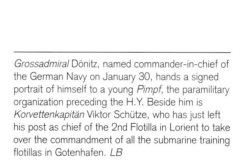

Grossadmiral Dönitz, named commander-in-chief of the German Navy on January 30, hands a signed portrait of himself to a young *Pimpf*, the paramilitary organization preceding the H.Y. Beside him is *Korvettenkapitän* Viktor Schütze, who has just left his post as chief of the 2nd Flotilla in Lorient to take over the commandment of all the submarine training flotillas in Gotenhafen. *LB*

On February 6, 1943, U-123 returned from a two-month patrol in the Azores and to the east of Newfoundland. Its new commander, Horst von Schroeter, has added to the old wound badge insignia on each side of the conning tower, the insignia of his naval officers' class—the *Crew 37b*—that represents a vertical glaive on a black shield. *LB*

Following in the wake of its escort, U-123 is about to pass in front of the citadel at Port Louis. It has sunk a 3,385-ton ship and damaged another. *LB*

Arriving in the Scorff on February 6, U-123's crew discovers a landscape totally different to the one they had left behind on their last departure from Lorient in May 1942! The U-boat is rapidly put into the shelter of a concrete pen. *LB*

U-123's commander, Horst von Schroeter, and its chief engineer, Reinhard Koenig, who had been awarded the German Cross in Gold on December 12, 1942, travel to the Château de Pignerolles, near Angers. The chief of U-boats in the West, *Kapitän-zur-See* Hans-Rudolf Roesing, gives them their decorations. All promotions, decorations and changes in the submariners' personnel in the five bases built along the French coast, pass through his administrative service. *UBA*

Because their former barracks is uninhabitable, the crew of U-123 is taken by bus to *Lager Lemp*. The following evening after their arrival, British bombers returned to Lorient in greater numbers than before: 296 planes drop another 254 tons of bombs! *LB*

The crew of U-505, having crossed the Atlantic to Lorient in a badly damaged U-boat incapable of diving, is given leave in the Wolf Hotel (*U-Boot Sportheim*) at the Bad Wiessee ski resort. The crewmembers have changed jackets but have kept their garrison caps featuring the insignia of their U-boat, a small metal hatchet. These are the insignia made from the aluminum debris from the aircraft that had attacked them in November 1942. *LB*

There is nothing left of the barrack rooms on the upper story of the *Saltzwedel Kaserne*; even the metal bed frames have been deformed by the heat of the flames. *LB*

This submariner from U-505 must feel safer here in these snowy mountains than in his U-boat or under the bombs in Lorient. The change of space between a submarine crowded with torpedoes, food supplies and fifty men during two months, and these vast silent mountains must be very impressive. *LB*

The crew of U-505 also visit Schliesee, their patron town. This photo was taken in front of the town hall with Commander Peter Zschech in the middle. At the same time, part of the crew from U-128 visits Ulm, its patron town. But the best part for them is the day-long stopover in Paris on their way back with a guided tour of the Parisian cabarets given by the members of the *Todt Organisation*! *LB*

February 13, 1943, U-124 returns from a particularly successful patrol to the east of the Caribbean and along the coast of Guinea, with five ships sunk for a total of 28,282 tons. It is immediately put into shelter in the small base on the Scorff. *LB*

On February 12, 1943, U-514 arrives in Lorient, returning from a patrol in the Caribbean then in the Azores sector as part of the *Delphin* Wolfpack. It displays two pennants for one 7,177-ton ship sunk, and one ship damaged. *LB*

Outside the base, U-124's commander, Johann Mohr, chats with Ernst Kals, his flotilla chief, who advises him to do as he has done and take a post on land so that other commanders can benefit from his experience. *UBA*

In the conning tower, the four machine guns pointed towards the sky, proves the ever-present danger from enemy aircraft. In the center is U-514's commander, Hans-Jürgen Auffermann, former watch officer aboard U-69 in 1941, with two port pilots. The wave shield has disappeared during the patrol. *Ulf-Normann Neitzel*

U-124's commander, Johann Mohr, was awarded the Oak Leaves to the Knight's Cross on January 13. Before he goes to Germany to receive it, he and his comrades celebrate at *Lager Lemp* with cigars and good alcohol! What is somewhat unusual is that he has always navigated on the same U-boat, aboard which he rose in rank little by little since October 1940: second watch officer, watch officer, and then commander. *LB*

With music from an accordion, an army soldier, invited by the submariners, teaches them a Russian dance! *LB*

In the night of February 13-14, the RAF led a new attack with 422 planes dropping over 500 tons of bombs on the town! A major part of the civilian population has already been evacuated. *UBA*

During the air raid in the night of February 16-17, British planes drop 462 tons of explosive bombs, of which many are incendiary bombs. Evacuation was by bus in the *rue des Remparts*. Out of 46,000 people in the census of 1939, only about 500 remained in certain sectors of the town miraculously spared.

Burial of a German *KMW Lorient* worker in Kerentrech; a chaplain reads the funeral eulogy. *LB*

To help German laborers keep their determination, they are praised in *Generaladmiral* Marschall's agenda on February 16, 1943. Marschall was the commander-in-chief of the Naval Group Command in the West. *LB*

U-508's crewmembers, who arrived in Lorient on January 6, give a hand in clearing up operations in the ruins of a hut built over a bunker. The bombs had hit just beside it and caused several impacts in the reinforced concrete, but the damage isn't deep enough to penetrate the two-meter thick walls. *LB*

U-508's crewmembers are housed in blockhouses in Kernével, near the former French redoubt. Like the three villas at the Kernével Point, this sector situated at only 1.5km from Kéroman, was almost completely spared by the Allied air raids. *LB*

Members of U-508's crew resting in mid-February 1943 at Kernével Point. In the background is the citadel of Port-Louis. *LB*

Preparing for the departure of U-508. The cases are retrieved from a storeroom sheltered from bombs. *LB*

They are then loaded into a truck and brought to the U-508. *LB*

On February 22, with its newly painted camouflaged conning tower and insignia belonging to the 10th Flotilla, U-508 leaves for the Azores. *LB*

On February 26, U-508 was damaged to the northeast of the Azores during an attack by a B-24 Liberator from the 244th Squadron, flown by Wing Commander Peter J. Cundy. The crew couldn't repair the damage and the U-boat returned to Lorient, arriving on March 15. *LB*

On February 24, 1943, U-175 under Commander Heinrich Bruns returns after a three-month patrol along the African coast, with only one pennant for an American cargo ship sunk off the Ivory Coast. During the last five days of its approach to Lorient, U-175 navigated submerged during the day and on the surface at night. The crew, who had left Lorient on December 1, 1942, return to find a landscape in ruins; they will be billeted in the *Hundius Kaserne*'s bunkers. On March 27, with all the shore personnel of the 2nd and 10th Flotillas, they are be taken by bus to *Lager Lemp* to hear a speech by *Grossadmiral* Dönitz. Commander of a T3 torpedo boat in 1940, Bruns stayed for two months in hospital from October to December 1940, following the destruction of his ship by British aircraft in Le Havre Port in September. He then followed an officer submariner-training course in 1941. He was killed in the conning tower of his U-boat on April 17, hit by shrapnel during a final attack. *UBA*

On February 28, in the pen 1-2 at the small base on the Scorff, Kals, chief of the 2nd Flotilla, has come to shake hands with each crewmember of U-130—his former submarine! He carried out five patrols with them along the North and South American coats, and along the African coast to Freetown. He couldn't possibly imagine that in less than fifteen days, the fifty-three crewmembers would all be lost. Behind him is the new commander, Siegfried Keller, second watch officer aboard U-190 for a year, and who, for a year after finishing his commander's training course, stayed on for an extra year to train in the Baltic Sea. *LB*

Newly painted in camouflage colors, U-130 leaves Lorient on its last patrol. After having simultaneously sunk four British cargo ships in the XK 2 convoy on March 5, it was sunk in turn eight days later with all its crew, hit by six charges launched by an American destroyer. *LB*

March 1943: Twenty-seven U-boats Present at the End of the Month

Movements: Twenty arrivals, thirteen departures, number of U-boats present at the end of the month: twenty-seven. A total of seven U-boats left Lorient for the last time in March. They were all sunk before the end of August, such as U-163, lost only three days out of Lorient. Even the "ace" of the 2nd Flotilla, Johann Mohr, commander of U-124 and decorated with the Knight's Cross with Oak Leaves, and who refused a post on land when Dönitz offered him one, was lost at sea with all hands only seven days after leaving his base. However, these U-boats were replaced by the massive arrival of eleven others arriving for the first time in this port; this brought the number of boats to twenty-seven by the end of the month. These reinforcements were mainly Type VIIs of the 6th, 7th and 9th Flotillas normally based in

St. Nazaire and Brest; bases which were overcrowded and subjected to endless air attacks.

Observations: From March 1-12, 1943, a conference was held about the convoys in Washington, DC, with representatives of the American, British, and Canadian navies. The plans for the Battle of the Atlantic for the coming month were organized. The Americans would no longer escort convoys in the North Atlantic; these would be protected exclusively by the British and Canadians. Rear-Admiral Murray was named Commander-in-Chief Canadian Northwest Atlantic. The Canadian escorts would protect convoys along the American coast to the "chop-line" vertical to Iceland, where the British would take over their protection. Henceforth, the American escorts would ensure the protection

convoys in the mid- and south Atlantic. The construction of numerous escort aircraft-carriers, to make up for the lack of planes in the "gap" in the Atlantic, was programmed for May, as well as those for the independent escort groups. It was also decided to double the volume of materiel across the Atlantic before the end of the month. The Allies had remarked that the work of an escort was the same for large convoys as for small ones. The convoys would be doubled in size for an increase of only 30% in the escort ships.

For the convoys in the North Atlantic, March was the most violent month of the entire war. A first convoy, SC 121, scattered by a storm, was attacked by twenty-seven U-boats and lost thirteen ships between March 7-11. From March 10-19, Allied decoding services were unable to decode

U-BOAT	TYPE	FLOT.	COMMANDER	ARRIVAL	DEPART	NOTES
Departures						
U-67	IXC	2	Günther Müller-Stöckheim		3	Departure South Azores.
U-105	IXB	2	Jürgen Nissen		16	Departure for ninth and last patrol, in the Freetown sector; sunk 6/2/43 by French plane based in Dakar, no survivors, fifty-three dead. Results: twenty-two cargo ships and one corvette sunk.
U-108	IXB	2	Ralf-Reimar Wolfram			Being repaired February 24 - April 1, 1943.
U-117	XB	12	Hans-Werner Neumann		7	Departure for Brest, then mine-laying operation off the Moroccan coast; return to Bordeaux then fifth and last re-supply mission; while re-supplying U-66 whose commander, Markworth, had been wounded, an officer of U-117 boarded U-66; the two U-boats were attacked by planes, U-117 sank 8/7/43, no survivors, sixty-two dead. Only the officer transferred to U-66 survived. Results: 0 ships sunk, two damaged by mines.
U-123	IXB	2	Horst von Schroeter		13	Departure for south of the Canaries.
U-124	IXB	2	Johann Mohr		27	Departure for twelfth and last patrol, Freetown sector; sunk the 4/3/43 by depth charges launched by two British ships, no survivors; fifty-three dead. Results: forty-six merchant ships, one cruiser and one corvette sunk, four ships damaged.
U-125	IXC	2	Ulrich Folkers			In maintenance February 19 – April 13, 1943.
U-126	IXC	2	Siegfried Kietz		20	New commander, departure for sixth and last patrol, Freetown sector; sunk 7/3/43 during the night in Biscay Bay by a Liberator equipped with a search light; no survivors; fifty-five dead. Results: twenty-six ships sunk and five damaged.
U-128	IXC	2	Hermann Steinert			In maintenance January 15 – April 6, 1943.
U-129	IXC	2	Hans-Ludwig Witt		11	Departure for the American coast.
U-154	IXC	2	Oskar Kusch		20	Departure for the Cape Verde Islands and Freetown sector.
U-159	IXC	10	Helmut Witte		4	Departure for the South Azores.
U-161	IXC	2	Albrecht Achilles		13	Departure for a patrol escorting blockade runners with U-174 west of the Azores, then off the American coast opposite New York.
U-163	IXC	10	Kurt Engelmann		10	Departure for third and last patrol; sunk by a corvette 3/13/43 off the Spanish coast; no survivors; fifty-seven dead. Results: three ships and one gunboat sunk.
U-174	IXC	10	Wolfgang Grandefeld		18	New commander, departure for third and last patrol, direction the American coast with U-161; sunk 4/27/43 by depth charges launched by plane; no survivors; fifty-three dead. Results: five ships sunk.
U-175	IXC	10	Heinrich Bruns			In maintenance February 24 – April 10, 1943.
U-176	IXC	10	Reiner Dierksen			In maintenance February 8 – April 6, 1943.
U-505	IXC	2	Peter Zschech			Being repaired December 12, 1942 – July 1, 1943.
U-514	IXC	10	Hans-Jürgen Auffermann			In maintenance February 12 – April 15, 1943.
U-524	IXC	10	Walter *Freiherr* von Steinaecker		3	Departure for second and last patrol, direction south of the Azores; sunk 3/22/43 by a Liberator; no survivors; fifty-one dead. Results: two ships sunk.
Arrivals						
U-525	IXC	10	Hans-Joachim Drewitz	3		First time in Lorient; put into service 7/30/42. Arrives from its first combat patrol against convoys in the North Atlantic; sank one ship of 3,454 tons. The day before its arrival it had been attacked during the night by a Wellington equipped with a searchlight and could no longer dive; escorted to Lorient by three trawlers and two Ju 88 planes.
U-264	VIIC	6	Hartwig Looks	4	5	First time in Lorient; put into service 5/22/42. Arrives from a patrol escorting the German fuel tanker *Hohenfriedberg*, which was sunk by a British cruiser on April 26; U-264 arrived with seventy-five survivors; damaged propeller repaired; departure the next day for its base in St. Nazaire which it reached at 12:10.
U-186	IXC-40	10	Siegfried Hesemann	5		First time in Lorient; put into service 7/10/42. Arrives from its 1st combat mission in the North Atlantic, with three ships sunk for 18,782 tons.
U-382	VIIC	7	Herbert Juli	8		First time in Lorient; put into service 4/25/42. Arrives from the Gibraltar and Azores sectors where it damaged two ships. Change of commander, Juli named instructor at the U-boat school.

U-BOAT	TYPE	FLOT.	COMMANDER	ARRIVAL	DEPART	NOTES
U-511	IXC	10	Fritz Schneewind	8		Arrives from a six-week patrol between the Azores and the Canaries, with one 5,004-ton ship sunk.
U-303	VIIC	7	Karl-Franz Heine	8		First time in Lorient; put into service 7/7/42. Arrives from its first combat patrol in the North Atlantic, with one 4,959-ton cargo ship sunk.
U-135	VIIC	7	Heinz Schütt	10		New commander affected in St. Nazaire. Arrives empty-handed from a patrol in the North Atlantic, the U-boat was damaged by a Liberator.
U-226	VIIC	6	Rolf Borchers	10		First time in Lorient; put into service 8/1/42. Arrives empty-handed from its first combat patrol in the North Atlantic.
U-759	VIIC	9	Rudolf Friedrich	14		First time in Lorient; put into service 8/15/42. Arrives empty-handed from its first combat patrol in the North Atlantic.
U-508	IXC	10	Georg Staats	15		Returns from north of the Azores where it was damaged by a Liberator, four days out of Lorient; the crew tried without success to repair the damage at sea.
U-634	VIIC	9	Eberhard Dahlhaus	23		First time in Lorient; put into service 8/6/42. Arrives from its first combat patrol in the North Atlantic, with one 7,176-ton ship sunk.
U-66	IXC	2	Friedrich Markworth	24		Arrives from a seventy-five-day patrol off the African coast, with one trawler and one cargo ship sunk for 4,425 tons.
U-504	IXC	2	Wilhelm Luis	24		Arrives empty-handed from a patrol of over two months in the Azores and Canaries sectors. Fired eleven torpedoes without success, had to crash dive 135 times, and was damaged during several air attacks off Gibraltar, a diesel motor had broken down.
U-103	IXB	2	Gustav-Adolf Janssen	25		Returns empty-handed from the Azores and Gibraltar sectors where the Allied air presence has been highly reinforced.
U-107	IXB	2	Harald Gelhaus awarded the Knight's Cross March 26, 1943.	25		Returns from the Azores and Gibraltar sectors; six ships sunk: four from the OS 44 convoy during the night of March 12/13, totaling 37,588 tons.
U-521	IXC	2	Klaus Bargsten	26		Returns from a seventy-day patrol between the Canaries and the Azores; one anti-submarine trawler and one 7,176-ton cargo ship sunk.
U-410	VIIC	7	Horst-Arno Fenski	27		First time in Lorient; put into service 2/23/42. Arrives from its second combat patrol between the Azores and Gibraltar, with one 7,133-ton ship sunk and one damaged.
U-664	VIIC	9	Adolf Graef	28		First time in Lorient; put into service 6/17/42. Arrives from its third combat patrol in the North Atlantic, with two ships sunk from the ONS 167 convoy for 13,466 tons.
U-91	VIIC	9	Heinz Walkerling	29		First time in Lorient; put into service 1/28/42. Arrives from the North Atlantic where it took part in the largest wolfpack attack with a total of forty U-boats against the HX 229 convoy (New York to Liverpool), that lost twelve ships out of thirty-eight between March 16-18. U-91 sunk three ships for 21,238 tons.
U-190	IXC-40	2	Max Wintermeyer	30		First time in Lorient; put into service 9/24/42. Arrives from its first combat patrol in the North Atlantic with one 7,015-ton ship sunk.
U-43	IXA	2	Hans-Joachim Schwantke	31		Returns from its fourteenth combat patrol between the Canaries and Azores, with one 9,131-ton ship sunk, and a Liberator shot down by the DCA; and by mistake, on March 3, the German blockade runner *Doggerbank* taken for a British steamer; it sank within three minutes with its precious cargo from Japan; fifteen crewmembers managed to escape, and only one was still alive on March 29, picked up by a Spanish fuel tanker. The blockade runner was in a zone that had been prohibited three weeks before its due arrival.

German radio messages as the result of the Germans bringing in a new short weather report! The next convoy attacked, HX 228, which for the first part of its journey had been protected by the escort aircraft carrier USS *Bogue,* transporting twelve Wildcats and eight Avengers, only lost four cargo ships and one destroyer after its departure; two U-boats were sunk by the corvette FNFL *Aconit.* But being unable to decode the German radio messages cost the following two convoys dearly. Between March 6-20, forty U-boats relentlessly attacked convoys HX 229 and SC 122. This was the most important wolfpack attack of the entire war. In four days, twenty-one ships were sunk for the loss of a single U-boat. U-603 and U-758 used the new German *Falke* torpedo with great success;

these torpedoes had a speed of twenty knots and were equipped with an explode on contact device.

Around the Azores, two wolfpacks also continued their attacks. It was there, on March 3, that U-43 sank, by mistake, an isolated ship it took to be a British liner. The German general staff only found out a short time after the war was over, that it was in fact the blockade runner *Doggerbank*, which had entered the prohibited zone 3 weeks before its due date. On board were the survivors of the supply tanker *Uckermarck* and the raider *Thor*; only one survivor was picked up on March 29. Still in the Azores sector, on March 5, U-130, with its new commander Siegfried Keller, sank four ships in the XK2 convoy heading north, while on March 13, U-107 sank four cargo

ships in the OS 44 convoy heading south. Before the end of the month, these U-boats from the *Robbe* Wolfpack returned to Lorient for maintenance. After eight weeks without having found a single convoy out of the USA for Gibraltar, the convoy UGS 6 was spotted on March 12 in the mid-Atlantic. The Type IXs on their way to the American coast regrouped and attacked. But, even if the convoy didn't have aerial protection, the U-boats were systematically picked up on the escort ships' radar and stopped from coming nearer than ten miles of the convoy. A new tactic was adopted: underwater attacks. A total of four cargo ships were sunk before the battle ended on March 19. Much farther south, near Cape Town, the *Seehund* Wolfpack also had several good results, notably U-160, which sank four ships and damaged two others in the DN 21 convoy in a single day. The monthly report of the British Admiralty noted: "The Germans had never been so close to breaking communications between the Old Continent and the New as they were during the first twenty days of March 1943." But during the last ten days of the month, the convoys HX 230 and SC 123 in the North Atlantic, each protected by an aircraft carrier and several escort ships, managed to get through. By the end of the month, the U-boats had sunk 108 Allied ships representing 585,404 tons, and damaged twenty-three others. Among those destroyed, seventy-one were part of a convoy—a record!

In February 1943, the first Wellington bombers equipped with centimetric radar and *Theigh-Light* searchlights, appeared in Biscay Bay; a first was recorded against U-268 that was sunk on February 19. From March 20-28, thirty-six *Theigh-Light* equipped planes replaced Liberators at night chasing U-boats on the surface. Of the twenty-six U-boats spotted during these nights, fifteen were attacked. On March 27, Dönitz ordered U-boats to cross the Bay of Biscay underwater during the night, and only to surface for short times during the day to recharge their batteries. This security measure, which meant they couldn't use their diesels on the surface, delayed their arrival in the theater of operations.

On March 31, the German U-boat Corps general staff left Paris and set up in Charlottenburg, a district of Berlin, which meant they could work more closely with the other Admiralty departments and be nearer to Dönitz. On the same day, the chief of the Kriegsmarine signed an agreement with Albert Speer, the Minister of Armaments; henceforth, Speer's ministry would take charge of the shipyards that had been independent until then. In spite of Allied bombardments on the shipyards in Germany, and thanks to production being widely dispersed, the number of U-boats being built would continue to increase until 1944.

Allied reactions: Even though Lorient was nothing more than a field of ruins, four Allied attacks took place until the end of May. The first took place on March 6, 1943, with sixty-five planes from the 8th US Army Air Force that dropped 162.5 tons of bombs. The SIPEG reported that the bombings had resulted in 200 dead among the civilians, and at least twice that number wounded since the beginning of the year. Seeing the number of air raids since the summer of 1940, and the tonnage of bombs dropped on the town, civilian losses would have been much higher if it hadn't been for the concrete shelters built by the Todt Organization in the town center. In comparison, a single raid on Nantes, on September 16, 1943, caused the loss of 1,000 civilians. In the town center, over 2,000 buildings had been destroyed. The surrounding communities had also been hit, such as Lanester where between 500 and 600 houses had been demolished. The French arsenal had been badly hit, and part of the work force had been billeted a long way from the town. In the French shipyards, work on the cruiser *De Grasse*, which had begun in September 1939, had almost come to a halt, and two 850-ton minesweepers started in March, were still only half completed, because these ships were now claimed by the Germans. At the beginning of March, the Germans repatriated 1,000 French workers who had been given notice by the French director of the arsenal. They were put to work on the bases in Kéroman and on the Scorff, but individually to avoid sabotage: which is to say, neither in groups nor with their managers. Jacques Stosskopf, vice-director of the arsenal, and second to Renvoisé, director and chief engineer, objected to this individual work method. Finally, in May, 700 workers were sent, but keeping their French supervision. By aligning the salaries of the French with that of the German workers, and by applying a bonus system, the number of workers in the arsenal had fallen by about 1,500 men, while a total of 4,300 French workers and employees were directly hired by the German Navy in Lorient. Several cases of sabotage were carried out by French workers during this time, notably a periscope damaged while being transported by crane-driver Marcel Mellac in 1942, and the regular sabotaging of torpedo cones in the Tréfaven workshop by section head Barse. Coastal Command carried out two mine-laying operations with a total of eight planes.

On March 4, 1943, U-264 returned to Lorient, bringing with it the seventy-five survivors of the German fuel tanker *Hohenfriedberg*. In the conning tower on the left is the watch officer of this tanker, sunk by a British cruiser on February 26. The interior of the Type VII U-boat must be particularly overcrowded. After having its propeller repaired, U-264 left the next day for its base at St. Nazaire. *UBA*

Mines are charged aboard U-117, a Type XB U-boat that left on March 7 for Brest, which it left at the end of the month for a minelaying operation off the Moroccan coast. *UBA*

On March 6, sixty-five 8th US Army Air Force B-17s dropped 162.5 tons of bombs on Lorient and Lanester. *NA*

The arsenal sector is the most badly damaged as well as the quarters alongside it. Above: the Priatec fuel-oil tanks, burnt in June 1940. On the right: the former aviation factory used by the *Kriegsmarine* as a material depot. *NA*

Several barrack rooms in the *Hundius Kaserne* have been destroyed. The maritime hospital and the railroad have been hit, as well as the arsenal's installations on each side of Guesdon Bridge. The Germans said that because of the attack, the drinking water was no longer potable, as it caused diarrhea or a sort of dysentery, a sickness that the submariners humorously nicknamed "Lorientitus!" *NA*

The ruins of the *rue du Lycée*, between the *Café de la Halte* and the arsenal door. *Michel Quettier*

The Rex Cinema, *rue Française*, seen from the quay. *Michel Quettier*

On March 8, U-382 arrives in Lorient for the first time, returning from the Gibraltar and Azores sectors where it damaged two ships. The insignia on its conning tower represents British Prime Minister Winston Churchill being hit in the head by two fish-headed torpedoes with the lucky number 13 written on them. Just above Churchill's hat is a tiny insignia painted by the naval shipyard with the inscription "*Frontreif,*" which signifies that the submarine was delivered ready for combat. *UBA*

In U-382's conning tower, watching the coast, from left to right: Jakubowski, Commander Herbert Juli and Watch Officer Sigurd Seeger who is wearing a miniature of his U-boat's insignia on his cap. *UBA*

During the month of March, the crew of U-382 was billeted at Kernével Point in one of the three blockhouses used by crewmembers. Above the bunker's door under a stairway, a wooden panel bears the word "August," in reference to the Commander's name "Juli" (July). This type of code, used between submariners and German *KMW* workers, meant that they didn't use or write the number of the U-boats anywhere near French workers in touch with the Resistance could see or hear. *LB*

Crewmembers from U-382 in their bunker at Kernével. In contrast to their U-boat where the "hot bunking" principle reigns, here everyone has his own bed—a luxury! *LB*

Toilets have been set up directly on the beach, opposite the former French redoubt. This complex of bunkers wasn't only reserved for U-boats coming from bases other than Lorient, such as U-382 of the 7th Flotilla, but was commonly used by the crews of the 10th Flotilla, like U-508 in February and U-513 in April. A total of six U-boat crews could be billeted in these three bunkers. *LB*

U-382's crewmembers take advantage of the end of March sun! In the background is the Kernével redoubt surrounded by camouflaged bunkers. Those not on leave in Germany are taken six days a week to Kéroman by bus to help the laborers work on their U-boat, and also to go to *U-Bootsheim* where films are shown. *LB*

Sunbathing aboard a U-boat could prove dangerous. On March 8, U-156 was surprised by an American *Catalina* aircraft 300 miles to the east of Barbados in the Caribbean Sea, while members of the crew were sunbathing on the bridge. Coming from out of a cloud, the plane dropped four Torpex bombs on the U-boat, which broke in three and immediately sunk. The plane continued to circle and spotted eleven survivors swimming in the water. It dropped a dinghy and food. It then took this photo of five crewmembers who managed to reach the dinghy. In spite of an extensive search, no survivors were ever found. *NA*

Once it returned to base, Lieutenant E. Dryden, pilot of the *Catalina* from VP-53, painted the silhouette of U-156 on the cabin. Painting its silhouette after the destruction of a U-boat was also done on Allied escort ships. *NA*

On March 10, U-163 left Lorient for its third and last patrol. It was sunk with all its crew three days after leaving Lorient, probably by depth charges launched from a corvette, after having succeeded in getting by the danger represented by Allied planes patrolling the Gulf of Gascony. *Bernd Siepert*

After having done most of its technical calls at St. Nazaire or Brest, U-135 from the 7th Flotilla arrives in Lorient on March 10. It hadn't had any success against the convoys in the North Atlantic and was damaged by a *Liberator*. Several members of the crew were decorated in front of the *Hundius Kaserne*. The presence once more of submarines that were normally based in Brest or St. Nazaire was explained by the fact that at that time all the bases in the Gulf of Gascony were overcrowded. Only Lorient, with its capacity of thirty sheltered pens, could offer the U-boats protected accommodations. *UBA*

At 1700, on March 13, 1943, U-123 leaves Lorient for its twelfth patrol along the African coast. *LB*

In front of U-123 is U-161, heading for the Azores sector for a meeting with blockade-runners before crossing the Atlantic to the east of New York! The two U-boats follow each other in the wake of escorts to avoid the risk of hitting a mine. *LB*

The lookouts aboard U-123 survey the horizon, their machine guns ready for action in the event of an aerial attack. This is supposed to be avoided by using the *Metox* radar detector, whose antenna of retractable wood can be seen; the crew called it the "*Biscaye Kreuz* – the Gascony Cross" because of its permanent use in this very dangerous sector.

On March 16, U-105 left the small base on the Scorff for its tenth and last patrol, heading for the African coast and Freetown. Its third commander, Jürgen Nissen, had chosen a new insignia, a sword passing through a submarine. The fifty-three crewmembers were lost at sea on June 2 when U-105 was sunk by depth charges launched from *Antarès*, a Potez-type seaplane belonging to the 141st Squadron formed by the Free French Air Force. *Ulf-Normann Neitzel*

U-107 arrives in Lorient on March 25, returning from the Azores and Gibraltar sectors. Some of the crew who have come up for fresh air in the conning tower celebrate their six successes by singing a song accompanied by an accordion. *UBA*

The day after its arrival, and following his mission report, U-107's commander Harald Gelhaus is awarded the Knight's Cross. *UBA*

At *Lager Lemp*, accompanied by his chief of U-boats in the West, *Kapitän-zur-See* Hans-Rudolf Rösing inspects the crew of U-124. Although he has been awarded the Knight's Cross with Oak Leaves, Commander Johann Mohr has stubbornly refused to take a land based job. The entire crew is in battle dress because the submarine will be leaving in a few hours. All of them will be lost at sea seven days later. *UBA*

On March 27, 1943, *Grossadmiral* Dönitz lands in Vannes-Meucon to visit his submariners in Lorient, and particularly to see Johann Mohr, the most decorated member of the 2nd Flotilla. He has also come to see a group of officer candidates who have just arrived from Germany; he wants to shake their hands personally. *LB*

A party on March 27 takes place in the *Wilhelm Bauer Kaserne* in Hennebont. Renowned for his singing talent, Chief Engineer Ernst Turck of U-621 has come from Brest specially to sing one of his songs, in which he ironically asks Dönitz to supply them with new U-boats that would be invincible. *Sabine Turck*

The Admiral likes the song. He is with his faithful Rösing and Kals, the chief of the 2nd Flotilla, who is sitting next to Adalbert Schnee (in the foreground on the right) former commander of U-201, now with the Submarine Corps General Staff as a specialist in the fight against convoys. Also at the table is a rather elderly NCO who has just joined the 2nd Flotilla's brass band stationed at the Hennebont barracks. When Dönitz went to congratulate the band that had just finished playing, he noticed that one of the musicians wore a decoration of the submariners of 1914-18 on his chest; he asked him which submarine he had served on and the musician answered with a number…. "What!" exclaimed Dönitz. "You were on *my* boat!" The NCO immediately replied "*Jawohl, Herr Grossadmiral!*" and Dönitz invited him to his table! *UBA*

On March 31, U-43, a veteran of the 2nd Flotilla, arrives once again in Lorient. This Type IXA U-boat, commanded by Hans-Joachim Schwantke, is returning from its fourteenth war patrol since its first mission in November 1939! *UBA*

April 1943: The Port Empties When the Type IXs Leave to Hunt Convoys

Movements: Fourteen arrivals, twenty-one departures, number of U-boats present at the end of the month: twenty. After the arrival of U-109 on April 1, the base in Lorient reached its peak of U-boats present in the port with twenty-eight. This number didn't stop decreasing in the following months. Of the twenty U-boats leaving Lorient in April, only five came back to port. On April 6, the U-boat Corps general staff changed strategies: to keep an significant number of U-boats in the North Atlantic, it was decided that all of the Type IXs already at sea heading south should turn to the North Atlantic. Also, most of them ready to leave Lorient should head for the same sector. Out of twelve Type IXs leaving in April, this concerned nine U-boats; for four of them, this would be their last patrol. Since March, the British had been using the new *Mark XXIV* depth charges, which were more powerful, and when they exploded the torpedo containers under the submarines' bridge were immediately flooded. During April, while the Type IXs were three times less numerous than the Type VIIs to attack convoys, their losses were twice as high. This would be the only attempt at using Type IXs in wolfpacks for attacking convoys in the North Atlantic. Henceforth, these long-range U-boats would return to hunting individually in remote oceans, like lone wolves.

On April 14, 1943, a second U-boat was sunk by a mine just off Lorient: U-526, a Type IXC-40. Commanded by Hans Möglich, this U-boat had left on its first combat patrol in the North Atlantic on February 11. It participated in the attack on the convoys SC 121 and SC 122 but hadn't been successful and was driven off by either planes or escorts. On April 14, at 0655, it was southwest of Groix Island at the "Laterne" rendezvous point where it met up with its escorts, the *Sperrbrecher 135* and the UJ-1404 submarine chaser. U-513 arrived at 0907 and took its place following U-526 that advanced, as was customary, 300 meters behind the *Sperrbrecher*. The submarine chaser came last. The precautionary measures were all the more necessary because following repeated mine-laying by British planes, seen from lookout posts on land on April 13, the 10th Flotilla sent the following radio message: "Escort for Rüggeberg and Moeglich at Laterne point on April 14—danger of mines on the seabed, wait for the blockade runner." A Ju 52 equipped with an anti-magnetic mine system flew over them during their approach which took ninety minutes. The commander of U-526 knew Lorient well as he had been there twice: in December 1941 and February 1942 as watch officer on U-130. In port, a welcoming committee had gathered to receive them. The two escorts and the two U-boats crossed the shallows indicated by the buoys at 1032, only three miles from the platforms on the Scorff. The commander of U-526 let U-513, commanded by an officer with a superior rank, overtake him on the starboard side. Suddenly, at only 1,500 meters off Larmor Plage, an explosion rocked U-526! It had hit a mine, resting on the seabed at a depth of twenty-five feet. The men on the bridge were thrown overboard. The explosion made a hole in the hull just behind the conning tower, instantly killing most of the crewmembers. U-526 sank backwards, as a few men managed to escape through the conning tower's hatch. In fifteen minutes, the submarine chaser picked up eight survivors, five seriously wounded, and three slightly wounded. U-513 picked up two others. Wolfgang Hirschfeld, a former crewmember on U-109, was among the welcome committee in Lorient and had come to greet his former chief engineer Martin Weber with whom he had carried out several patrols. As chief engineer transferred to U-526, Weber had been awarded the German Cross in Gold the day before and was to be decorated on his arrival. Wolfgang Hirschfeld recalls: "While several of my friends from the 10th Flotilla and I waited on the platform Isère, a motorboat suddenly pulled up alongside, a man with a loudhailer shouted: 'Stop the music! Clear the platform! U-526 has exploded during its arrival'! It was like being hit over the head with a club!" Chief of the 10th Flotilla Kuhnke was also in the welcome committee and he quickly requisitioned a small boat to direct rescue operations. Later, thanks to help from French divers who managed to open the rear hatch of the U-boat, settled on the seabed at only twenty-five feet, three last submariners were saved. The

U-BOAT	TYPE	FLOT.	COMMANDER	ARRIVAL	DEPART	NOTES
Departures						
U-43	IXA	2	Hans-Joachim Schwantke			In maintenance March 31 – July 13, 1943.
U-66	IXC	2	Friedrich Markworth	28	27 29	After a first departure on the twenty-seventh, returns to Lorient because smoke from the diesel motors filled the boat. After repairs, departure on April 29 for the coast of Florida; ninth patrol.
U-91	VIIC	9	Heinz Walkerling		29	Departure for fourth patrol, then returns to its base in Brest; sunk by three frigates 2/25/44; sixteen men taken prisoner, thirty-seven dead. Results: four ships and one destroyer sunk, two damaged.
U-103	IXB	2	Gustav-Adolf Janssen		24	Departure for the North Atlantic, tenth patrol.
U-107	IXB	2	Harald Gelhaus		24	Departure for the North Atlantic, tenth patrol.
U-108	IXB	2	Ralf-Reimar Wolfram		1	Departure for eleventh and last patrol in the North Atlantic; arrived in Germany, and turned into ship school in September 1943. Sunk 4/11/44 by American aircraft, refloated and regulated 7/17/44, scuttled 4/24/45. Results: twenty-five ships sunk.
U-125	IXC	2	Ulrich Folkers		13	Departure for seventh and last patrol, direction the North Atlantic; rammed 5/6/43 by a first destroyer, sunk by a second; no survivors; fifty-four dead. Results: sixteen ships sunk.
U-128	IXC	2	Hermann Steinert		6	Departure for fifth and last patrol in the South Atlantic; forced to surface after an aerial attack, commander ordered U-128 abandoned when two destroyers approached it 5/17/43; three killed during the attack, four wounded and later died, forty-seven survivors. Results: twelve ships sunk and one damaged.
U-135	VIIC	7	Heinz Schütt			Repairs after an air attack March 10 – June 7, 1943.
U-175	IXC	10	Heinrich Bruns		10	Departure for third and last patrol, direction the North Atlantic, forced to surface, under fire from several ships from a convoy and sunk 4/17/43; commander and twelve men killed, forty-one men taken prisoner. Results: ten ships sunk.
U-176	IXC	10	Reiner Dierksen		6	Departure for third and last patrol in the Antilles sector; sunk 5/15/43 by a combined attack from an American plane and a Cuban patrol boat; no survivors; fifty-three dead. Results: eleven ships sunk.
U-186	IXC-40	10	Siegfried Hesemann		17	Departure for second and last patrol in the North Atlantic; sunk 5/12/43 by destroyer; no survivors; fifty-three dead. Results: three ships sunk.
U-190	IXC-40	2	Max Wintermeyer			In maintenance March 30 – May 1, 1943.
U-226	VIIC	6	Rolf Borchers		10	Departure for second mission, then returns to St. Nazaire and Brest; sunk 11/6/43 by corvettes; no survivors; fifty-one dead. Results: one ship sunk.
U-303	VIIC	7	Karl-Franz Heine		1	Departure for the Mediterranean; passage Gibraltar during the night of April 9/10; sunk 5/21/43 during trials off Toulon by a British submarine; nineteen dead, ten survivors. Results: one ship sunk.
U-382	VIIC	7	Theopold Koch		8	New commander, departure; numerous missions out of St. Nazaire, La Pallice; then transferred to Norway then Germany; sunk during the bombardment of Wilhelmshaven in January 1945; refloated 3/20/45 and regulated; scuttled 5/3/45. Results: two ships damaged.
U-410	VIIC	7	Horst-Arno Fenski		26	Departure for the Mediterranean, passage Gibraltar during the night of May 5/6; numerous missions out of La Spezia and Toulon, badly damaged during American bombardment 3/11/44, regulated 3/22/44. Results: seven ships, one cruiser and one LST sunk, one ship damaged.
U-504	IXC	2	Wilhelm Luis		21	Departure for the North Atlantic and then returns to Bordeaux; sunk 7/30/43 by ships from the 2nd Support Group; no survivors; fifty-three dead. Results: sixteen ships sunk.
U-505	IXC	2	Peter Zschech			Being repaired December 12, 1942 – July 1, 1943.
U-508	IXC	10	Georg Staats			Being repaired March 15 – May 29, 1943, after an air attack.
U-511	IXC	10	Fritz Schneewind			In maintenance March 8 – May 10, 1943.
U-514	IXC	10	Hans-Jürgen Auffermann		15	Departure for the North Atlantic.
U-521	IXC	2	Klaus Bargsten			In maintenance March 26 – May 5, 1943.
U-525	IXC	10	Hans-Joachim Drewitz		15	Departure for the North Atlantic.

U-BOAT	TYPE	FLOT.	COMMANDER	ARRIVAL	DEPART	NOTES
U-634	VIIC	9	Eberhard Dahlhaus		15	Departure for second patrol direction the Atlantic then return to Brest; departure for third and last patrol destination the Caribbean; sunk 8/30/43 by depth charges launched by British ships; no survivors; forty-eight dead. Results: one ship sunk.
U-664	VIIC	9	Adolf Graef		29	Departure for fourth patrol in the North Atlantic then return to Brest; departure fifth and last patrol in the mid-Atlantic; sunk 8/9/43 by air attack, commander gave the order to abandon ship on the surface; eight dead; commander and forty-three men taken prisoner. Results: three ships sunk.
U-759	VIIC	9	Rudolf Friedrich			In maintenance March 14 – June 7, 1943.
Arrivals						
U-109	IXB	2	Joachim Schramm	1	28	Returns empty-handed from a month-long patrol in the Azores sector. New commander, because Bleichrodt, who was ill, disembarked in St. Nazaire 1/23/43. Returning prematurely after propeller problems, its fuel was transferred to three other U-boats. New departure; sunk 5/4/43 northeast of the Azores by depth charges dropped by a Liberator; no survivors; fifty-two dead. Results: thirteen ships sunk and one damaged.
U-106	IXB	2	Hermann Rasch	4		Returns empty-handed after a patrol of nearly two months between the Azores and Canaries, had to crash dive 105 times! Change of commander: Hermann Rasch affected to the general staff of Navy Operations.
U-642	VIIC	6	Herbert Brünning	8		First time in Lorient; put into service 10/1/42. Arrives from its first combat patrol in the North Atlantic, sunk one 2,125-ton ship, a straggler from the SC 121 convoy.
U-527	IXC-40	10	Herbert Uhlig	12		First time in Lorient; put into service 9/2/42. Arrives from its first combat patrol in the North Atlantic. Sank one 5,242-ton ship, which was carrying a 143-ton LCT assault craft, and damaged one other ship.
U-67	IXC	2	Günther Müller-Stöckheim	13		Returns empty-handed from a patrol between the Azores and Canaries. Patrol cut short after being damaged by a corvette on March 29.
U-513	IXC	10	Rolf Rüggeberg	14		Returns from a two-month patrol between the Canaries and Azores, without success. Brings back two survivors from U-526 sunk by a mine off Lorient on April 14. Change of commander: Rolf Rüggeberg named chief of the new 13th Combat Flotilla based in Drontheim, Norway.
U-510	IXC	10	Karl Neitzel awarded Knight's Cross on arrival.	16		Returns from a successful three-month patrol in the Caribbean, and off the coast of French Guiana. During the night of March 8/ 9, sank three ships for 18,240 tons, and damaged five others, all belonging to the BT 6 convoy. Change of commander: Karl Neitzel named interim chief of the 25th Training Flotilla based in Liepaja.
U-523	IXC	10	Werner Pietzsch	16		First time in Lorient; put into service 6/25/42. Arrives from its first combat patrol in the North Atlantic, with one 5,847-ton ship sunk; this ship was from the HX 229 convoy and had already been torpedoed by U-527 and abandoned by the crew.
U-172	IXC	10	Carl Emmermann	17		Returns from successful two-month patrol between the Azores and Canaries, with eight pennants. In reality, five ships were sunk, mainly from the UGS 6 convoy, totaling 29,165 tons.
U-530	IXC-40	10	Kurt Lange	22		First time in Lorient; put into service 10/14/42. Arrives from its first combat patrol in the North Atlantic, with two ships sunk from the convoys SC 121 and HX 231, for 12,063 tons.
U-159	IXC	10	Helmut Witte	25		Returns after a six-week patrol between the Azores and Canaries, with one 5,449-ton ship sunk. Returns to Lorient with half of the crew from U-167, which, after being damaged, was scuttled off Gran Canary on April 6. The rest of the crew had been picked up by U-455.
U-518	IXC	2	Friedrich Wissmann	27		Returns from a seventy-five-day mission off the coast of Brazil, with four ships sunk for 22,598 tons.
U-155	IXC	10	Adolf Piening	30		Returns from a seventy-five-day mission off the coast of Florida and in the Gulf of Mexico, with two ships sunk for 7,973 tons.

casualties were treated in the Maritime Hospital bunker because of the unending bombardments. Commander Möglich died just after his arrival, and six days later the second watch officer died from his wounds. Forty-two crewmembers (including the commander) died and most of them were buried in Kerentrech Cemetery; there were eleven survivors. Several crewmembers of U-504, on R&R at Larmor-Plage where they were billeted, were on the beach at the time and saw the explosion. Seconds before it happened, *Obermaat* Walter Wiese who had watched the two U-boats approaching the port had said to his friends: "They managed to get through, the lucky dogs!" After receiving first aid in Lorient, the wounded were sent to Ste. Anne-d'Auray Hospital Annex for convalescence on April 20. The dead submariners recovered from the sea were buried in Kerentrech Cemetery, and then after the war moved to Pornichet Cemetery. In September 1943, the two halves of the U-boat were moved: the back half was taken out of the water and dismantled in Kéroman III, and the remainder was dumped in the Kernével mud pits, from where it was removed by the

Marine Nationale in 1948, and put into a dry dock and dismantled.

Two U-boats of the 7th Flotilla left Lorient in April for the Mediterranean, where they managed to cross the Strait of Gibraltar. Five U-boats out of other French bases failed between May and November, four of them were sunk in the strait, and one damaged but managed to turn back. Because of the installation of Allied radar along the North African coast at the beginning of 1943, German U-boat action in the Mediterranean was almost non-existent. As soon as a U-boat surfaced off the North African coast, Allied planes or destroyers appeared within less than thirty minutes! A saying started to circulate among the U-boat commanders: "Idiots sail in the Atlantic, and total fools in the Mediterranean." Between July 10 and mid-August, the Allies invaded Sicily; there were only a dozen U-boats left in the Mediterranean by the end of 1943.

Observations: The rhythm of attacks against convoys decreased during the first days of April as a lot of U-boats had to return to their bases, after the hard month of March, for maintenance, or for fuel and torpedoes. In the North Atlantic, three convoys got through with only seven ships sunk for three U-boats lost. Six U-boats were off Freetown. U-515, commanded by Henke, surprised the TS 37 convoy. In twenty-four hours, he sank seven ships for a total of 43,255 tons, equalizing the record held by Schepke! For the few Type IX U-boats operating in remote waters, along the American and Brazilian coasts, the results were small except for U-129 that managed to sink two ships. Allied air patrols were so extensive that the U-boats couldn't remain on the surface near the coast. The U-boats' results fell by half in April with forty-nine ships sunk for a total of 266,274 tons. On April 23, U-191 was the first German U-boat sunk by a new *Hedgehog* weapon installed on the British destroyer *Hesperus*. This forward-launching weapon could launch twenty-four small spigot mortar bombs at the same time that exploded on contact with the submarine. They sank three times faster than traditional depth charges that weighed 270kg and were programmed to explode at a predetermined depth.

The Indian Ocean, where three Type IXD-2 U-boats had patrolled for the first time from the beginning of November to mid-December 1942, was once again patrolled by the same type U-boats at the beginning of April 1943. The first was U-180 on a special patrol that consisted of transferring the Indian Independence leader Chandra Bose to the Japanese submarine I-29 on April 27. Along with seven others, they sank a total of thirty-six ships until August 17, 1943, for the loss of the U-197. U-178 left for Penang in Malaysia, the others returned to Bordeaux at the end of their patrol. U-196, with 225 days at sea, held the record of the longest U-boat patrol without call.

In April 1943, a new Allied naval force appeared that caused big problems in the U-boat ranks: the Support Groups. These were groups of escort ships independent from convoys, contrary to the former Escort Groups charged with staying near convoys in the event of attacks. The five support groups could intervene immediately in the event of an attack against a convoy to reinforce the initial convoy, and above all remain behind after the passage of a convoy to destroy any lingering U-boats when they were forced to surface after twenty hours underwater to charge their batteries. Certain support groups specialized in permanently searching for U-boats, totally independent from convoys. This was the case of the famous 2nd Support Group commanded by Captain F.J. Johnnie Walker in the Bay of Biscay. This unit was credited with the destruction of twenty-two U-boats by the end of the war! These new groups were the brainchild of Admiral Max Horton, commander-in-chief of the Western Approaches, based in Liverpool. In action in the Atlantic, an initial formation of six ships of the same type (destroyers, sloops or corvettes) could be complemented by adding an escort aircraft carrier.

Allied reactions: The Royal Air Force carried out its last bombardment of the year on Lorient during the night of April 2/3, with forty planes out of the forty-eight planned that dropped 117 tons of bombs. The Americans took over on April 16. Fifty-nine B-17s dropped another 147 tons of bombs. Mine-laying operations intensified: eight were carried out at night during April with an average of five Wellingtons each time.

Canadian Rear-Admiral Leonard W. Murray. As a lieutenant during the last two years of World War I, he was in charge of the convoy escorts crossing the Atlantic. On June 13, 1941, he commanded the entire Newfoundland Escort Force, charged with protecting the convoys leaving New York to a rendezvous point with the British escort ships south of Iceland. Based in Halifax, he was named officer commanding the Atlantic coast on September 9, 1942, with 322 ships to ensure the success of his missions. Following the conference on the organization of the convoys held in March 1943, he was named commander-in-chief Canadian Northwest Atlantic. *RCN*

The fifty-three crewmembers of U-167 found refuge in Las Palmas on Gran Canary Island on April 6 1943, when their commander decided to scuttle their U-boat, badly damaged after an attack by two *Hudson* planes. Fifty-one of them were picked up two weeks later by U-455 and then divided between this U-boat and U-159 for their return to France. Commander Kurt Sturm left by plane a little later, while Second Watch Officer Ernst Semmel stayed for six months on the island, charged with diving to the U-boat and recovering all the documents on board and destroying them! U-167 hadn't sunk very deep and was raised by Spain in 1951 and used in several films. *UBA*

U-642 arrived in Lorient on April 8, 1943, after its first patrol in the North Atlantic, where it sank one ship. The antenna of the *Metox* radar detector had been set up while crossing the Gulf of Gascony. The watch crew was made up of four men, one of which was an officer. Each had a 90° sector to watch. In case of an attack the officer in charge sounded an electric alarm and had to go inside last to make sure that the hatchway was sealed. A U-boat would have a leakage problem if the antenna cable wasn't stowed properly before a dive. *UBA*

Commander Herbert Uhlig of U-527 made a great success of his first patrol. He arrived in Lorient on April 12 with a 5,242-ton ship transporting a 143-ton LCT landing barge sunk, and another ship damaged to his credit. Before attending a commander's training course he was watch officer aboard U-105 and had already been to Lorient four times between August 1941 and May 1942. *UBA*

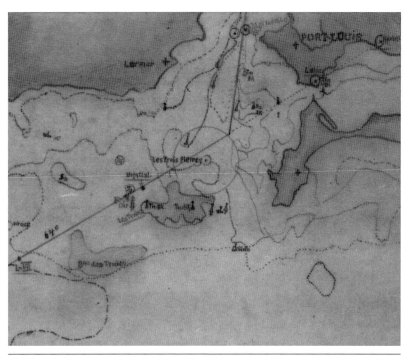

The spot where U-526 sank (*Unfallstelle*—accident position) after hitting a mine on April 14, fifteen kilometers from Larmor-Plage after it had just passed a seamark buoy. *BAMA-Freiburg*

Radioman Wolfgang Hirschfeld, formerly on U-109, affected in mid-January to the general staff bunker under the maritime prefecture, was among the welcome committee waiting to greet U-526 on A3 pontoon *Isère*. He recalls: "While we were waiting for the arrival of U-526, which had been announced, a motorboat approached, the pilot aboard told us to leave, the U-boat we were waiting for had hit a mine. I had wanted to congratulate Martin Weber, its chief engineer with whom I had once sailed with on U-109. Opposite my office in the prefecture bunker were several rows of lockers, each corresponding to a U-boat of either the 2nd or the 10th Flotilla. The index card with the number of the U-boat was inside each locker. Each time a U-boat was reported missing, I found the index card on my desk when I arrived in the morning. At the beginning of March 1943, I was sad to find U-522's card (sunk with all its crew on February 23). I had almost boarded that U-boat after meeting, during the welcome ceremony for it on December 2, 1942, an old friend from U-109 who had been transferred to U-522. Thanks to his invitation, I had spent the Christmas holiday with the crew of U-522 in Saltzwedel Kaserne and it was during that period that Commander Schneider asked me to join them for their next mission. Something must have told me that it would be wise to decline the invitation! Another day I found U-130's index card (sunk on March 13). Commander Keller had been second watch officer aboard U-109 with me in 1941. Previously, I had heard that U-520, commanded by Volkmar Schwartzkopff, the former watch officer aboard U-109, had been sunk at the end of October 1942. Thus, the two watch officers from U-109, with whom I had shared many missions, had disappeared during their first patrol as commander of a U-boat, both lost with their entire crew, including the chief engineer. Then on a day in June, I found the card of U-109 on my desk. All my former comrades were dead. I remembered the last drink I'd had with my friend Ferdinand Hagen, just before U-109 left on April 28. He told me that he had the feeling that he wouldn't return from the next trip and he charged me to personally break the news to his fiancée if his premonition should prove true." *UBA*

On April 16, 1943, U-510 returned from a successful three month patrol in the Caribbean and off the coast of French Guiana. During the night of March 8-9, it sank three ships for a total of 18,240 tons, and had damaged five others belonging to the BT6 convoy. *Ulf-Normann Neitzel*

Commander Karl Neitzel of U-510 is impatient to reach Lorient where he will receive the Knight's Cross, awarded on March 27. Opposite him is Chief Engineer Karl Beckmier, and on his right is *MatrOGef* Willy Märtens. *UBA*

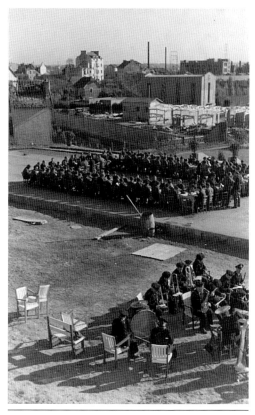

An open-air reception has been planned for U-510's crew between the *Hundius Kaserne's* two bunkers. The brass band has been invited to play during the light meal. In the background on the right is the cider making building and next to it, the electric factory's two small chimneys. *Ulf-Normann Neitzel*

Kuhnke, chief of the 10th Flotilla, stands up. On the left is the large officers' bunker that looks out over *Cours Chazelles.* *Ulf-Normann Neitzel*

After a welcoming glass of beer, U-510's crew assembles in the *Hundius Kaserne's* courtyard for the ceremony awarding the Knight's Cross to their commander. *Ulf-Normann Neitzel*

Kuhnke gives his congratulatory speech to U-510's crew. Sitting next to him is Commander Neitzel. *UBA*

Rösing, the chief of U-boats in the West has come from Angers specially to pin the decoration on Commander Neitzel. The latter will be leaving his U-boat as he has been named interim chief of the 25th Training Flotilla based in Liepaja.

Iron Crosses are then awarded to deserving crewmembers. *Ulf-Normann Neitzel*

After U-510's arrival in Lorient, on the same day between 1412 and 1414, the 8th US Army Air Force mounts a raid on the same sector where the reception had been held! The two preceding raids took place during the nights of March 6 and April 2-3. *NA*

A total of fifty-nine B-17s dropped another 147 tons of bombs, mainly on the northern quarter of the town. The maritime hospital was hit once again. *NA*

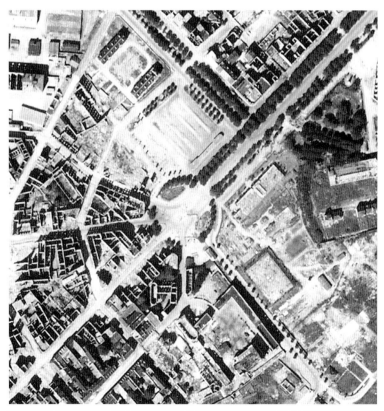

The wooden huts serving as lodging and mess in the *Hundius Kaserne* have disappeared. The stone buildings opposite the bunker have survived the attack better. *NA*

On April 17, 1943, in the North Atlantic, 400 hundred miles north of the Azores, U-175 was attacked by the escorts of the HX 233 convoy. The U-boat was spotted thanks to the escorts' *Huff/Duff* system. The main attacker was the Coast Guards' cutter *Spencer. NA*

A charge explodes. Will it force U-175 to surface in the middle of the American battleships? *NA*

The *Spencer* launches twenty-two depth charges towards U-175! *NA*

The U-175 surfaces, and the Coast Guard ships *Duane*, *Spencer* and *Dianthus* open fire while advancing on the U-boat, while the crew abandons it. Commander Heinrich Bruns is mortally wounded by shrapnel while in the conning tower. *NA*

A boarding party from the *Spencer* inspects the U-boat just before it sinks. We can clearly see the anti-aircraft gun on the rear platform; several members of U-175's crew attended the twelfth session of a formation between March 8 and 12 at the *Flak* School in Mimizan. *NA*

The forty-one survivors of U-175 swim towards the *Spencer* and the *Duane*. During the attack, the commander and twelve crewmembers were killed. *NA*

Midshipman Walter Wepplemann and 2nd Watch Officer *Leutnant-zur-See* Paul Möller. At thirty-four years of age he is one of the oldest members of the crew. A former commander in the merchant navy, he arrived in Lorient in April to board the U-boat for this last patrol. Equipped with their breathing apparatuses, they board the *Spencer. NA*

Helped aboard by a net. *NA*

Maschinengefreiter Otto Herzke aboard the USS *Duane. USCG*

These members of U-175's crew have been given blankets. *NA*

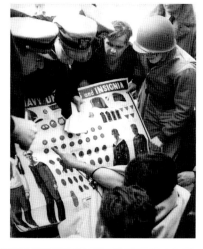

Once aboard, the Americans ask for their ranks, helped by an identification chart of *Kriegsmarine* personnel. *NA*

Once aboard, the Americans show them their magazines! *NA*

The US Navy marines celebrate their victory over U-175. *NA*

Commander Harold S. Berdine congratulates Captain Paul Heineman of the USS *Spencer* for the destruction of U-175. *USCG*

On April 17, 1943, U-172 heads for Kéroman III. It is returning with eight pennants from a successful two-month patrol between the Azores and the Canary Islands. On April 7, between 1420 and 1620, the U-boat took part in an attack on the surface against a bomber plane, using all its guns, including its 105mm gun on the bridge! It managed to hold the plane off. *UBA*

On April 20, 1943, following its return from patrol, the ceremony for awarding decorations to U-172's crew is held in the *Hundius Kaserne's* courtyard. *UBA*

Watched by Commander Emmermann, Kuhnke, chief of the 10th Flotilla, awards the Iron Cross to deserving crewmembers of U-172. *Bootsmannmaat* Herbert Plottke recalls: "Two days after our arrival, half of the crew left on leave. I was part of the second group and we shifted everything out of the U-boat so that we could have some free time. No matter what, an NCO and four marines had to remain with the U-boat while it was in the shipyard to guard against sabotage. When it was my turn on night duty, I found a way to sleep in my bunk for a while. I tied a length of rope to my foot and gave one end to the men on guard in the conning tower. If anything happened, all they had to do was to pull on the rope to wake me! Maintenance in the shipyards takes about four weeks when there isn't any particular damage to be seen to. When the first group on leave came back, it was the turn of the second group and we came back a few days before departure to help with loading supplies on board. The last days before our departure we went out a lot and we drank a lot as well, because none of us knew if this patrol would be our last." *UBA*

Commander Emmermann (on the right) accompanied by Rösing, chief of U-boats in the West, Kals, chief of the 2nd Flotilla and Commander Schwantke of the U-43 go to see *Grossadmiral* Dönitz in Brest. On the way they stop off to visit the beautiful town of Locronan. *UBA*

U-66 crewmembers salute their comrades on land. They left Lorient on April 27 for the coast of Florida. *LB*

The tug *Priatec* helps U-66 maneuver to leave the small base on the Scorff. In the foreground is Commander Friedrich Markworth. *LB*

The *Auray* wing in the maritime hospital where the survivors of U-526, sunk by a mine on April 14, spend their convalescence. In this photo, taken in 1995, we can still see the traces of the Red Cross painted on the roof. *UBA*

In the gardens adjoining the *Ste. Anne d'Auray* wing. From left to right: Sister Margarete, Karl Stachelhaus, *Fähnrich-zur-See* Wilhelm Daude, unknown, Konrad and *San. Uffz.* (Medical Officer) Wagner. *Uwe Stachelhaus*

The survivors of U-526 who weren't wounded arrive at the *Ste. Anne d'Auray* wing to visit their comrades. From left to right: Karl Metz, Karl Bongartz, Karl Stachelhaus and Dickhaus in front of the "*fontaine aux vœux*" (wishing fountain). Behind them is the War Monument for the Bretons who died in action during World War I. *Uwe Stachelhaus*

The final stage of convalescence for the survivors of U-526 is spent at Marburg in Germany. From left to right: Robert Maschauer, Peters, Wilhelm Daude, Karl Metz and Konrad. *Uwe Stachelhaus*

On April 29, 1943, U-664, commanded by Adolf Graef, left Lorient for its second-to-last patrol in the North Atlantic. According to the interrogation of the crew after their capture, the commander wasn't much liked by his crew, but who nevertheless admired his ability to locate a convoy. A supplementary crewmember named Dobberstein boarded the U-boat in Lorient before its departure, with a false rank of artillery quartermaster. In reality, he was a specialist of B-*Dienst*, the German service in charge of deciphering Allied radio messages, and trained in Belgium! It was the first mission of this kind aboard a U-boat. Thanks to a *Telefunken* receiver, he listened to the convoys' radio traffic in English, which he immediately translated on paper. On his arrival in Brest after the patrol, Dobberstein headed directly for Berlin. His notes helped to understand certain codes used by long-range aircraft, the number of planes used to cover a convoy, and also the arrival of a new Allied weapon against the U-boats, called the *Hedgehog*, a mortar/bomb launcher. During its next and last patrols, U-664 took on board two new operators from B-*Dienst* who were captured along with the rest of the crew when the U-boat was taken. They were quickly unmasked by the Americans. *UBA*

May 1943: Forty-One U-boats Sunk, North Atlantic Abandoned

Movements: Sixteen arrivals, eleven departures, number of U-boats present at the end of the month: twenty-five. Between May 4-11, three U-boats of the *Seehund* Wolfpack that had left for Cape Town at the end of December 1942 – beginning of January 1943, returned to Lorient; the fourth, U-160, went to Bordeaux. They obtained good results with a total of twenty ships sunk for only one loss: U-182, commanded by the experienced Nicolai Clausen. Almost all of the Type IX U-boats returned from attacking convoys in the North Atlantic empty-handed; five of them had been lost in April. On May 5, it was decided to stop using the Type IXs for chasing convoys in the North Atlantic. The rare departures on operation were for patrols along the North and South American coasts, after receiving supplies in the Azores sector.

Observations: On May 4, 1942, the ONS 5 slow convoy heading west, with a reduced escort, entered the *Fink* Wolfpack sector. During the night, six ships more or less scattered, were sunk. The next day, attacks by submerged U-boats sank four more cargo ships. Just before nightfall, fifteen U-boats were approaching when a sudden thick fog saved the convoy. Guided by their centimetric radar, the escorts kept the U-boats from attacking and sank four of them; a record number. In the morning of May 6, thanks to the arrival of a support group, two more U-boats were sunk. With the loss of a U-boat sunk by an aircraft on May 4, and the collision of two others, this brought the U-boat losses up to nine. For the first time, the escorts had managed to stop a U-boat threat on their own. The following convoys sustained fewer losses, while a U-boat was destroyed nearly every day. The SC 130 convoy marked the peak of Allied victims. When four wolfpacks were sent in its direction, between May 18-20, no ships were sunk, whereas three U-boats were lost, including U-954 aboard which was one of *Grossadmiral* Dönitz's two sons. On May 22, the U-boats were ordered to remain submerged in case of bad visibility. On May 24, 1943, Dönitz admitted defeat in the North Atlantic and ordered the surviving U-boats to temporarily leave the theatre of operations and head for the southwest of the Azores. It was the turning point in the Battle of the Atlantic. While, during the first half of 1942, the loss of one U-boat was offset by the destruction of 220,000 tons of Allied ships, this number had fallen by 55,600 tons for the second half of the year; 31,700 tons were sunk during the first three months of 1943, and fell to 5,600 tons in May 1943.

Returning from a combat patrol in the North Atlantic in May 1943 was already an achievement in itself, as former radio operator aboard U-533 Gottfried Zestermann, then aged eighteen, recalls: "When it was put into service we thought our U-boat was invincible, with a 105 mm gun in front of the conning tower, its 37 mm rear gun, and its anti-aircraft guns. Most of the crewmembers had never sailed in a U-boat; we were all so young! But after four months training in the Baltic Sea, we were finally ready to leave. After calling in Kristians and Norway for the rest of our fuel supplies, we left on April 17. On the 24th, the first alert sounded: a Stirling that finally didn't notice us. But at the end of the afternoon, we were attacked by another

plane flying out of the sun that dropped three depth charges in our direction! Everything on board was tossed about, but we held on. The next day, April 25, we were south of Iceland, where the sea was very rough with a force seven wind. At 1600 we surfaced, but only an hour later, an approaching Stirling forced us to dive. At 2329, we surfaced again to use the diesels; things were getting serious. Suddenly, a Sunderland seaplane flew straight at us out of a cloudbank, and it was too late to dive! The lookout crew dashed to the anti-aircraft guns while the seaplane made a half-turn. In spite of our defenses, it fired at us and dropped four 250 kg depth charges that exploded very close to us on level with the conning tower. We were tossed about but managed to dive; three crewmembers were wounded. They were given first aid by the commander, and radio operator Proft. Two of them received treatment in Lorient and were able to leave on the second patrol, the third, a young man called Fekken, had to stay longer in the hospital. On April 27, along with fifteen other U-boats, we received the radio order to get into line and try to find a convoy. Each of us had a lookout sector of twenty-five miles, our group controlled between 350-400 miles of ocean. At that moment, of the sixteen U-boats concerned, U-710 commanded by Carlowitz was already missing; sunk on April 24. Little by little, as the days passed, we lost U-192 commanded by Happe on May 6, U-209 commanded by Brodda the next day, U-528 commanded by Rabenau on the 11th, U-381 commanded by Pückler, U-954 commanded by Löwe on the 19th, and then U-258 commanded by Massenhausen the next day. Apart from U-528, the U-boats sank with their entire crew. I should mention here that we young sailors didn't have any idea that about 200 submarines had been sunk since the beginning of the war! During the day of April 27, we were forced to dive twice when approaching Catalinas were spotted, but they didn't drop any bombs. The next day we were in position between Iceland and Greenland, and had to crash dive after the sudden appearance of a destroyer coming out of the fog. Finally, three ships sailed over us, searching for us, but we managed to avoid detection. During the day, we had to crashdive four more times because of Sunderland seaplanes. At 2045 we received a message from U-650 commanded by Witzendorf: 'convoy found!' Suddenly, two destroyers came out of the fog only 1,000 meters from us! We turned and left at full speed, and half an hour later they abandoned the chase. When we returned into sight of the convoy's escort ships, another destroyer turned towards us and we dove when we were about 2,000 meters from it. It arrived over us and dropped seven depth charges, but they didn't cause any damage. A handling problem caused about seven tons of water to leak into the control room, but the chief engineer managed to solve the problem. On April 29, at 0205, we came across another destroyer and decided to attack. But, just before we fired, it turned in our direction and we were forced to leave. After about twenty-five minutes, it turned back towards the convoy. At 0359, we tried to slip along behind the leading escort ship, but once again a destroyer headed towards us and we had to dive; it too dropped seven depth charges which didn't do us any damage either. But it

remained over us until a search group arrived. They tried to situate our position with their localizing equipment and dropped about 100 depth charges. We managed to escape and surfaced at 0814 to try to find the convoy. We were now east of Greenland, and the sea was still stormy with a force seven wind. At 0100 on April 30, we saw the convoy on our port side, but once again a destroyer forced us to abandon the chase. At 0600 the fog was getting thicker and we came across the escort again, but had to crash dive to avoid depth charges. But the convoy was there so we prepared torpedo launching tubes 1 to 4, but a handling mistake prevented us from firing. By the time it was repaired, the convoy had passed and we only saw the last escort ship! We surfaced at 1242; we had missed it. That day it was Commander Helmut Hennig's twenty-ninth birthday, and the cook had baked a cake with the drawing of a sinking destroyer on it. At the very moment, he carried it into the officers' quarters a huge wave rocked the U-boat and the cake ended up on the floor! Was this a bad omen? On May 1, we were southwest of Greenland in a force eight wind, and the sea even more stormy. At 0243, we were forced to dive by a destroyer that greeted us with seven depth charges. When we rose to periscope depth at 0800, the commander spotted the destroyer on our port side, about 1,100 meters away. Now the storm had reached force ten, and it was impossible for us to attack. At 2142, we received a message ordering the wolfpack to stop the chase. On May 2, we were in the middle of what was almost a hurricane, when the commander authorized the personnel still inside, to spend quarter of an hour in the conning tower in small groups. I'll never forget what I saw: our tiny U-boat rolling in the middle of this wild sea, waves reaching twelve to fifteen meters high and crashing down on us. So that we could eat in peace at midday, we dived to forty meters below the surface but the U-boat still pitched about; it was better at sixty meters. The 'Old Man' let us listen to records. On May 2, we set out in the direction of a new convoy; because of the storm, our top speed was nine knots. The following morning, we had another alert because of a destroyer coming out of a fog bank. On May 4, at 0305, our anti-radar detection system sounded when suddenly a plane appeared above us with its searchlight turned on. This was a "Leigh Light" that in the submariners jargon was called *Leichenlicht* (corpse light). It fired at us, and inside we could hear the impacts against the hull. Miraculously, it appeared that he was out of depth charges! We were able to dive. Until daybreak, there were two more air raid alerts. At 0800, we surfaced again and spotted a distant convoy; at 1600 we started approach maneuvers, at a distance of fifteen miles from the convoy. At 2000, we spotted eight more ships in the AJ 9174 square. Visibility had deteriorated a lot, and, at 2330, we tried to approach; with the rain, visibility had fallen to 200 meters. At 0130, we dove to listen for propeller sounds; we heard sounds made by the Asdic and detonations from far off. At 0655, I was sitting quietly at my post in front of the radio when I heard a shout from the conning tower to the control room: 'Searchlight on the port side!' A destroyer came out of the fog, straight at us, at full speed and opened fire! Our watch officer, who arrived last in

U-BOAT	TYPE	FLOT.	COMMANDER	ARRIVAL	DEPART	NOTES
Departures						
U-43	IXA	2	Hans-Joachim Schwantke			In maintenance March 31 – July 13, 1943.
U-67	IXC	2	Günther Müller-Stöckheim		10	Departure for eighth and last patrol, east of the Caribbean; ten weeks without success, attacked and sunk on the way home 7/16/43 by an American plane; three survivors; forty-eight dead including the commander. Results: thirteen ships sunk and five damaged.
U-106	IXB	2	Wolfdietrich Damerow			In maintenance April 4 – July 28, 1943. New commander.
U-135	VIIC	7	Heinz Schütt			Being repaired after an air attack, March 10 – June 7, 1943. Change of commander: Schütt took command of U-294 in October.
U-155	IXC	10	Adolf Piening			In maintenance April 30 – June 10, 1943.
U-159	IXC	10	Helmut Witte			In maintenance April 25 – June 12, 1943. To date, U-159 survived a total of 700 depth charges! Change of commander: Witte very ill and sent to hospital for three months and then six months' convalescence; later named chief of the *Panther* Group comprising small attack U-boats.
U-172	IXC	10	Carl Emmermann		29	Departure for fifth patrol, in direction of the coast of Brazil, at the same time as U-508 and U-530.
U-190	IXC-40	2	Max Wintermeyer		1	Departure for second patrol, off the American coast.
U-505	IXC	2	Peter Zschech			Being repaired December 12, 1942 – July 1, 1943.
U-508	IXC	10	Georg Staats	31	29	Returns with technical problems.
U-510	IXC	10	Alfred Eick			In maintenance April 16 – June 3, 1943. New commander, former second watch officer aboard U-176.
U-511	IXC	10	Fritz Schneewind		10	Departure for fourth patrol, destination Japan! Aboard: the German Ambassador in Japan, the Japanese Naval Attaché in Germany, and *Kriegsmarine* engineers; arrival in Kure (Hiroshima) 8/7/43, and crew disembarked. U-511 ceded to the Japanese Navy and renamed RO 500; surrendered to the Americans August 1945 and scuttled 4/30/46. Results: five ships sunk and one damaged.
U-513	IXC	10	Friedrich Guggenberger		18	New commander, departure for fourth and last patrol, direction the South Atlantic; sunk by a plane 7/19/43; seven survivors including the commander; forty-six dead. Results: six ships sunk, two damaged.
U-518	IXC	2	Friedrich Wissmann			In maintenance April 27 – June 24, 1943.
U-521	IXC	2	Klaus Bargsten		5	Departure for third and last patrol, direction American waters; sunk 6/2/43 by an American ship; only the commander survived; fifty-one dead. Results: three cargo ships and an anti-submarine ship sunk.
U-523	IXC	10	Werner Pietzsch	26	22	Attacked by a plane two days after departure; damaged by six depth charges and had to turn back.
U-527	IXC-40	10	Herbert Uhlig		10	Departure for second and last patrol, in the Antilles sector; sunk 7/23/43 by aerial attack, commander and twelve men taken prisoner; forty dead. Results: one merchant ship and one LCT sunk, one cargo ship damaged.
U-530	IXC-40	10	Kurt Lange		29	Departure direction south of the Canaries as a re-supply ship. Then sent to Bordeaux and La Pallice before returning to Lorient in February 1944.
U-642	VIIC	6	Herbert Brünning		4	Departure for the North Atlantic then return to St. Nazaire; left for the Mediterranean, passage Gibraltar night of November 2/3, 1943; damaged during the American bombardment of Toulon 2/4/44 and then 7/5/44. Two crewmembers killed; regulated 7/12/44. Results: one ship sunk.
U-759	VIIC	9	Rudolf Friedrich			In maintenance March 14 – June 7, 1943.
Arrivals						
U-188	IXC-40	10	Siegfried Lüdden	4		First time in Lorient; put into service 8/5/42. Arrives from its first combat patrol in the North Atlantic. Fired six torpedoes at the ON 176 convoy, thought to have sunk four ships; in fact only one 1,190-ton British destroyer was hit. Two days before arriving in Lorient, it was attacked by a plane; the commander and a crewmember were wounded.
U-516	IXC	10	Gerhard Wiebe	4		Returns a long patrol of over five months off the coast of South Africa, to Cape Town; *Seehund* Wolfpack. Sank four ships for 25,586 tons.

U-BOAT	TYPE	FLOT.	COMMANDER	ARRIVAL	DEPART	NOTES
U-68	IXC	2	Albert Lauzemis	7		Returns from a three-month patrol in the Caribbean, with two ships sunk for 10,292 tons.
U-506	IXC	10	Erich Würdemann	8		Returns from a long patrol of over five months off the coast of South Africa to Cape Town; *Seehund* Wolfpack. Sank two ships for 9,980 tons.
U-509	IXC	10	Werner Witte	11		Returns from a long patrol of over five months off the coast of South Africa to Cape Town; *Seehund* Wolfpack. Sank two ships for 12,066 tons.
U-183	IXC-40	2	Heinrich Schäfer	13		Returns from a patrol of over three months in the Caribbean, with one ship sunk for 2,493 tons.
U-532	IXC-40	2	Otto-Heinrich Junker	15		First time in Lorient; put into service 11/11/42. Arrives empty-handed from its first combat patrol of nearly two months in the North Atlantic; attacked several times by depth charges, and missed its attack on an escort ship.
U-168	IXC-40	2	Helmuth Pich	18		First time in Lorient; put into service 9/10/42. Arrives from its first combat patrol in the North Atlantic. No success in spite of firing six torpedoes at the HX 232 convoy.
U-514	IXC	10	Hans-Jürgen Auffermann	22		Arrives empty-handed after a month-long patrol in the North Atlantic.
U-533	IXC-40	10	Helmut Hennig	24		First time in Lorient; put into service 11/25/42. Arrives empty-handed from its first patrol in the North Atlantic; managed to arrive safely after being rammed by a British corvette during the night of May 5/6.
U-525	IXC	10	Hans-Joachim Drewitz	26		Arrives damaged after an aerial attack by a Wellington equipped with a searchlight while returning from a five-week patrol in the North Atlantic, during which it sunk a 3,454-ton cargo ship separated from its convoy.
U-103	IXB	2	Gustav-Adolf Janssen	26		Arrives empty-handed from a month-long patrol in the North Atlantic. Arrives in Lorient with three British officers from the cargo ship *Fort Concord*, sunk on May 11 by U-456.
U-107	IXB	2	Harald Gelhaus	26		Returns from a month-long patrol in the North Atlantic, with one 12,411-ton ship sunk west of Ireland at the beginning of the patrol.
U-129	IXC	2	Hans-Ludwig Witt	29		Returns from a seventy-five-day patrol off the American coast, with three ships sunk for 26,590 tons. A crewmember lost overboard on May 21.

the control room, said drolly, 'Get ready for forced labor cutting wood in Canada!' We crash dived, but at a depth of eight meters, we were rammed by the corvette *Sunflower* (I learned that afterwards; at the time, we called anything that chased us a destroyer!). It hit us at the back of the conning tower and I was thrown forward onto my radio. The sound of the shock was awful, and then it dropped a depth charge right next to our boat. Our chief engineer took us down to a depth of 250 meters at full speed. Smoke was pouring out of a diesel motor that had caught fire; breathing in that air became unpleasant. We were ordered to move towards the front, and order was restored. We heard a few more charges far-off. Later we learned that we had confronted the ONS 5 convoy, which lost twelve cargo ships, but whose escort had sunk six U-boats with their entire crews, and had damaged five others. Two cargo ships were sunk for a U-boat destroyed—it was our worst result ever. At 0800, we heard more explosions from far off. When we surfaced at 1117, we were in the middle of an empty sea. Our antenna was out of order, our 37 mm rear gun was on the bottom of the seabed; a torpedo-launching tube had also been destroyed with a torpedo inside it. A diesel engine was damaged, and we had an oil leak that was repaired at 1800. During the days that followed, until May 11, nothing special happened. Then we were in the sector of a new convoy and we met up with U-569, commanded by Johannsen, at 1700. At about 2130, two U-boats arrived in our sector, chased by a

destroyer! We immediately moved off at full speed, but because of the damage we had sustained, the two other U-boats were faster than us! The destroyer approached us and opened fire at a distance of about 7,000 meters! We were finally forced to dive twenty minutes later after the arrival of a whole group of hunters! They dropped depth charges all round us for seven hours! They found us each time with the Asdic—I'll never forget that sound! But we hung in there, and none of us broke down. We heard each impact of the charge hitting the water, then we counted the seconds; at a depth of 180 meters, by example, we knew that we had a thirty to thirty-five second wait between launching the charge and its exploding. Our commander didn't stop changing direction and depth. All of a sudden, we heard a charge hitting the conning tower and then rolling along the deck; luckily, we were rising at the time and it exploded well below us! We had released 'Bold' decoys by the VII tube; perhaps that had helped us. In any case, in the early hours of the morning, when we no longer heard the sound of propellers, we surfaced at 0758. Three tanks had been torn open and were leaking; it took seven hours to pump them out by hand. On May 15, we were on the way home, and found ourselves northwest of the Azores. After transferring a part of our fuel, in difficult conditions, to U-621, commanded by Kruschka, we headed towards Lorient on May 17 using the electric motors, and then the diesels. At 2130, the alarm sounded at the approach of a plane, but it didn't drop any bombs.

May 18 and 19 went well. We repaired our anti-aircraft guns that were important when crossing the Bay of Biscay; we prepared the shells. On May 21, a Sunderland was spotted that our alarm system hadn't located (it must already have been equipped with a centimetric radar, but we didn't know that at the time). We crash dived to thirty meters; four bombs exploded. The next day, on May 21, we were west of the Bay of Biscay, and, during the day, we dove a dozen times either because of planes, or because our anti-radar alert kept going off. On May 22, we signaled our approach and continued underwater. The next day, we heard the English propaganda radio program 'U-Bootsender Atlantik' which was broadcast in German. It was the kind of propaganda that didn't impress us all that much, but it annoyed us to hear the commentator giving out the names of the survivors from U-569, commanded by Johannsen, and destroyed the day before, which we had met up with ten days earlier. Sometimes they sent personal messages to a particular crewmember! On May 24, at 0230, we reached the 'Kern' rendezvous and continued submerged to 'Laterne' point where we met up with our escort at 1510. We spotted the French coast, and all the crewmembers who weren't busy went up onto the bridge. We saw the clean beaches, the green countryside, white houses and all that under a blazing sun. We began to realize that we were leaving Hell behind us. Only a few days ago we heard depth charges exploding! We had survived, most of us, our first baptism of fire! For me personally, it was as it was ten Christmas Days at once! At 1650, we entered the number 13 pen in Kéroman III, happy to have this thick slab of concrete over our heads! Of course, we hadn't had a victory, but nevertheless we were proud to have become real submariners who had seen combat."

Radio operator Gottfried Zestermann, who recounted this mission, was transferred to U-155 and survived the war. The rest of the U-533 crew was lost during its next patrol in the Indian Ocean, apart from one survivor: torpedo mechanic Günther Schmidt. He had been on the bridge smoking a cigarette when a plane appeared; the U-boat crashed dived. He just had enough time to get into the upper part of the conning tower with the watch officer before the dive and both of them had still been in the upper part when a depth charge dropped by a plane hit the hull that immediately filled with water. Without survival equipment, the two men nevertheless managed to open the upper hatch, and get out of the U-boat, which then sank to a depth of 180 feet. They swam to the surface, where the officer passed out. The mechanic swam alone for thirteen hours and managed to reach the coast where he was taken prisoner.

The Allies now had fifty long-range planes based on each side of the Atlantic, England, and Newfoundland, Canada, as well as Catalina's in Iceland. With these aircraft, they were able to totally protect the convoys in the Atlantic. Also, the Allies improved the depth charges dropped by plane: a new adjustment permitted them to explode in shallow depth, which quadrupled their chances of success. On May 23, for the first time, rockets were fired against a U-boat plane from the British escort aircraft carrier *Archer*. U-752, already damaged, was scuttled. Since the end of 1942, certain planes had been armed with four 76.2mm rockets under each wing. The planes also had a new weapon of which 500 models had been

produced: the Mk.24 *Fido* acoustic torpedo which homed in on a U-boat trying to make a diving escape. On May 25, U-467 was the first German U-boat sunk by an acoustic torpedo of this type. Finally, in May, the convoys were accompanied by escort aircraft carriers throughout their voyage. A total of eighteen *Bogue*-class escort aircraft carriers were put into service in 1942-43, and then twenty-four *Repeat Bogue*-types during 1943. On May 20, the Americans created the Xth Fleet, a general staff in charge of commanding and coordinating all the American anti-submarine operations. Directed by Rear-Admiral Francis S. Low, named on April 6, chief of staff 10th Fleet. Low had authority over all the long and extra-long range planes, the support groups comprising an escort aircraft carrier and escort ships, the Anti-submarine Group of the Atlantic Fleet, the ASWORG (Anti Submarine Warfare Operations Research Group) composed of scientifics, and the Bureau of Shipping Lanes and Convoys. From June on, this unit published a monthly "Report of the Anti-submarine War." Widely distributed, it outlined the views and conceptions of the ship commanders and aircraft pilots involved in anti-submarine warfare. Setting up this command unit against the U-boat corps played a determining role in the destruction of the German U-boat fleet in the following months. Until then, after eighteen months of combat, the American naval and aviation forces had only sunk thirty-two U-boats out of a total of 189. Henceforth, the American, British, and Canadian intelligence and operational services concerning U-boats worked closely together out of Washington, DC, London, and Ottawa. In three and a half months, the Allies had patiently put together an armada, both naval and aerial, that almost completely prevented U-boats from taking action on the surface in the Atlantic. All of Dönitz's strategies, and above all, wolfpack attacks at night,

depended on their mobility. Now, for the German U-boat corps, only their Type IX, long-range U-boats hunting in far-flung oceans stood any chance of success. The next step for the Allies was to destroy the re-supply U-boats, and prevent them from reaching their remote destinations where defenses were not yet completely operational. In May, the U-boats only sank forty-five ships for a total of 237,182 tons; almost the same number of U-boats was lost.

The aerial attacks carried out by Coastal Command, still numerous in the Bay of Biscay, managed to sink nine U-boats in May. To counter this in the shipyards, platforms behind the conning towers were equipped with quadruple 20mm anti-aircraft guns. This redoubtable *Flak Vierling* was capable of firing 1,800 rounds a minute! A total of seventy-two installations were planned for June, July, and August. On May 20, 1943, an order was given to turn ten U-boays into *Flak* U-boats. Only two days later, the first of these, U-441, left Brest; it was armed with two quadruple 20mm guns, a 37mm gun, and two simple 20mm guns! Its first aerial combat against a Sunderland ended in the destruction of the plane, but the U-boat sustained damage and had to return to base. On May 29, 1943, the U-boat Corps Command ordered its U-boats to cross the Bay of Biscay in groups during the day and on the surface, to confront the planes. This began on the same day in Lorient with the group departure of U-172, U-508, and U-530.

Allied reactions: The last bombardment on Lorient in 1943 was carried out on May 17 with 118 B-17s and B-24s dropping 289.5 tons of bombs. Coastal Command carried out four mine-laying operations with six Wellingtons and a fifth operation with only three planes.

On May 2, 1943, Commander Klaus Bargsten of U-521 receives the Knight's Cross from *FdU-West* Rösing. Spending leave with his family in Brême until April 28, Bargsten witnessed a very violent attack in full daylight by the Americans. On April 29, he returned to Lorient and discovered the next day that he had been awarded the Knight's Cross. A month later his U-boat sank and he was the only survivor. Bargsten, who had formerly taken part in four patrols as the commander of U-563, had been trained on U-99 under Kretschmer with whom he had undertaken seven patrols as watch officer. *Charita*

Commander Erich Würdemann of U-506, who arrived in Lorient on May 8, 1943, receives the Knight's Cross that he was awarded on March 14. This was the second U-boat of the *Seehund* Wolfpack patrolling around the Cape to return, after U-516 that had arrived on May 4. U-506 had travelled 19,624 miles without call during a patrol of 146 days! Like the others in his pack, he had been given supplies south of Saint Helena Island on the way out, and south of the Azores on the way back. The two ships sunk between March 7-9 pushed Commander Würdemann over the 100,000 tons that won him his decoration. During his next patrol, he and forty-seven members of his crew were lost at sea on July 12. *UBA*

Born in Padang in Sumatra, and just twenty-six-years-old, Commander Fritz Schneewind of U-511 left Lorient on May 10 for a very long trip to Japan!; with him were the plans for the Messerschmitt Me 262 jet aircraft. He also had several engineers taken on board in Lorient, as well as Dr. Ernest Woermann. the German Ambassador to Japan, the Japanese Medical Officer Sougita, and Vice-Admiral Nakouni Nomura, Japanese Naval Attaché in Germany, aged fifty-six. The latter recalls: "A few days before I left Berlin, Admiral Dönitz invited me to a reception and said to me 'I have the immense pleasure to inform you, who are about to leave our country, that our navy will soon be sending our U-boats to the Indian Ocean to cooperate with yours. This has been decided this afternoon. After returning his vessel to your country, the German crew of U-511 will board one of these U-boats which will take part in operations in the Indian Ocean.' On March 8, I left Berlin, full of souvenirs, for Lorient that I reached the next morning. The bombardments had caused a great deal of damage everywhere I looked. I spent the morning in barracks underground, consulting with German officers about U-511 that would be leaving on May 10. In the afternoon of May 10, at 1300, I boarded the U-boat to the national anthems of both countries. Commander Schneewind gave his orders in a piercing voice and his boat moved slowly away from the base. Deeply moved, the crew and the people who came to see it off, all saluted." During its long trip, U-511 was re-supplied by U-460 off Freetown. *UBA*

These three U-527officers, Second Watch Officer Heinrich Abel, Commander Herbert Uhlig and Chief Engineer Walter Lewandowski, have only been to Lorient once, at the end of their first patrol. U-527 left the port on May 10 for its second and last patrol. It managed to cross the Atlantic to patrol around Florida, but without result. Like many other U-boats at that time, it was sunk on its way back, in the Azores sector on July 23, during a re-supply operation. It was attacked by a Grumman Avenger launched from the American aircraft carrier USS *Bogue*. The commander and twelve other members escaped, two of who were these two officers. *UBA*

U-509 is the last submarine from the *Seehund* Wolfpack to return to Lorient on May 11, 1943. It had sunk two ships for 12,066 tons. On the slipway at Kéroman I, it is raised onto a wagon to be carried onto a mobile platform to a dry pen where it will be cleaned and repaired. In the sky behind is a group of barrage balloons to prevent low-altitude air attacks. *UBA*

These two U-509 crewmembers must be happy to be back on land after their departure from Lorient on December 14, 1942, five months earlier. Out of five U-boats sent to the Cape, four came back undamaged. U-182 was sunk on May 16 off Madeira when it had almost reached a base in the Gulf of Gascony. *UBA*

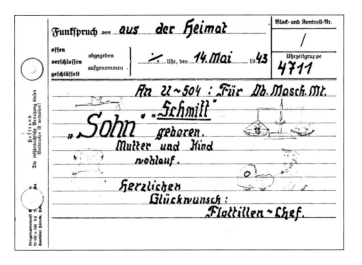

This radio message sent by the chief of the 2nd Flotilla in Lorient on May 14 must have made Machinist Schmit very happy. He was a member of U-504's crew on patrol against convoys in the North Atlantic. The chief congratulated Schmit on the birth of his son, and said that mother and child were well. A very personal message that, for once, wasn't of much interest to the British decoders in Bletchley Park! The radio message ended with little drawings: one of a stork carrying a baby and another of a woman pushing a pram. *UBA*

U-532 arrives in Lorient for the first time on May 15. The crewmembers discover the joys of the countryside at *Lager Lemp*, a lot calmer than the numerous depth charge attacks they suffered during their patrol. *UBA*

Weber, Weigelt, and Spalteholz from U-532 play cards at *Lager Lemp*. *UBA*

On May 16, 1943, U-108 arrived in Stettin, Germany. This U-boat of the 2nd Flotilla, put into service in October 1940, had just finished its eleventh and last combat patrol; it was later transformed into a U-boat school. The 187,000 tons of ships painted on the conning tower was an exaggeration; in truth it had sunk twenty-five ships for a total of 127,990 tons. Aboard was Officer-candidate Hans-Dieter Brunowsky. On his unique patrol on a U-boat, he recalls: "At the beginning of 1943, we, the officer-candidates, proudly carried our dirks after graduating from officer training school. A part of our class left immediately for the front. We submariners had one more commander's course at the Neustadt-in-Holstein school. We put on our *feldgrau* combat dress to act out the role of commander, one after the other. In the middle of the course sixteen of us were called to the secretary's office. We listened rather nervously as an adjutant read our names off a telex and then he suddenly announced: transferred to the 2nd U-boat Flotilla in Lorient! Filled with joy, we rushed off to our quarters. We handed in our *feldgrau* uniforms and filled our big aluminum case full of clothes that wouldn't be of any use aboard a submarine: white walking-out dress, brown overalls for apprentices. We wrote the number of the military post of the 2nd Flotilla on the case that was then taken to the station in a truck. We then presented ourselves dressed in coat, cap and dirk, to the company chief—we were ready for the

front! Two days later we arrived in Lorient. In the middle of a landscape in ruins, we saw a single truck. 'Are you the officer-candidates for the 2nd Flotilla?' demanded the driver. What planning! We got into the truck; our cases were already loaded. We passed buildings and houses in ruins for a long time, and then we left it behind and found ourselves in the countryside. When we had left Neustadt School in mid-March we had the impression that it was winter, but here it was already spring! At the gate leading to the camp our papers were controlled, even though we were in a truck belonging to the Kriegsmarine. We presented ourselves to the flotilla chief and then we were sent to our quarters in barracks reserved for officers. A pretty French girl who was making up her bed, said: 'My name is Simone if you need anything.' Good Heavens, it was like being in a hotel! In the officers' mess we could have anything, just by handing over coupons without having to pay. Anything we ate or drank was later taken out of our pay ... or sometimes it was free. For the next three days I ate eight fried eggs for breakfast! We were affected to different U-boats. I was supposed to be assigned to Mohr, who already had Oak Leaves to his Knight's Cross. Then I met Lieutenant Richard von Harpe, who is related to my mother-in-law. He managed to fix it so that I was on his boat, U-108, so that he could look after me. We later learned that Mohr had been sunk in the Gulf Of Gascony. I think that French agents must have passed on the information of this ace's departure to the British; once again I had been lucky! With my friend Harnak, who was an officer-candidate on U-108 too, we discovered our new sand-colored uniform. Were we going to the Caribbean or the west coast of Africa? We went with the officers to the base where there was an incredible amount of activity, a strong smell of diesel and the air was filled with shouting voices. My dream was about to come true— I was going to board a U-boat that would be leaving on patrol in a few days! While the officers were busy on board, the other officer-candidates and I visited the base, an incredible installation where the laborers could work night and day in this huge naval shipyard protected under concrete, safe from enemy air raids. That night we celebrated at *Lager Lemp*, notably at the Moulin Bar where officers met up every night during the days before leaving on patrol. For my part, the most impressive moment will always be meeting Admiral Dönitz on March 27 when he wanted to personally shake hands with each officer-candidate. During dinner with him we were given American Chesterfield cigarettes! Then things got serious: checking the food supplies, torpedoes and fuel. Tinned food was stocked everywhere, sausages were hung up and fresh bread was put into hammocks. In the front part of the submarine the crew had their bunks—over the greasy torpedoes. The officer-candidates' bunks were in the part reserved for NCOs. Suddenly, it was departure time! We lined up on the bridge, von Harpe reported to the commander who called out 'Greetings men!' We replied so loudly that it echoed round the bunker: 'Greetings *Herr Kaleu*' (abbreviation for *Kapitänleutnant*.) He gave a short speech then it was time to go to maneuvering stations. The diesel motors coughed into life, the boat slowly left the bunker for the open air and then prow-first we headed for the Atlantic. On the port side we passed an old fortress, the sea lay before us, we were on combat patrol. After a few eventful weeks, we arrived in Stettin where we were separated. Commander Ralf-Reimar Wolfram was killed aboard U-864 off Bergen on February 9, 1945. Our Watch Officer Richard von Harpe, who became commander of a Type XXI U-boat, was killed on March 2, 1945, when his boat hit a mine. None of the crew of these two U-boats survived. My friend Harnak who had become a sub-lieutenant, died in 1945." U-108 didn't survive the war either; it was sunk during an American attack on Stettin on April 11, 1944. *UBA*

The Allies carried out their last bombardment of Lorient in 1943, on May 17. Among the planes that participated in this raid was the famous B-17 *Memphis Belle*. This plane took part in four raids on Lorient in 1943: January 23, March 6, April 16, and May 17. *NA*

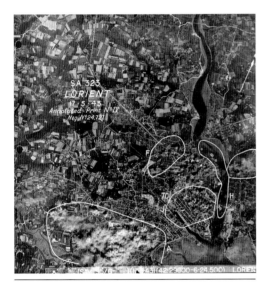

The Kéroman zone was the most damaged area, but part of the 289.5 tons of bombs dropped by the 118 B-17s and B-24s fell on the town center again. *NA*

Plan of the bombs dropped in the Kéroman sector. On the right: the Kéroman submarine bases, in a half circle. The torpedo bunkers in Kérolay were linked to the bases by railroad. *NA*

The submariners' hostel in Kéroman has been badly hit, however, the part on the right which still has its roof would be used until the end of the war. *LB*

In the morning of May 17, 1943, U-128, which had been tracking a convoy spotted during the night, showed up on the *Huff/Duff* systems aboard two *Mariner* planes, which attacked twenty kilometers off the Brazilian coast. *NA*

U-128 crash dived, but was hit during the maneuver; it sank to 220m! After an emergency ballast tank blow, it rose to the surface but was attacked again by the planes. This time it was seriously damaged by charges and could no longer dive. *NA*

Two hours after the attack, two destroyers approached U-128 and opened fire, forcing Commander Hermann Steinert to order his crew to abandon ship. It was sunk by gunfire from the destroyers, which later picked up fifty-one crewmembers out of fifty-four; later four survivors died from their wounds. When U-128 left Lorient on April 6, the watch officer, *Kapitänleutnant* Siegfried Sterzing, held a higher rank than Commander Steinert, who was only an *Oberleutnant*; the commander was finally promoted on May 1, 1943, a few days before the destruction of his U-boat. *NA*

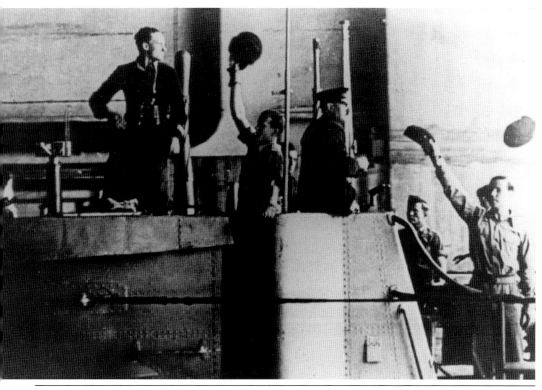

U-513 was the first of the three to leave. It left the small base on the Scorff on May 18. Most of the crewmembers were enthusiastic that their commander, Rüggeberg, had been replaced a few days earlier by this ace. They had grown tired of being called the "Failure Crew!" Re-supplied by U-460 off Freetown, their U-boat crossed the Atlantic for the coast of Brazil, where it sank four ships and damaged five others before being sunk in turn by aircraft on July 19. Only seven survivors, one of which was the commander, were fished out of the sea and taken prisoner. Commander Guggenberger, after having his wounds treated in hospital, was sent to the camp in Papago Park, Arizona, from which he escaped twice: on February 12 with four other commanders, but they were quickly caught; the second time on December 12, 1944 with twenty-four others. This time he was caught on January 6, 1945, only four miles from the Mexican border. The second ace to leave on patrol on June 2 was Cremer aboard the U-333. He returned from his patrol unsuccessful after having been attacked by planes; the third ace, Kuppisch, left the base aboard U-847 at the end of July. He and his entire crew were lost at sea a month later. *UBA*

Commander Friedrich Guggenberger arrived in Lorient by train to take over the command of U-513 and left on patrol on May 18. Following the large number of U-boats lost during the first weeks of May 1943, the U-boat Corps General Staff decided to send three aces to the Atlantic. If they succeeded in their mission, it would be an example for all the younger and less experienced commanders that represented the highest part of the losses. Therefore, on May 14, Dönitz organized a meeting with his general staff in Berlin and asked for three volunteers among the officers to leave on mission. As all the officers qualified to command a submarine stepped forward, he chose: Peter "Ali" Cremer of U-333, who had already survived being rammed by a fuel tanker and a surface combat against a corvette, and who had been decorated with the Knight's Cross; Friedrich Guggenberger, decorated with the Knight's Cross with Oak Leaves, who had sunk the British aircraft carrier *Ark Royal* in the Mediterranean while commanding U-81; and Herbert Kuppisch, former commander of U-94, aboard which he had won the Knight's Cross.

U-523 commanded by Werner Pietsch left Lorient on May 22 at 1530. Two days later it had to return after being damaged by an aerial attack northwest of Cape Ortegal. *UBA*

American Commander Kenneth Knowles, Officer in Charge "Atlantic Section" Tracking Room, in the 10th Fleet. This Special Anti-submarine Service, formed on May 20, 1943, within the US Navy, integrated the OP-16-W, a "Special Warfare Branch" created in December 1942 and part of the Office of Naval Investigation (ONI). The OP-16-W's task was to undermine German submariners' morale by using propaganda. *NA*

These U-514 crewmembers, who arrived in Lorient on May 22 at 1602, must have crossed the crew of U-523, which was leaving. U-514 had no success during its patrol against convoys in the North Atlantic, but it returned undamaged to its base, which was lucky at that time. *UBA*

Submariner Ernst Droese of U-525 at *Lager Lemp*. Unlike most of the Type IX U-boats that came back empty-handed from their patrols in the North Atlantic at the end of May 1943, U-525 had sunk a cargo ship that that been separated from its convoy. *UBA*

U-533 crewmembers on the corner of *rue du Maréchal Joffre* and *Cours Chazelles,* in the *Hundius Kaserne* sector, in front of one of the few buildings in the area still intact—the *Soldatenheim* (soldiers' hostel). Their first mission, leaving Kiel on April 15 to arrive in Lorient on May 24, was particularly difficult. They suffered a dozen air raid alerts, resulting in four aerial attacks against their submarine, and seven attacks from escort ships with several dozen depth charges launched against them, and having the conning tower rammed! *UBA*

At Kernével, on the balcony of Villa Sevenne, end of May 1943: Kuhnke, chief of the 10th Flotilla, greets Ramcke, general in the *Fallschirmjäger*. On the right: Commander Neitzel of U-510. *Ulf-Normann Neitzel*

U-103 returned empty-handed from its tenth patrol in the North Atlantic where it had been confronted by aircraft carriers escorting the convoys. They brought back British Navy officers from the *Fort Concord* cargo ship, sunk on May 11 by U-456. Put into service in July 1940, this U-boat stayed for three months in the naval shipyard for a complete overhaul. On the front of the conning tower, the Olympic Rings were added to the earlier insignia to remind everyone that Commander Gustav-Adolf Janssen graduated as an officer in 1936. *UBA*

Commander Burkhard Hackländer of U-454, which arrived at La Rochelle on May 23, an officer of the Luftwaffe, *Leutnant-zur-See* Hoffmann, watch officer aboard U-172, and Commander Georg Staats of U-508. These two commanders are due to leave on patrol on May 29. *UBA*

Officers of U-172 take advantage of the sun on Lamor beach before their next departure on May 29. In the center, in uniform next to Commander Emmermann in sunglasses, is Helmut Berndt, the war correspondent who had participated in the previous patrol. *LB*

Last moments of respite in Lamor for the officers of U-172. In the background: "*La Maison des Espagnols*" on the "*Pointe des Blagueurs.*" UBA

Commander Kurt Lange of U-530. At thirty-nine years of age, he is a veteran figure amongst the commanders of combat U-boats. *UBA*

U-530 performing water tightness tests in the Scorff, before its departure on May 2. *UBA*

Commander Emmermann of U-172 in sand-colored uniform, and like most of the U-boat commanders at that epoch, wearing his Knight's Cross. As his U-boat leaves, he salutes his friends on land who have come to wish him good luck. *LB*

U-172 prepares to cross the Gulf of Gascony; a crewmember is already folding away the flag. Just below him is a new platform installed in the naval shipyard, for an extra anti-aircraft gun. This new patrol is along the coast of Brazil. *LB*

U-508 had left two days earlier but had to return to the small base on the Scorff on May 31 due to a technical problem. It also has a Type IV conning tower with two rear platforms. *UBA*

With the help from three tugs from *KMW*, U-172 left the small base on the Scorff at 1345 for a new patrol. To face the danger posed by Allied planes while crossing the Gulf of Gascony, it left Lorient accompanied by U-508 and U-530. *Bootsmannmaat* Herbert Plottke, detailed the submarine's armament in coordination with the 10th Flotilla: "First of all, helped by crewmembers, the Torpedo Mechanic loaded 22 to 24 torpedoes in the fore and rear compartments, and reserve tubes on the bridge. All of this was checked by the watch officer who was responsible for the torpedoes. The technical crew, under orders from the chief engineer and the mechanics, checked that the fuel, oil and drinking water were loaded. The helmsman, who was one of the first to know where our patrol will head, arrived with his charts. After that, the second watch officer oversaw the ammunition being loaded on board. Shells in tubes on the bridge, but cases are also loaded on board anywhere there was a place for them. As well as shells for the U-boat's guns, there were rounds for individual weapons: two MG34 machine guns, two submachine guns, six 7.65mm Mauser pistols for officers, and two NCOs. The foodstuffs only arrived when everything else was loaded, under the responsibility of the helmsman and the chef. Everyone was called upon to help out with the cargo that took up the last spaces, even in the two toilets. Everything had to be battened down in case of bad weather at sea. We loaded several tons of various materiel, food and fuel for a patrol of at least three months." *Anthony Guychard*

June 1943: Dangerous Crossing of the Biscay Bay

Movements: Seven arrivals, eleven departures, number of U-boats present at the end of the month: twenty-one. On June 8, U-758, the first combat U-boat equipped with a *Flak Vierling*, succeeded in confronting several plane attacks keeping them at a distance of 2,000 meters, but eleven crewmembers were wounded. A new, more powerful 20mm shell called *Minengeschoss* was available for the U-boats on June 1; in the following month it was used in combination with perforating and homing shells. Almost all the U-boats leaving on patrols left Lorient in groups of three to cross the Bay of Biscay in full daylight in order to counter the danger from Allied aircraft. This worked quite well during the first two weeks, but the Allies quickly found the solution. A plane spotting a group of U-boats didn't attack but remained at a distance radioing other planes, who then attacked in groups to force the anti-aircraft U-boats to dive. This was the case for U-68 and U-155, damaged by four Mosquitos on June 14 and forced to turn back. As in the previous months, several U-boats heading for remote destinations, such as the African coast and the Caribbean, still benefited from receiving their last supplies south of the Azores.

Observations: The principal theater of operations for the U-boats that had survived May became the sector southwest of the Azores. The U-boat Corps Command hoped that the sixteen U-boats in the *Trutz* Wolfpack would find convoys on the United States-Gibraltar route while staying safe from planes. But these convoys weren't even spotted, although the U-boats were systematically attacked by fighter planes from an escort aircraft carrier. During the first ten days of June, Wildcats and Avengers from the USS *Bogue* kept the U-boats away from convoys GUS 7A and UGS 9, which passed 100 miles south of their position. As soon as the convoys were out of danger, and after decoding the *Enigma* messages giving the rendezvous point of submarines' re-suppliers, the American fighters started sinking all of the supply U-boats in the sector, the first being U-118 destroyed on June 12. The situation was repeated between June 16-22, a UG convoy heading west passed 300 miles south of the wolfpack. U-488, a Type XIV, was the supply ship for this group of U-boats; it was the last successful transfer of provisions southwest of the Azores. The U-boats tried to approach the convoy but when they neared the African coast, aerial activity became too intense. By the end of the month, five U-boats from the *Trutz* Wolfpack had been sunk while no ships had been lost; the survivors were allowed to rejoin a base in France. Hunting convoys southwest of the Azores was abandoned and never resumed.

At the end of May, six U-boats that didn't have enough fuel to reach the Azores remained in position in the North Atlantic. At the beginning of June, their mission was to send numerous radio messages to make their enemies believe that the sector was still active, but the Allies weren't fooled. Once these U-boats had been sunk or had returned to their base, there were no longer any U-boats in the waters between Newfoundland and the British Isles during the two months of summer. In June 1943, German U-boats only sank twenty-one ships for 78,316 tons. The last time the score was this low was in November 1941, although the tonnage had been far superior.

In June 1943, the Allies intensified their offensive of destroying U-boats while crossing the Bay of Biscay. This time, the operation was carried out conjointly by twenty squadrons from Coastal Command based in England and Gibraltar, American planes based in Morocco, and ships from a support group protected by at least one cruiser. The planes that didn't manage to sink a U-boat on the surface, signaled its dive position to the ships in the 2nd Support Group. Once in place, this group of U-boat hunters nearly always managed to hit its target. The first zone (called *Seaslug*) to be controlled was 200km wide by 400km long and situated 400km off Cape Finisterre northwest of Spain. The following patrol zone (called *Musketry*) was towards the east, at about 100km from this cape, and mounted vertically to the level of Lorient that allowed them to intercept all of the U-boats out of the bases on the Atlantic. On June 24, the group sank both U-119 and U-449.

On June 10, the Allies complicated their radio messages coding system. They adopted the Naval Cipher 5 code for all messages between warships in the Atlantic concerning convoy protection. This new code was never broken by German intelligence services. The only source of information about convoys left to the German general staff was deciphering the codes from commercial ships: the Merchant Ships Code. But in December 1943, the Allies introduced a new encrypting alphabet for their positions that rendered the MSC obsolete. This meant that after January 1944, the Germans knew nothing more about anything.

Allied reactions: June 1943 marked a clear increase of mine-laying operations off Lorient. A total of sixteen missions were carried out with between four and nine planes.

Off the American coast, on June 2, 1943, U-521 was attacked by the USS *PC 565,* an American submarine chaser, which sent five depth charges in its direction. The explosions damaged the U-boat and forced it to surface. Commander Klaus Bargsten was the first to open the hatch and climb into the conning tower, ordering his men to abandon ship as the U-boat was sinking headfirst. At that same moment, the patroller launched another bomb and the rest of the crew went down with the U-boat, not having time to escape. Commander Bergsten, the only survivor, talked with Lieutenant Flynn, the patroller's captain. During his interrogation by American ONI agents, he told them that the officer-candidates at the U-boat school had to pass an exam surfacing the false nose of a submarine from a depth of twenty meters. Those who succeeded were given a humorous diploma "*W.C. Schein*"("certificate of the john") which describe in an amusing way their exploit! The Americans noted in their report that he must have been an excellent officer, very patriotic but not at all politically inclined. He listened attentively to their questions about security but was pleasant to question, being a very good raconteur with a lively sense of humor! He told them one particular story about what he had said to his watch officer during an attack on the surface against a corvette under a full moon: "I feel like a man walking nude down a city street!" *NA*

U-BOAT	TYPE	FLOT.	COMMANDER	ARRIVAL	DEPART	NOTES
Departures						
U-43	IXA	2	Hans-Joachim Schwantke			In maintenance March 31 – July 13, 1943.
U-68	IXC	2	Albert Lauzemis	16	12	Departure with U-155 and U-159; these U-boats were joined by U-257, U-600 and U-615 out of La Pallice to cross Biscay Bay together. The fourteenth: attack by four Mosquitoes from a Polish squadron in the RAF; U-68 and U-155 had to turn back after being damaged. A man was lost from U-68, the commander and two other crewmembers were wounded.
U-103	IXB	2	Gustav-Adolf Janssen			In maintenance May 26 – July 21, 1943.
U-106	IXB	2	Wolfdietrich Damerow			In maintenance April 4 – July 28, 1943.
U-107	IXB	2	Harald Gelhaus			In maintenance May 26 – July 28, 1943. Change of commander: Gelhaus affected to the General Staff of the *Kriegsmarine* Command.
U-129	IXC	2	Hans-Ludwig Witt			In maintenance May 29 – 27 July 27, 1943. Change of commander: Witt affected to the general staff of the U-boat Corps.
U-135	VIIC	7	Otto Luther		7	New commander; departure for seventh and last patrol, direction the mid-Atlantic; crossed Biscay Bay with U-508 and U-759; 7/15/43, forced to surface after ninety depth charges launched by three ships; gunfire exchanged; new aerial attack by four depth charges, and then rammed by a corvette; five dead; forty-one survivors including the commander, taken prisoner. Results: three ships sunk, and one damaged.
U-155	IXC	10	Adolf Piening	11 16	10 12 30	After a technical problem during its first departure, U-155 left Lorient with U-68 the twelfth. After an aerial attack on the fourteenth, where five crewmembers were wounded, returns to Lorient on the sixteenth. New departure on June 30 for the Canaries, then the Cape Verde Islands where in July it was charged with re-supplying a U-boat from the *Monsun I* Wolfpack leaving for the Indian Ocean.
U-159	IXC	10	Heinz Beckmann		12	New commander; departure for fifth and last patrol, direction the Caribbean; attacked and sunk by plane 7/15/43, no survivors; fifty-four dead. Results: twenty-three ships sunk and one damaged.
U-168	IXC-40	2	Helmuth Pich			In maintenance May 18 – July 3, 1943.
U-183	IXC-40	2	Heinrich Schäfer			In maintenance May 3 – July 3, 1943.
U-188	IXC-40	12	Siegfried Lüdden		30	Change of Flotilla; departure for the Indian Ocean, first of the *Monsun I* Wolfpack; carried out operations out of Penang and then returns to Bordeaux on June 19, 1944; because it didn't have any batteries and couldn't leave before the Liberation of Bordeaux, it was regulated and scuttled in the U-boat base 8/25/44. Results: fifteen ships and one destroyer sunk, one damaged.
U-505	IXC	2	Peter Zschech			Being repaired December 12, 1942 – July 1, 1943.
U-506	IXC	10	Erich Würdemann			In maintenance May 8 – July 6, 1943.
U-508	IXC	10	Georg Staats		7	Departure for the African coast, Gulf of Guinea.
U-509	IXC	10	Werner Witte			In maintenance May 11 – July 3, 1943.
U-510	IXC	10	Alfred Eick		3	Departure for the African coast, Gulf of Guinea.
U-514	IXC	10	Hans-Jürgen Auffermann			In maintenance May 22 – July 1, 1943.
U-516	IXC	10	Gerhard Wiebe			In maintenance May 4 – July 8, 1943. Change of commander: Wiebe named battalion chief of the naval school in Schleswig.
U-518	IXC	2	Friedrich Wissmann		24	Departure for the Atlantic; attacked on June 27 by a Sunderland seaplane and damaged; during its return to Bordeaux, attacked a second time on June 30 by another Sunderland; the plane was damaged by the U-boat's DCA. Arrived for repairs in Bordeaux on July 3.
U-523	IXC	10	Werner Pietzsch			Being repaired after an aerial attack, May 26 – August 1, 1943.
U-525	IXC	10	Hans-Joachim Drewitz			In maintenance May 26 – July 25, 1943.
U-532	IXC-40	2	Otto-Heinrich Junker			In maintenance May 15 – July 3, 1943.
U-533	IXC-40	10	Helmut Hennig			Being repaired after being rammed by a corvette; May 24 – July 3, 1943.
U-759	VIIC	9	Rudolf Friedrich		7	Departure for second and last patrol, destination the Caribbean; sunk 7/26/43 by aerial attack; no survivors; forty-seven dead. Results: two ships sunk.

U-BOAT	TYPE	FLOT.	COMMANDER	ARRIVAL	DEPART	NOTES
Arrivals						
U-264	VIIC	6	Hartwig Looks	1		Arrives after a patrol of nearly two months in the North Atlantic, with two ships sunk from the ONS 5 convoy for 10,147 tons.
U-161	IXC	2	Albrecht Achilles	7		Arrives after a three-month patrol, starting with a rendezvous with two blockade runners in the Azores sector to transfer radar equipment and instructions; then off the American coast where only a 255-ton Canadian sailing ship was sunk.
U-123	IXB	2	Horst von Schroeter	8		Returns from a successful patrol of nearly three months off the African coast to Freetown, during which five ships and a submarine were sunk, totaling 28,855 tons. The submarine was the British P 615, built for Turkey under the name of *Uluc Ali Reis*, and taken back by the Royal Navy at the beginning of the war.
U-515	IXC	10	Werner Henke awarded Oak Leaves to his Knight's Cross on July 4, 1943.	24		Returns from a very successful patrol of nearly four months off the African coast to Freetown, with ten ships sunk totaling 58,456 tons (for a declaration of twelve ships for 71,401 tons).

June 6, 1943: The day before their departure the petty officers aboard U-508 get ready. They must especially make sure that nothing on board is missing. On the right: *Obermachinist* Max Henschler. *UBA*

On June 7, U-508 left the small base on the Scorff with the crew aligned on the bridge. It leaves accompanied by U-135 and U-759, following in the wake of a blockade runner, with aerial support from six Junkers Ju 88 planes of V./KG 40 up to point "*Kern*," the 100m line. *UBA*

U-508 was headed for the African coast where, with five other U-boats, it formed a reconnaissance line to the Ivory Coast, but without success. In the background is the former forge that was badly damaged during air attacks. *UBA*

On June 8, Commander Horst von Schroeter, of U-123, brought his U-boat home to Lorient after a successful three-month patrol along the African coast to Freetown. Like the rest of his crew, he wore his lifejacket for the few hours of navigation on the surface to point "*Laterne*," where he met up with the ship that escorted him to Lorient. *LB*

U-123's conning tower with the insignia of Commander von Schroeter's graduation as an officer of the navy. During this patrol, he sank five ships and a British submarine. *LB*

June 12: U-155 leaves for its sixth combat patrol accompanied by U-68 and U-159 to avoid crossing the Gulf of Gascony alone. It passes by the Kéroman III bunker. We can clearly see that its conning tower has been elongated to take on new anti-aircraft weapons. On each side of the conning tower is the blazon of its patron town of Schwelm, along with the insignia of the 10th Flotilla to which it belongs. In the background are the installations in the fishing port. The three U-boats managed to repel several attacks by individual aircraft until June 14, when they were attacked by four Mosquitoes from the 307 Squadron, piloted by Polish crews. U-68 and U-155 were damaged and had to turn back; five members of U-155's crew were wounded. *UBA*

U-118 was sunk by bombs dropped from several American planes; the commander and forty-three crew members were killed during the attack. The survivors all said that Commander Czygan had been a father figure and was highly respected and admired by his crew. Among the fifteen survivors were the wounded from U-758 that the supply boat had picked up earlier.

On June 12, 1943, U-118 was the first supply boat to be sunk off the Azores by planes from the aircraft carrier *USS Bogue*. This was the beginning of a long series of German supply U-boat sinkings by the Allies until the end of the war, thanks to the Enigma decoders that revealed the rendezvous points where supplies were to be handed over. *NA*

A member of U-118's crew, Hans Wosnitza, was Polish. He told the Americans aboard the USS *Osmond Ingram* destroyer, that he had been recruited into the German army by force and put in the U-boat corps. He had never really become an accepted member of the crew, but the commander regularly invited him to play chess, even though Wosnitza won every time!

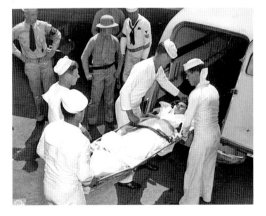

Immediately separated from the rest of the survivors, he was extremely co-operative with the Americans in charge of his interrogation, eager to answer all their questions. He said he wanted to stay in the United States to help them free Poland. *NA*

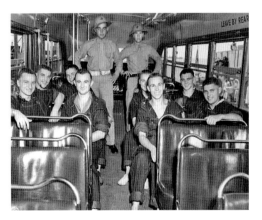

Eight of the fifteen submariners who survived the attack on U-118. At the back on the left: Werner Drechsler, who worked for the Americans and was in charge of interrogating the German prisoners at the Interrogation Service at Fort Hunt. For seven months, under two false identities, he mingled with several crews from the U-boats who had just been taken prisoner to get information out of them for the Americans. Instead of being kept apart after working for this service, he was sent to the prison camp at Papago Park on March 12, 1944. Immediately recognized by several submariners he had tried to get information out of, he was found hanged in the showers. The Americans investigated the crime, which resulted in the trial of seven submariners, who were found guilty and executed together at Fort Leavenworth, Kansas. This was the last mass execution to take place in the United States. *NA*

A summer fête on June 21, 1943, in the Pont-Callec Chateau's park for the crew of U-518, which will be leaving on patrol in three days. Two adversaries, standing in a barrel with their eyes blindfolded and wearing boxing gloves have to try to knock the other down! *Walter Wittig/UBA*

The game stands in the chateau's park. *UBA*

On June 16, U-68, damaged during the attack by four Polish Mosquitoes two days earlier, arrives in Lorient. In the center is Commander Albert Lauzemis who was wounded during the attack and who had been temporarily replaced by his watch officer for the return journey. Commander Lauzemis, who asked Dönitz not to send the U-boat out again until he was recovered, was awarded the German Cross in Gold, along with the chief engineer who had managed to keep the U-boat going for its return journey, in spite of the serious damage caused by enemy fire, notably to the exterior tanks. *UBA*

Radioman Walter Wittig playing table tennis in front of Pont-Callec Chateau. *Walter Wittig/UBA*

On June 24, U-515, under Werner Henke, returns from a very successful patrol of over four months along the African coast to Freetown, with ten ships sunk for a total of 54,456 tons. *LB*

For the return of this successful mission, and with the halt in the air raids on Lorient, U-515 is welcomed with great pomp in the Scorff, as in the days before mid-January 1943. Off Freetown during the night of April 30/May 1, U-515 surprised the TS 37 convoy and sank seven ships in twenty-four hours, thereby equalizing the record set by Commander Schepke on U-100. In the background the buoys maintain the netting to stop British submarines infiltrating the Scorff. *UBA*

Kuhnke, chief of the 10th Flotilla, comes onto the bridge to congratulate U-515's crew. Among the officers, on the right is *Leutnant-zur-See* Heinrich Niemeyer, who has just taken part in his first combat patrol aboard a U-boat, and who has just celebrated his thirty-third birthday. He recalls the curious circumstances that led him to the U-boat corps: "Before the war, I worked aboard large passenger ships for various maritime companies, which took me to Australia, New York, and even Peru. At the beginning of World War II, I hadn't had any military training; I was captain on a fishing boat getting ready for the next season. On October 3, our fishing boats were requisitioned by the Kriegsmarine; after being armed at the end of four or five months, they were operational as submarine chasers or patrollers. We were given special ranks—as a captain I was named *Feldwebel Sonderführer*. Our first mission started on April 1, 1940, in Norway; we escorted fifteen cargo ships from Świnoujście to Oslo. I won the Iron Cross 2nd Class for that, on April 28. After that, we returned to the shipyards in Königsberg where each ship had to give up its second watch officer. I was affected to the Vp 1507 patroller as watch officer; our newly formed flotilla—the 15th Vorp.-Flotilla—was charged with coastal security between the Hook of Holland and Cherbourg in the Channel, with Le Havre as our home base. We were often attacked by British planes and their fast speedboats. On November 28, 1940, I was awarded the Minesweeper War Badge—a decoration common to minesweepers, submarine chasers and protection units. In March 1941, I was named commander of the Vp-507 with the rank of *Steuermann Sonderführer*. In June, while we were escorting a large fuel tanker from Cherbourg to the Hook of Holland, I was seriously wounded when we were attacked by a plane off Dunkirk. I was awarded the Iron Cross 1st Class. Promoted to R.O.A (*Reserve Offizier Anwärter*) I went to a naval NCO training course in Glücksburg which lasted until December 9, 1941. At the beginning of 1942, I was sent to supervise the transformation of a fishing boat, 'La Lorientaise' into a patroller. On July 1, 1942, I was promoted to *Leutnant-zur-See der Reserve* (Sub-Lieutenant Reserve). It was at that moment that I participated in a discussion between the patrol commanders and our flotilla chief, in the 15th Flotilla's base in Fécamp. He explained: 'I have here a Telex from the Division; each flotilla must give two navigators to the U-boat corps, if possible with some experience at sea. Volunteers, stand up!' When no one stepped forward, he said: 'I'm surprised! None of you want to join the Kriegsmarine's elite? Very well, I will choose: the two youngest officers will leave to join the U-boat corps!' Although not being among the youngest, I had just been named an officer! That's how I found myself in a course for watch officers at the U-boat training facility in Pillau, after my former patrol flotilla chief had granted me ten days special leave. It was a long course from August 3 to September 27, 1942, in Pillau, with courses and training aboard a U-boat school, and then torpedo training at Mürwik from September 28 to November 21, using real torpedoes in the Baltic Sea. After that, naval transmission school and courses about tactics for attacking convoys from November 22, 1942, to January 6, 1943, followed by artillery and anti-aircraft firing at Świnoujście from January 7 to February 21, 1943. Ten officers were then sent to Lorient. I was affected to the 10th Flotilla and U-515 under Commander Heinke, who had already received the Knight's Cross after two patrols. My first operational mission aboard U-515 was a 124 day patrol at sea, and twelve ships torpedoed." Two patrols later, and having followed commander training course in Danzig, Heinrich Niemeyer returned to Lorient in April 1944 to take over the command of U-547. *UBA*

A welcome-home meal is offered to U 515's crew in front of the huts that link the two rear wings of Gabriel House's pavilions, rapidly rebuilt and camouflaged after the air raids. They are built on the roof of a large bunker. *UBA*

U-515 crewmembers are given their mail, which has accumulated in the 10th Flotilla's secretary's office since their departure four months earlier. *UBA*

Commander Werner Henke of U-515 has the Oak Leaves added to his Knight's Cross on July 4, 1943, becoming the most decorated member of the 10th Flotilla. He shakes hands with his men after the decoration is awarded next to the officers' bunker in *Hundius Kaserne*. *UBA*

Five members of U-515's crew tour Lorient after being awarded their decorations. Apart from the submariners' hostel in Kéroman, distractions have become rare. *UBA*

To keep fit after an aerial attack on June 14 forced them to turn back, a part of U-68's crew take a long walk in the Caudan countryside. *UBA*

U-68 crewmembers take advantage of a well-earned rest at *Lager Lemp* at the end of June 1943. *LB*

Comrades of U-68 in front of the kiosk situated just above Kersalo Lake at *Lager Lemp*. *UBA*

The U-boats leave their shelter in KIII for the dangerous crossing of the Gulf of Gascony. On the base's roof is the framework of the future DCA blockhouses. *LB*

July 1943: The First Wave of Departures for the Indian Ocean

Movements: Thirteen arrivals, eighteen departures, number of U-boats present at the end of the month: sixteen. Nearly all the U-boats leaving in July had been in maintenance in the shipyards since May to be fitted with their quadruple 20mm gun. After sending two groups of Type IXD-2s to the Indian Ocean, since October 1942, between July 3–8 1943, a total of eight Type IXs left in turn for this sector. With the departure of U-188 on June 30, the *Monsun I* Wolfpack (code name "Monsoon" because the U-boats were to arrive just after the rainy season in September), that comprised nine U-boats, was supposed to be bound for Penang. But three of them were sunk in the Bay of Biscay, between July 8-15. U-487, which was to carry supplies to them, was sunk on the thirteenth thanks to Allied decoding of Enigma messages, so a fourth U-boat was forced to give its fuel to others and turn back. Of the remaining U-boats, one was sunk in the Indian Ocean in October, and so only four reached their new base in Malaysia with a total result of six Allied ships sunk just before their arrival. Once again, a previous successful sector for U-boats had been reinforced by the Allies, who could now sink U-boats and protect their own cargo ships.

Observations: Considering the regular losses of submarine suppliers, the two Type IXs, U-129 and U-525, left Lorient in July for simple supply missions, that weakened the number of combat U-boats; U-525 didn't return. Considering the Allies' deciphering the supply rendezvous points at sea south of the Azores, with an escort aircraft carrier on permanent patrol nearby, carrying out this type of operation several times proved to be more dangerous than taking part in a combat mission alone! For the first time in July 1943, following the creation of the Xth Fleet three months earlier, the Americans succeeded in destroying more U-boats than the British: twenty-three out of thirty-eight.

Most of the American successes were due to planes off the aircraft carriers *Bogue*, *Card*, *Core*, and *Santee*. On July 7, U-951 had been literally cut in two by the explosion of a new depth charge dropped by plane: the Mk.37, using *Torpex*, an explosive 50% more powerful than the TNT used until then. The loss of U-514 on July 8, five days after its departure from Lorient, was particularly significant of the Allies' progress in air delivered weapons. Northwest of Cape Finisterre, the U-514 was attacked on the surface by a Liberator equipped with a searchlight, which fired eight rockets at it, then dropped eight depth charges before finishing it off with a **Fido** acoustic torpedo.

Few Type IXB U-boats put into service in 1939-40 arrived in Lorient at that time. Two of them were destroyed in July, notably the veteran of the 2nd Flotilla, U-43, put into service in August 1939 and that had been on its fifteenth combat patrol; a mine-laying operation off Port Lagos, Nigeria. U-107 left fifteen days later, and had better luck laying its mines off Charleston Port, SC, USA. Because of the lack of results with torpedoes, the U-boat Corps Command general staff had programmed eleven mine-laying operations for June-July. Eleven U-boats left from different bases with this objective, only five managed to carry out their mine-laying mission! The results of the 113 mines laid off Halifax, Dakar, Norfolk, and Charleston were so insignificant that the general staff wondered if the mines used hadn't been defective.

The British maintained pressure on the Bay of Biscay. On July 30, three U-boats, two being precious Type XIV suppliers, were spotted on the surface; U-462 and U-504 were destroyed by ships from a support group, and U-461 by Sunderland seaplane. In July, the Germans started using two solutions for continuing sailing on the surface: *Aphrodite*, a three-foot diameter balloon filled with hydrogen, attached to a raft by a fifty-meter line which had three aluminum strips of foil tied to it which produced an echo similar to the radar used on a conning tower; and *Thetis*, a buoy that played the same role as a decoy, but on the water's surface.

To have a chance of spreading the offensive in the Atlantic, on July 8, 1943, the U-boat Corps Command general staff agreed to the production of new, more modern U-boats: the XXI and XXIII types. Their construction was done in sections in different shipyards to economize a third of the working hours. This method would produce forty units a months by the spring of 1944. The diving speed of the Type XXI, up to eighteen knots, should give it more mobility against convoys.

In July 1943, U-boats sank forty-nine Allied ships for a total of 263,037 tons, a success mainly achieved in remote waters by attacking alone. Indeed, thanks to the transfer of supplies to the Azores sector two months earlier, several U-boats carried out their last attacks in zones less frequented the past few months where their appearance created a momentary surprise. A peak of thirty U-boats present in these remote zones was reached on July 20: seven in the Caribbean, seven between Trinidad, and the mouth of the Amazon, five on the north coast of Brazil to Rio, nine on the African coast from Dakar to the Niger estuary, and two between the Bahamas and Cape Hatteras on the American coast. Several successes were recorded. However, everywhere, the Allied air defenses had been considerably reinforced, particularly off the coast of Brazil, where of the seven U-boats engaged in July-August, only U-172 reached Lorient in September. The problem surviving U-boats that operated in these far-flung waters faced when they arrived in the Azores sector during August was finding fuel to enable them to reach their bases.

Allied reactions: At night during July, groups of seven or eight Wellingtons carried out a total of six mine-laying operations in Lorient Harbor.

JULY 1943

U-BOAT	TYPE	FLOT.	COMMANDER	ARRIVAL	DEPART	NOTES
Departures						
U-43	IXA	2	Hans-Joachim Schwantke		13	Departure for fifteenth and last patrol, mine-laying operations off Lagos (Nigeria); sunk south of the Azores on 7/30/43 by an acoustic torpedo launched by an American plane from an escort aircraft carrier; no survivors; fifty-six dead. Results: twenty-three ships sunk and one damaged.
U-68	IXC	2	Albert Lauzemis			Being repaired after an air attack; June 16 – August 1, 1943.
U-103	IXB	2	Gustav-Adolf Janssen	26	25	Left with U-525 and returned the next day with it. No more patrols until September.
U-106	IXB	2	Wolfdietrich Damerow		28	Departure for tenth and last patrol; damaged by an aerial attack in the morning of 8/2/43 after crossing Biscay Bay; rendezvous with three torpedo boats for its return to base; when the torpedo boats approached, U-106 surfaced and was sunk by two planes that immediately arrived; twenty-five dead; thirty-five crewmembers and commander saved by the torpedo boats. Results: twenty-one ships sunk and three damaged.
U-107	IXB	2	Volker Simmermacher		28	New commander; departure for a minelaying mission off the American coast.
U-123	IXB	2	Horst von Schroeter			In maintenance June 8 – August 1, 1943.
U-129	IXC	2	Richard von Harpe		27	New commander; departure south of the Azores as a re-supplier for other U-boats.
U-161	IXC	2	Albrecht Achilles			In maintenance June 7 – August 8, 1943.

U-BOAT	TYPE	FLOT.	COMMANDER	ARRIVAL	DEPART	NOTES
U-168	IXC-40	2	Helmuth Pich		3	Departure for the Indian Ocean (*Monsun I* Wolfpack with U-183, U-188, U-506, U-509, U-514, U-532 and U-533) where it carried out numerous operations; sunk 10/6/44 by Dutch submarine; twenty-three dead; twenty-seven men and commander survived. Results: two ships and one repair-ship sunk, two damaged.
U-183	IXC-40	2	Heinrich Schäfer		3	Departure for the Indian Ocean where it carried out numerous operations; sunk 4/23/45 by an American submarine while U-183 was flying the Japanese flag; one survivor; fifty-five dead. Results: five ships sunk.
U-264	VIIC	6	Hartwig Looks			In maintenance June 1 – August 4, 1943.
U-505	IXC	2	Peter Zschech	2 13	1 3	Departure for the Atlantic after more than six months being repaired. On July 8, the U-boat was attacked by a plane; their *Metox* radar detector was out of order. Then on the same day, U-505 was attacked by destroyers that launched depth charges; the commander decided to turn back following the Spanish and French coasts.
U-506	IXC	10	Erich Würdemann		6	Departure for fifth and last patrol, direction the South Atlantic and Indian Ocean; sunk 7/1/43 by a Liberator based in Port Lyautey; forty-eight dead including the commander, six survivors picked up by a British destroyer three days later and taken prisoner. Results: fourteen ships sunk and three damaged.
U-509	IXC	10	Werner Witte		3	Departure for fourth and last patrol, direction the Indian Ocean; sunk 7/15/43 by two planes from an American escort aircraft carrier; acoustic torpedoes hit the U-boat; no survivors; fifty-four dead. Results: six ships sunk and three damaged.
U-514	IXC	10	Hans-Jürgen Auffermann	2	1 3	Departure for fourth and last patrol, direction the Indian Ocean; sunk 7/8/43 by a Liberator using rockets, depth charges and a *Fido* torpedo; no survivors; fifty-four dead. Results: seven ships sunk and one damaged.
U-515	IXC	10	Werner Henke			In maintenance June 24 – August 21; 1943.
U-516	IXC	10	Hans Tillesen		8	New commander; departure for the Indian Ocean. Served as re-supplier for others in the group north of the Cape Verde Islands, and then turned back to Lorient, which it reached on August 23.
U-523	IXC	10	Werner Pietzsch			Being repaired after an air attack; May 26 – August 1, 1943.
U-525	IXC	10	Hans-Joachim Drewitz	26	25 27	After a round-trip with U-103 on July 25–26, departure for third and last patrol. Used as a re-supplier in the Atlantic; sunk 8/11/43 by two planes from an American aircraft carrier escort; depth charges and an acoustic torpedo were launched at the submarine; no survivors; fifty-four dead. Results: one ship sunk.
U-532	IXC-40	2	Otto-Heinrich Junker		3	Departure for the Indian Ocean where it carried out numerous missions; returns with a cargo of strategic equipment on January 13, 1945. At sea on May 4, 1945, at the end of hostilities, U-532 surrendered in Liverpool on 5/10/45. Results: eight ships sunk and two damaged.
U-533	IXC-40	10	Helmut Hennig		6	Departure for second and last patrol, direction the Indian Ocean; sunk 10/16/43 in the Gulf of Oman sector by a British plane; one survivor managed to reach the coast after swimming for thirteen hours; the commander and fifty-one others dead. Results: 0.
Arrivals						
U-154	IXC	2	Oskar Kusch	6		Arrives after a 105-day patrol off the coast of Africa near Freetown, and then off the coast of Brazil and French Guiana. The first torpedoes fired against a ship were defective; the others only damaged three American ships, which were towed to the port; three cargo ships and a petrol tanker sunk, one petrol tanker damaged.
U-170	IXC-40	10	Günther Pfeffer	9		First time in Lorient; put into service 1/19/43, with the former crew of U-171 that was sunk by a mine off Lorient in October 1942. First U-boat put into service in 1943 to arrive in Lorient; used as a re-supplier during its patrols.
U-536	IXC-40	2	Rolf Schauenburg	9		First time in Lorient; put into service 1/13/43. Arrives from its first combat patrol as a re-supplier. On July 5, while crossing Biscay Bay with U-535 and U-170, the three boats were attacked by a Liberator, and U-535 was sunk.
U-420	VIIC	11	Hans-Jürgen Reese	16		First time in Lorient; put into service 12/16/42. Out of Kiel on June 12, U-420 and five other U-boats were ordered until July to pass a lot of radio messages in the Atlantic to make the Allies believe that the sector hadn't been abandoned. It was badly damaged by an aerial attack on July 3; two crewmembers were killed. Remained in the shipyards until October.
U-211	VIIC	9	Karl Hause	16		First time in Lorient; put into service 3/7/42. After the abandonment of the North Atlantic, the U-boat was sent with others to hunt in the Azores sector, intercepting convoys between the USA and the Mediterranean, but without success.
U-271	VIIC	1	Kurt Barleben	16		First time in Lorient; put into service 9/23/42. Ordered to pass a lot of radio messages in the Atlantic. Later turned into a *Flak-Boat*.

U-BOAT	TYPE	FLOT.	COMMANDER	ARRIVAL	DEPART	NOTES
U-336	VIIC	1	Hans Hunger	17		First time in Lorient; put into service 2/14/42. Arrives from a fruitless patrol in the Azores sector. Re-supplied at the beginning of June by U-488; this was the last successful re-supply operation by a "milk-cow" south of the Azores; during the first week of July, air attacks were so frequent that the commanders were authorized to return to bases on the French coast.
U-228	VIIC	6	Erwin Christophersen	19		First time in Lorient; put into service 9/12/42. Arrives empty-handed from the North Atlantic, and later the Azores.

After more than six months in Lorient, while U-505 was being repaired, Commander Zschech's warrant officers get ready to leave for *Lager Lemp*. From left to right: the new Second Watch Officer Kurt Brev, Watch Officer Paul Meyer (former second watch officer) Dr. Bernd Rosemeyer, the U-boat's doctor, and Chief Engineer Josef Hauser. *UBA*

As good as new, with a Type IV conning tower, and painted light gray, U-505 left for a new patrol on July 1, 1943. For the departure ceremony, no brass band, but accordions. The U-boat returned the next day following a technical problem, and then left again on July 3 with five other U-boats. On July 8, it was attacked by a plane as its *Metox* radar detector had broken down. Then, on the same day, it was attacked by destroyers that launched depth charges; the commander decided to turn back, along the Spanish and then French coasts. It was the only one of the six U-boats that left on July 3 to reach Lorient, but with a lot of technical problems discovered during their short patrol. *UBA*

At the beginning of July, *Oberleutnant (Ing)* Otto Ranke, former chief engineer aboard U-154, promoted to second engineer of the 2nd Flotilla on January 1943, watches U-168 during diving trials. In the background, the KIII base with camouflaged *Flak* towers. On the right, the coal cranes in the fishing port. *Ranke*

Aboard a boat, *Oberleutnant* Ranke watches U-168 dive; it will be leaving on patrol on July 3. *Ranke*

Departure of six U-boats on July 3. U-168, under Helmut Pich, leaves its pen in Kéroman III for the Indian Ocean as part of the *Monsun* Wolfpack (U-183, U-509, U-514 and U-532 leave at the same time; U-506 and U-533 left Lorient three days later). It carried out numerous patrols in the Indian Ocean before being attacked on the surface by a Dutch submarine on October 1944. Most of U-168's crew sank with it to a depth of 120 feet, but managed to escape through the conning tower and reach the surface, where they found the survivors who had been in the conning tower when the U-boat exploded. The Dutch submarine picked up twenty-seven survivors. It kept five on board, notably four officers who were taken as prisoners to Australia. The twenty-two others were disembarked on land occupied by the Japanese. *UBA*

U-509 left in turn. Behind it, berthed in front of the pens, is the cruiser *Strasbourg* to prevent air dropped torpedoes from penetrating the base. U-509 was sunk twelve days after its departure by two planes from an American escort aircraft carrier that dropped homing torpedoes on it. There were no survivors. *UBA*

In the base on the Scorff, before its departure on July 3 too, U-183's commander, Heinrich Schäfer, chats with his officers. *UBA*

U-532 leaves the Scorff: KIII on the starboard side. It carried out patrols in the Indian Ocean and then surrendered to the British in Liverpool on May 10, 1945. *UBA*

Kals, chief of the 2nd Flotilla, gives a speech to the crew of U-183. *UBA*

U-183 leaves for the Indian Ocean, where it carried out numerous patrols before being sunk by an American submarine in April 1945. To ward off bad tuck, it was traditional that flowers offered at departure were thrown overboard as the Breton coast disappeared. *UBA*

U-154 arrived in Lorient on July 6, returning from a three-and-a-half-month patrol along the coast of Africa off Freetown, and then along the coasts of Brazil and French Guiana. It brought back five pennants, but in reality none of them represented a ship sunk. The first was spotted on May 8 and four torpedoes were launched at it; two of them missed and the third hit without exploding. The four other ships, hit by six torpedoes between 0443 and 0446 on May 28, had been repaired, while the commander's report signaled three cargo ships and a petrol tanker sunk, with a second tanker damaged. *UBA*

Commander Oskar Kusch of U-154 leaves the small base on the Scorff with the chiefs of the 2nd and 10th Flotillas. *UBA*

Kusch chats with Kals, his flotilla chief. On his cap we see a star—the insignia of U-154—and the victory rune of U-103 aboard which he had been watch officer. *UBA*

After his arrival in *Lager Lemp*, Commander Kusch organizes an awards ceremony for the members of his crew. *UBA*

Studio portrait of Günther Pfeffer, aged twenty-eight, commander of U-170. He previously commanded U-171, which was sunk by a mine off Lorient on October 9, 1942. He returned to Lorient on July 9, 1943, with a new U-boat. *UBA*

Half of the crew of U-515 takes advantage of Carnac Beach during a day off, while the other half is on leave in Germany. Those left behind have to go to the naval shipyards six days out of seven to supervise the work the laborers at *KMW Lorient* are doing on their U-boat. *UBA*

Commander Werner Henke of U-515 has returned from his trip to Germany where he was awarded the Oak Leaves to his Knight's Cross; the decoration had been awarded on July 4. *Charita*

U-43, veteran boat of the 2nd Flotilla, commanded by Hans-Joachim Schwantke, left on July 13 for its fifteenth and last patrol. At the end of the month, to the south of the Azores, an American plane from an escort aircraft carrier fired a homing torpedo at the U-boat. All hands were lost. *UBA*

On July 14, following the destruction of two cargo ships totaling 12,243 tons a few days earlier off Lagos in Nigeria, that added to his credit list, the commander of U-508 received a radio message that he was awarded the Knight's Cross. While waiting for the real award that would be presented when he returned to Lorient in September, the crew made him a provisional version. *UBA*

On July 16, Williams, the American pilot of the Avenger, which had just sunk U-67 to the west of the Azores, is interviewed for the program "This Nation at War." From left to right: Lt. Cdr. Charles Brewer, commander of VC-13, Captain Marshal Greer, commander of the *USS Core* and Lieutenant Robert P. Williams. *NA*

U-271, a Type VIIC U-boat of the 1st Flotilla in Brest, arrives at the base in the Scorff after its first patrol sending out false radio traffic in the North Atlantic to make the Allies think that numerous U-boats were on patrol there. It was later transformed into a *Flak-Boat* in Lorient. *UBA*

On July 21, U-662 was sunk off the coast of Brazil by a Catalina. Its three survivors were picked up by an American patrol boat seventeen days later. One of them was Commander Heinz-Eberhard Müller, badly wounded, who was repatriated to Germany on March 1944, during an exchange of invalid prisoners. This was made possible by the Articles 68 to 74 of the Geneva Convention of July 27, 1929, concerning the treatment of prisoners of war. *NA*

On July 24, at Penang, the German crew of U-511 salutes the new Japanese crew who is taking over their U-boat; offered to the Japanese Navy and re-baptized RO 500. The Germans will stay in Penang, where they will serve to complement the crews of U-boats arriving from France. In August 1945, under the Japanese flag, the RO 500 will surrender to the Americans. *UBA*

A Japanese guide takes the former U-511 crewmembers to see what life is like in the Far East. *UBA*

Commander Hans-Joachim Drewitz, of U-525, left Lorient on July 27. Aged thirty-seven, he was lost at sea fifteen days later, leaving behind him in Germany, his wife, his son and his future daughter who was born in March 1944. Most of his papers and photos, which he had left behind on his departure because he had a premonition that he wouldn't return, were destroyed when the town was bombed. According to legend, his hair had suddenly turned white during trials in the Baltic Sea when his U-boat was trapped on the seabed for twenty-four hours. *Hans-Jürgen Drewitz*

U-532 leaving for the Indian Ocean on July 3, 1943. *UBA*

August 1943: The Departure of U-536 for Operation Kiebitz

Movements: Thirteen arrivals, sixteen departures, number of U-boats present at the end of the month: thirteen. Up to twenty-seven at the end of March 1943, the number of U-boats present in Lorient had halved in five months.

Observations: On August 2, faced with the losses during the two previous months in the Bay of Biscay, *Grossadmiral* Dönitz ordered the U-boats not to sail on the surface during the day and only to resurface at night to recharge their batteries. On August 14, the U-boat Corps Command general staff ordered their U-boats not to use their *Metox* radar detectors. For several weeks, German radar specialists had been asking themselves questions about the U-boats losses due to air attacks; it turned out that *Metox* radar detectors themselves gave off echoes that guided Allied planes to them: twelve miles off for a plane flying at an altitude of 500 meters, to twenty-five miles at an altitude of 2,000 meters! They were quickly replaced by the new *Wanze* (*Hagenuk-Wellenanzeiger*) radar detector that had just been delivered to bases in the west. Covering a large waveband browsed automatically, it came with an optical indicator. U-523 was the first U-boat in Lorient to be equipped. Like the others leaving in August, it would be efficiently protected from surprise attacks from the air, but not from escort ships. The second Allied offensive in the Bay of Biscay ended on August 27, when a squadron of Luftwaffe Dorniers Do 217s armed with Henschel Hs-293A radio-controlled glide bombs attacked a group of British ships off Vigo on the Spanish coast. The sloop *HMS Egret* was the first Allied ship sunk by this new weapon, a cruiser was also damaged.

On August 23, while waiting for the Type XXIs to be put into service the following year, Dönitz organized a meeting with the various flotilla chiefs from the Brest and Bordeaux bases at Château de Pignerolles, at the HQ of *FdU-West Kapitän-zur-See* Rösing. They unanimously decided to continue the battle, even with a technical inferiority, in order to keep the thousands of Allied ships and planes involved in anti-submarine warfare in the Atlantic busy, or they would be deployed elsewhere. This decision was mostly motivated by a message deciphered by *B-Dienst* where they learned that two groups from British Coastal Command, until then occupied with the battle against U-boats, had participated in bombardments on Hamburg between July 24 and August 3, which had claimed many lives. However, during the meeting at Pignerolles, Dönitz wanted to give his commanders hope for the future: the Type VII and IX U-boats were to receive, in addition to their new radar detector, a new weapon that would allow them to resume the offensive. This was an acoustic torpedo with a speed of 24.5 knots, and a range of 5,700 meters that would destroy their principal enemy: the escort ships whose low draft and high speed helped them escape from classic torpedoes. Called the *T5 Zaunkönig*, the first eighty models were delivered by train to the bases in the west at the beginning of August. Thanks to Albert Speer, head of the armaments industry, specialists were also sent from Germany to the bases on the Atlantic in order to look after the torpedoes and make sure they were operational after their long railroad trip. Their mechanisms were so complex, that the least shock during transport was enough to cause damage.

On August 8, the British signed an agreement with the Portuguese government that authorized Allied planes to use two airstrips on the Azores Islands. Two squadrons arrived in October, which permitted the Allies to effectively control the entire airspace over the Atlantic. At the end of August, as they had forecast, the Allies had sunk, in four months, nine supplier U-boats in the Azores sector and Bay of Biscay. These losses now prevented most of the combat submarines from reaching remote destinations. By the end of August, the U-boat corps only had three supply U-boats left: two Type XIVs and a Type XB.

In August 1943, the German U-boats sank twenty-six cargo ships for 93,069 tons. A total of twenty-four U-boats were lost during the month, thirty-eight had been lost the previous month; considering the small number of U-boats in operation, the percentage of losses was higher in July-August than in May, over 35%! Above all, during these two months, a total of 64% of the U-boats lost weren't destroyed in their combat zones, but on the route taking them there!

On August 29, U-536 left Lorient on a special mission known only to Commander Rolf Schauenburg: Operation Kiebitz. The outline had been given to him at the beginning of the month, while he was at the U-boat Corps Command General Staff HQ in Berlin: Schauenburg learnt that the former commander of U-99 Otto Kretschmer, a prisoner in Canada, had communicated with Dönitz by encoding the letters exchanged by his former watch officer and his wife in Germany. Kretschmer told Dönitz that he planned to escape with several other officers and they would need a U-boat to pick them up on the east coast of Canada. Kretschmer was the leader of a group that called themselves "The Lorient Espionage Section" that would help with the escape. Since the beginning of 1943, over 150 prisoners had been taking turns night and day to dig three tunnels passing the barbed wire of the surrounding walls; the earth was mostly hidden above the ceiling in the dormitories. Other prisoners made false papers and civilian clothes. After four months, only the third tunnel was continued; reaching over 300 meters in length, and by the beginning of August it was more-or-less finished. Through a new encoded letter, Kretschmer informed Dönitz. Having a small atlas of Canada in his possession, he also gave the place where a U-boat could pick them up, in a bay on the east coast. In his reply, Dönitz told him that a U-boat would surface off the bay every night from September 26 onwards. To avoid any possible leaking of the information before leaving Lorient, the crew of U-536 hadn't been informed until they boarded on August 29. Reaching the Azores on September 12, the U-boat received the radio order to begin Operation Kiebitz. The commander could now open the sealed envelope containing very precise charts and the last instructions. U-536 should wait off Pointe Maisonnette, on Chaleur Bay, on September 26. Each night for a maximum of two weeks, he should surface for two hours until he could pick up four escaped U-boat officers: Kretschmer, ace of the U-boat corps and former commander of U-99; Hans-Joachim von Knebel-Doberitz his watch officer on U-99 and former personal adjutant of Admiral Dönitz; Horst Elfe former commander of U-93; and Hans Ey former commander of U-433. While U-536 was crossing the Atlantic to carry out its special mission, the initial plan was upset by two incidents in Camp 30 at Bowmansville. A week before the date fixed for the escape, the ceiling in one of the dormitories fell in; it was too weighed down by the earth from the tunnels. The first two tunnels were discovered by camp guards, but the third tunnel was the only one that came up outside the walls. Even though Kretschmer thought that the discovery might compromise their escape, he nevertheless decided to try it that same night! But during the day, the ground caved in under the feet of a prisoner who was digging up a bit of earth for his flowerbeds near the fence! The guards therefore found the third tunnel. The former commander of U-434, Wolfgang Heyda wanted to take his chances in spite of everything, drawn by the possible arrival of U-536. He proposed an audacious individual escape plan and Kretschmer accepted it. During the night, equipped with hob-nailed boots, he climbed a loudspeaker-pole against the outer wall, then using a canvas chair he managed to get hold of the second loudspeaker pole by rocking back and forth, and then he climbed down on the outside of the camp without being seen! Wearing civilian clothes and armed with false papers, he took a train and then walked to the rendezvous point with the U-boat, which he reached on September 26—the planned date! After passing two identity controls without any problem during his 770-mile trip, he was arrested by guards on the beach in Chaleur Bay. He was taken to the lighthouse on Pointe de Maisonnette, the exact place from where he would have sent signals with a lamp to U-536. While being interrogated (he was finally unmasked because of the German Red Cross chocolates in his pocket), he saw that the lighthouse was being used by the Canadians as a command post and that they had set up radar on the ground on each side of the bay, and had sent a fleet to sink U-536! On September 25, the Canadian Royal Navy placed a destroyer, four corvettes, five minesweepers, and motorboats to trap the U-boat in the bay. In fact, the details of Operation Kiebitz had been known by the Allied intelligence service since the very beginning! The encoded letters to and from Camp 30 in Bowmansville had all been deciphered, and the detailed chart of Chaleur Bay had been found in a package from Germany addressed to one of the prisoners. A special listening device, installed underground in the prison camp, had even permitted the Allies to listen to the prisoners digging their tunnel! Finally, deciphered Enigma radio messages had also given

U-BOAT	TYPE	FLOT.	COMMANDER	ARRIVAL	DEPART	NOTES
Departures						
U-68	IXC	2	Albert Lauzemis	3 15	1 14	Recalled the day after its first departure, returns rapidly from the second.
U-103	IXB	2	Gustav-Adolf Janssen			In maintenance July 26 – 18 September 18.
U-123	IXB	2	Horst von Schroeter	5	1 16	After returning early because of technical problems, left for its fourteenth patrol, direction the coast of French Guiana and the Antilles.
U-154	IXC	2	Oskar Kusch			In maintenance July 6 – September 23, 1943.
U-161	IXC	2	Albrecht Achilles		8	Departure for sixth and last patrol, on a special mission: rendezvous with the Japanese submarine I-8 in the Azores sector; two German officers with the radar detector *Wanze* board the I-8; after that U-161 heads for the coast of Brazil, and was sunk by a plane 9/27/43; no survivors; fifty-two dead. Results: seventeen ships sunk and seven damaged.
U-170	IXC-40	10	Günther Pfeffer		29	Departure for the coast of Brazil.
U-211	VIIC	9	Karl Hause			In maintenance July 16 – September 23, 1943.
U-228	VIIC	6	Erwin Christophersen			In maintenance July 19 – September 18, 1943.
U-264	VIIC	6	Hartwig Looks		4	Departure for the base in St. Nazaire; after an aborted passage in the Mediterranean, and damage following air attacks, remained in St. Nazaire from 10/15/43 to 2/5/44 where the first *Schnorchel* was installed; during its fifth and last patrol, it was forced to surface 2/19/44 after depth charges were launched by a destroyer; scuttled; fifty-one survivors. Results: three ships sunk.
U-271	VIIC	1	Kurt Barleben			In the shipyards from July 16 to September 14, 1943, being turned into a *Flak-Boat*.
U-336	VIIC	1	Hans Hunger		26	Departure for Brest then fourth and last patrol; sunk 10/5/43 by a plane using rockets; no survivors; fifty dead. Results: one ship sunk.
U-420	VIIC	11	Hans-Jürgen Reese			Being repaired July 16 to October 7, 1943, after being damaged during an air attack.
U-505	IXC	2	Peter Zschech	2 15 22	1 14 21	Trials; returns each time after strange sounds were heard when it dove to fifty meters.
U-515	IXC	10	Werner Henke	22	21 29	After a round trip, departure for the Azores.
U-523	IXC	10	Werner Pietzsch	3	1 16	Departure for third and last patrol, direction the North Atlantic; first U-boat to be equipped with the *Wanze* radar detector; sunk 8/25/43 after being chased for four hours by a British destroyer and corvette; thirty-five survivors taken prisoner; twenty dead. Results: one ship damaged.
U-536	IXC-40	2	Rolf Schauenburg		29	Departure for second and last patrol, special mission: rescuing four former U-boat commanders after they escaped from prison in Canada. On November 20, 1943, northwest of the Azores, U-536 was attacked by a corvette and frigate that sent it to a depth of 240 meters, and then attacked it when it reached the surface; the commander and sixteen men taken prisoner; thirty-eight dead. Results: 0.
Arrivals						
U-306	VIIC	1	Claus von Trotha	11		First time in Lorient; put into service 10/21/42. Arrives from a two-month patrol off the African coast. On July 16, attacked the SL 133 convoy and declared four ships sunk and one damaged; in fact only one ship was damaged.
U-155	IXC	10	Adolf Piening	11		In the Cape Verde sector, re-supplied U-168, U-183 and U-188 that were leaving for the Indian Ocean.
U-190	IXC-40	2	Max Wintermeyer	19		Returns empty-handed from a three-month patrol off the American coast; was attacked by a Liberator.
U-516	IXC	10	Hans Tillesen	23		Initially due to leave for the Indian Ocean, but used in July in the Cape Verde sector to re-supply U-532 and U-533 after their re-supplier had been sunk.
U-510	IXC	10	Alfred Eick	29		Returns from a three-month mission off the coast of French Guiana, with three ships sunk for 18,865 tons and one damaged, from the TJ 1convoy.

information about the operation to the Allied intelligence service. But they hadn't let on about what they knew, in the hope of easily capturing the U-boat when it arrived at the rendezvous—or sinking it! Without knowing anything about the Allies' trap or that the escape attempt had failed, U-536 arrived off Chaleur Bay on the same day as Wolfgang Heyda and surfaced during the night; it was immediately detected by land radar. An unlit corvette approached to try to capture the U-boat intact. U-536 received the message, "Komm, komm! – come here, come here!" But the message wasn't the one agreed on and Commander Schauenburg became suspicious and decided to dive and leave! As soon as they heard the propellers, the Canadian battleships started launching depth charges but not in the right spot! Taking advantage of the shallow depth of the bay to hide on the seabed, U-536 managed to escape the trap without being damaged. But, after having re-crossed the Atlantic, it was finally sunk on November 20, 1943, northwest of the Azores.

Allied reactions: In August 1943, groups of four to seven Wellington bombers returned nine times in August to lay mines in Lorient Harbor; roughly once every three days.

Early in the morning of August 2, 1943, U-106, which had left Lorient five days earlier was attacked and damaged by a *Wellington* off the Spanish coast. The crew made some hasty repairs and the submarine dived; a rendezvous was fixed with T-22, T-24 and T-25 torpedo boats to escort it back to a French base. When U-106 resurfaced, thinking it heard the torpedo boats' propellers, it was attacked again by two Sunderlands that sank it with depth charges. The commander and thirty-five crewmembers were picked up by the torpedo boats at the end of the afternoon. Among the survivors was Radioman Erich Oberquelle who recalls: "I joined the Navy on January 1, 1938. After my radio operator's course, I was affected to U-58 a 250-ton U-boat, at the beginning of January 1939. When war broke out, we were already off the Scottish coast. I took part in twelve relatively short patrols, one of which took us to the first bases in Lorient at the end of July 1940. U-58 returned to Germany, and I was sent on a petty officer course at the transmissions school in Flensburg-Mürwik. After that, I was transferred to the general staff of the U-boat Corps in Kernével. In mid-July, I was once again affected to a U-boat—the 900-ton U-106 belonging to the 2nd Flotilla in Lorient. We carried out long patrols, even to the Gulf of St. Lawrence in Canada. On August 2, U-106 was sunk leaving the Gulf of Gascony; twenty-one crewmembers were killed by a Sunderland seaplane's guns. I was lucky to be rescued by a torpedo boat after four hours in the water. After a few days' leave to get me on my feet again, I was affected to U-122, a U-boat fitted with a Snorkel underwater-breathing apparatus. Aboard this U-boat, we left for a long patrol of 128 days, about 115 underwater using the Snorkel! Even though I hadn't done anything particularly heroic, I was awarded the German Cross in Gold at the beginning of 1945, for having participated in at least 500 days of combat, and the destruction of at least 100,000 tons of Allied ships. I was happy to serve in the U-boat corps as a radioman, and even happier to have survived the war. My wish for the future: No more wars!" *IWM*

Damaged by the first bomb and incapable of diving, U-117 remained alone on the surface and was sunk by depth charges dropped by two additional Avengers that had arrived on the scene. There were no survivors. In the report sent by U-66 once it had dove, they signaled that they had heard five detonations followed by cracking sounds, which signified the destruction of their supplier. *NA*

On August 7 to the west of the Azores, U-117 and U-66 were surprised on the surface during a re-supply operation by an Avenger from the aircraft carrier *USS Card*. U-66 had already been attacked by a plane four days earlier and Commander Markworth had been wounded. The two U-boats had met up the day before on August 6 and the U-boat's medic, Dr. Schrenk and *Oberleutnant-zur-See* Paul Frerks had been transferred from U-117 to U-66; the former to treat the wounded, the latter to take command for the return trip. During fuel transferring operations on August 7, they were surprised by the appearance of a plane that attacked and dropped a bomb between the two U-boats, right near U-117's conning tower. U-66, on the left of the photo, crash-dived and disappeared under the surface. *NA*

Lieutenant A.H. Sallenger, pilot of the Avenger and turret gunner Hogan were decorated for their part in the destruction of U-117. *NA*

On August 8, 1943, U-161 under Commander Albrecht Achilles, left for its sixth and last patrol. Before reaching the Brazilian coast, it had a mission to complete: on August 20, in the Azores, it transferred two German officers equipped with the new radar detector *Wanze*, only recently delivered to the French bases, aboard the Japanese I-8 submarine, so that it could reach the port in Brest without damage in September. U-161 was sunk off the coast of Brazil on September 27 after an aircraft attack. There were no survivors. *UBA*

The officers of U-386, who arrived in St. Nazaire on July 8, stop off at Carnac sea resort, before they leave at the end of August, to see their friends based in Lorient. *UBA*

Crewmembers from U-386 at Carnac. The crews of the 6th and 7th Flotillas based in St. Nazaire usually spent their rest time at La Baule's sea resort. *UBA*

Off the coast of Brazil, U-604 was damaged, first by an aerial attack carried out by a Ventura on July 30, and then by depth charges from an American destroyer, before being rendered incapable of diving by an attack from a B-24 on August 3. Its commander decided to scuttle the U-boat, but first he wanted his men to be picked up by another boat. U-185 and U-172 received the radio order to the rendezvous point to pick them up. The three boats met up on August 11. While U-604 was transferring fuel to U-185, a Liberator appeared and attacked. The U-boats targeted by the bombs replied with their anti-aircraft guns. Those on U-185 finally managed to hit the plane and shoot it down, while U-172, whose anti-aircraft guns had been damaged, crashdived. The crew of U-604 scuttled their U-boat and were then transferred to U-185. Three days later twenty-two men from U-604 swam from U-185 to U-172, as their life rafts had been lost during the air attack. With eighty men aboard U-172, they still had to cross the Atlantic. The drinking water wasn't sufficient enough for the number of people aboard, which made the trip very difficult. They were rationed three cups of water per person, per day, which caused a lot of sickness on board. *UBA*

On August 23, crewmembers of U-516, equipped with their *Tauchretter*, sun bathe on the rear platform during their approach to Lorient. They were initially to go to the Indian Ocean, but with the destruction of most of the supply submarines by the Allies, they had to change plans and serve as supplier for U-532 and U-533 to the northwest of Cape Verde. *UBA*

During a meeting at Pignerolles between *Grossadmiral* Dönitz, and the flotilla chiefs based in the Gulf of Gascony on August 23, it was decided to continue the battle in the Atlantic, even if the force was technically inferior. However, Dönitz announced the arrival of a new armament to fight against the escort ships—the T5 homing torpedo. From left to right: Rösing, *FdU-West*, Kals, Dönitz, Scholtz, chief of the 12th Flotilla in Bordeaux, Schulz, chief of the 6th Flotilla in St. Nazaire, Winter, chief of the 1st Flotilla in Brest, Lehmann-Willenbrock, chief of the 9th Flotilla in the same port, and Kuhnke. *UBA*

Ten unharmed survivors from U-185 on the bridge of the USS *Core*. A total of twenty-seven members from U-185 and nine members from U-604 were rescued, but four of them died two days later—two from their wounds and two because they had inhaled too much chlorine. The Americans had a lot of trouble extracting information during interrogations, which always happened when the crew had an efficient commander who they respected. The only weak link in the crew's security proved to be a man who claimed to be a communist and he told them all he knew. At the beginning of this same mission in Hune, U-185 had already picked up eighteen survivors from U-564, sunk by an Allied plane, and had transferred them to the Z-26 destroyer! *NA*

On August 24, U-185 was surprised on the surface, 600 miles south of the Azores while it was heading to a rendezvous point to be re-supplied by U-847. It was attacked by four Avenger and Wildcat planes from the aircraft carrier USS *Core,* which dropped Telex and Mk.47 bombs. The U-boat started sinking backward after the crew tried to defend themselves with anti-aircraft guns. Commander Maus ordered the evacuation of the U-boat, but several men had been wounded or killed during the attack, while others were trapped inside and had been wounded by the explosions, or asphyxiated by the chlorine pouring from the batteries. Among those who never left the wreck was Commander Höltring of U-604, who had been picked up on August 11 after scuttling his U-boat. He went to the torpedo room just before the boat sank to help a man who had been wounded and unable to move; when the first odors of chlorine reached them, the man implored Höltring to kill him; the commander obeyed, before turning his arm against himself.

Three hours after the sinking of U-185, the destroyer USS *Barker* picked up thirty-six survivors, including Commander Maus. They were transferred to the USS *Core*, where a barechested Maus and watch officer *Leutnant-zur-See* Hans-Otto Rieve are given survival bags, offered by the American Red Cross. Interned at Papago Park, Maus was among the five U-boat commanders to escape on February 12, 1944, but was captured along with Guggenberger in Tuscon, Arizona. He also took part in digging a tunnel that helped twenty-five prisoners escape during the night of December 23-24. *NA*

Crewmembers of U-505 at *Lager Lemp* after their return to Lorient on August 22, following a third abortive departure that month. The first two attempts, on August 1 and 14, they had problems during diving trials before each departure; unusual sounds had been heard. They started seriously doubting the capacities of their U-boat and thought that it had been sabotaged. Effectively, the technicians at *KMW* found that important parts had been weakened and they were replaced. The third departure on August 21 started off well—no strange sounds at sixty meters—during diving trials, but when they regained the surface they found that they had left a long layer of oil behind them! The order was given to return to Lorient; the crew's morale was rockbottom and they decided to get drunk at *Lager Lemp* to drown their sorrows. *UBA*

On August 29, 1943, U-510 is welcomed in the Scorff by a large crowd gathered on the *Isere* pontoon. *UBA*

Nurses of the German Red Cross have brought bunches of flowers for the crew. In background on the left is the base on the Scorff. *UBA*

U-510 sank three boats for 18,865 tons, and damaged a fourth, mainly from the TJ-1 convoy northeast of Cayenne. *Wolfgang Ockert*

Even the band wears sand-colored uniforms. *UBA*

The crew goes ashore after a patrol of almost three months along the French Guiana coast. *UBA*

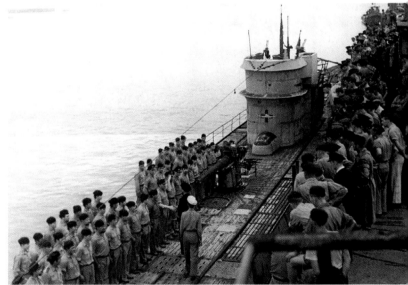

Kuhnke, chief of the 10th Flotilla, on the bridge of U-510 to shake hands with the crewmembers. *Wolfgang Ockert*

Kapitän-zur-See Rösing, the chief of U-boats in the West, has come to Lorient to welcome U-510's crew in *Hundius Kaserne's* courtyard. *UBA*

Several crewmembers are decorated by Rösing with the Iron Cross 1st Class. *UBA*

Rösing shakes the hand of each recipient. Behind him is Alfred Eick who has just returned from his first patrol as commander, and who has also received the Iron Cross 1st Class, and Kuhnke, chief of the 10th Flotilla. *UBA*

Commander Rolf Schauenburg of U-536 recalls how he was given a special mission: "In July 1942, I went to the U-boat Corps HQ in Paris to give my report on my first patrol in the North Atlantic, leaving Kiel on June 1 and arriving in Lorient on July 9. Dönitz said: 'Schauenburg, I've got something for you. A special operation on the Canadian coast. Are you interested?' I replied: 'Of course!' I was given eight days' leave and afterward I returned to my base in Lorient. Then Adi Schnee, the officer attached to the U-boat Corps HQ, arrived with instructions. He said 'Here's what you're going to do; what a super adventure!' 'Daddy' Kals, my flotilla chief, was a bit more precise: 'You have to rescue Kretschmer, von Knebel-Döberitz, Elfe and Ey.' Then he gave me the details of the astonishing escape plan Kretschmer had elaborated. A special courier arrived from Berlin with detailed charts of the point where I was to pick up the escapees. Meanwhile, my U-boat was fitted out. No one in Lorient knew of the plan, even my officers didn't know what it was about until we were off the Canadian coast."

U-536 left Lorient; the crew didn't yet know that Commander Rolf Schauenburg had received a special mission—to rescue the U-boat officers who had escaped from their camp in Canada. *UBA*

On August 29, U-515 under Commander Henke leaves for its sixth combat patrol. *UBA*

U-515 leaves the base on the Scorff heading for the Azores. *UBA*

CONCLUSION

In spite of the massive Allied bombardments at the beginning of 1943, maintenance and repairs continued in Lorient on the pens of the U-boat base. After having reached its peak with twenty-eight U-boats present on April 1, it held no more than thirteen at the end of August 1943. During the last two weeks of August, several U-boats left their bases in Biscay Bay with, as well as their classic torpedoes, four new T5 acoustic torpedoes. They were to gather in the middle of the North Atlantic on September 2 to form the *Theuthen* Wolfpack charged with attacking convoys once more. They were also equipped with 20mm

four-barrel anti-aircraft guns and the new *Wanze* radar detector. The U-boat Corps Command general staff were anxious for results.

In the next volume, covering the period from September 1943 to May 1945, you will discover the results of the last wolfpack attacks in the North Atlantic during the autumn of 1943. You will find details of the installation in Lorient of the *schnorchel*; the last solution found by the shipyards permitting U-boats to navigate at periscope depth with their diesel. It will explain the reasons why I-29, the last Japanese submarine, came to Lorient. It details the special missions

carried out by U-530 and U-537. You will learn about the last U-boat departures for the Indian Ocean, Freetown, the coast of Brazil, the Caribbean, and even the American coast; and the fewer returns to base where the welcoming ceremonies to greet the returning submarines flying pennants became rarer and rarer. You will also discover the U-boats' reaction to the landings in Normandy and their evacuation of the bases in Biscay Bay. The role the base played in the "Lorient Pocket" is also mentioned, as well as its capture and its restoration by the Marine Nationale.

BIBLIOGRAPHY

Bavendamm, Dirk, and Witte, Lothar, *Ursprünglich wollte Ich nur die Welt seh'n.* Auto-edition, 2007.

Blair, Clay, *Hitler's U-Boat War,* vols.1-2. Cassell & Co., 2000.

Bohn, Roland, *Raids aériens sur le Bretagne durant la deuxième guerre mondiale,* vols.1-2. Vanity Press, 1997-1998.

Bourguet-Maurice, Louis, and Grand Colas, Josyane, *Et la tanière devint le village.* Du Quantième, 1997.

Braeuer, Luc, *La base de submarines de Lorient.* Liv Editions, 2008.

Braeuer, Luc, *U-boote! Lorient June 40 – June 41.* Liv Editions, 2009.

Braeuer, Luc, *U-boote! Lorient July 41 – July 42.* Liv Editions, 2010.

Busch, Rainer, and Roll, Hans-Joachim, *Der U-boote Krieg,* vols. 1-5. Mittler Verlag, 1996-2003.

Catherine, Jean-Claude, *Articale in the Revue Historique des Armées,* No.195. 1994.

Chazette, Alain, *Articles in 39/45 Magazines,* No.241 and 243, 2007.

Dönitz, Karl, *Ten Years and Twenty Days.* Plon, 1959.

Dörr, Manfred, *Die Ritterkreuzträger der U-Boot-Waffe.* Biblio Verlag, 1988.

Estienne, René, *Article in Cols Bleus,* No.2121. 1991.

Fahrmbacher, Wilhelm, and Matthiae, Walter, *Lorient.* Prinz Eugen Verlag, 1956.

Farago, Ladislas, *La Xe Flotte.* Presses de la Cité, 1964.

Frank, Wolfgang, *U-boats contre les Alliées marines.* Arthaud, 1956.

Goebeler, Hans, and Vanzo, John P., *Steel Boats, Iron Hearts.* Wagnerian Publications, 1999.

Hague, Arnold, *The Allied Convoy System.* Vanwell Published Limited, 2000.

Herlin, Hans, *Les damnés de Atlantic.* France-Empire, 1960.

Hirschfeld, Wolfgang, and Brooks, Geoffrey, *The Story of a U-Boat NCO, 1940-1946.* Pen & Sword Books Ltd., 1996.

Högel, Georg, *Embleme Wappen Mailings.* Koehler Verlag, 1996.

Lange, Ulrich, *Auf Feindfahrt mit U-170.* Self-published, 2002.

Le Berd, Jean, *Lorient sous l'occupation.* Ouest-France, 1986.

Le Guen, A., *Lorient ville martyre.* Vanity Press, 1991.

Le Puth, L., *Quelques souvenirs de the vie Lorientaise de 1940 à 1945.* 1955.

Lukas, Yann, *Hennebont.* Palantines, 2006.

Malbosc, Guy, *The Battle of the Atlantic.* Economica, 1995.

Mallmann Showell, Jak, *U-Boats at War: Landings on Hostile Shores.* Ian Allan Publishing, 2000.

Milner, Marc, *Battle of the Atlantic.* The History Press, 2011.

Minister of the Defense, *SHAT,* 1978.

Neitzel, Sönke, *Die deutschen Ubootbunker.* Bernard & Graefe Verlag, 1991.

Plottke, Herbert, *Fächer Loos.* Podzun Pallas, 1994.

Rahn, Werner, *Kriegstagebuch der Seekriegsleitung 1939–1945.* Mittler & Sohn Verlag.

Rapports d'activité du XXVe Corps d'Armée German en occupation en Bretagne. Translated by Commandant Even, Roskill, S.W., Capt., *La flotte British en guerre.* Presses de la Cité, 1961.

Reberac, Fabien, *Article in Histoire de Guerre No.3 sur les U-boote dans l'Océan Indien.* 2000.

Schmeelke, Karl Heinz, and Schmeelke, Michael, *German U-Boat Bunkers.* Schiffer Publishing Ltd., 1999.

Stachelhaus, Uwe, *U-526.* Self-published, 2012.

The U-Boat War in the Atlantic. HMSO Publications Centre, 1989.

Theroux, Roger, *Le Morbihan en guerre.* Imprimerie de la Manutention, 1991.

Williamson, Gordon, *U-Boats vs. Destroyer Escorts.* Osprey Publishing, 2007.

White, John, *U-Boat Tankers.* Airlife Publishing, 1998.

Wynn, Kenneth, *U-Boat Operations of the Second World War.* Chatham Publishing, 1997.

COLOR GALLERY

RECENT VIEWS OF SUMMER 1942

Members of the 2nd Flotilla's ground personnel and civilians take advantage of the sun on the beach in front of the Port-Louis Citadel in the summer of 1942. *LB*

A concrete shelter was built after the summer of 1942. The citadel was to be used as a prison for the French Resistance. Sixty-nine of them were shot by the German army in June 1944, and their bodies discovered in a pit on May 23, 1945. A memorial was set up in 1959, with the names of sixty-two identified; seven remain unknown.

On August 7, 1942, joint meal between the crew of U-105 and the Japanese submariners of I-30 in front of the submariners' hostel in Kéroman, decked out in Japanese flags. *LB*

Recent view.

Crew of U-67 at rest during August 1942 in Carnac, in front of the Grand Hotel. *UBA*

Recent view.

Crew of U-67 in front of the bar *La Potinière*. *UBA*

Recent view.

Awards ceremony for U-509's crewmembers in the *Hundius Kaserne's* courtyard on September 13, 1942. *UBA*

Recent view.

Chief of the 10th Flotilla Günther Kuhnke hands out decorations to U-509 crewmembers. Commander Karl-Heinz Wolf holds the list of those awarded. *UBA*

Recent view.

On April 16, 1943, Commander Karl Neitzel of U-510 receives the Knight's Cross that he was awarded on March 27. Opposite him is *Kapitän-zur-See* Rösing, chief of U-boats in the West. *Ulf-Normann Neitzel*

Recent view.

End of May 1943: U-533 crewmembers on the corner of the *rue de Maréchal Joffre* and *Cours Chazelles*, in the *Hundius Kaserne* sector, in front of one of the only buildings remaining intact in the *Soldatenheim* (soldiers' hostel) district! *UBA*

Recent view.

RECENT VIEW OF THE U-BOAT BASE

November 1, 1942, members of the Flotillas' ground personnel installed in the "*caserne des 1000*" of KII. This space, equipped with every comfort and air-conditioning, is in the K6A pen, above the site reserved for stocking the two mobile platforms for carrying U-boats along the esplanade between KI and KII. *LB*

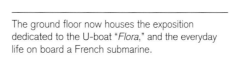

The ground floor now houses the exposition dedicated to the U-boat "*Flora*," and the everyday life on board a French submarine.

U-514 arrives at Kéroman III on February 12, 1943. *Ulf-Normann Neitzel*

Recent view.

On February 14, 1943, U-105 arrives at Kéroman III to berth in the double pen 17-18. *UBA*

Recent view.

On July 3, 1943, U-183 leaves the base on the Scorff for a mission. *UBA*

Recent view.

Rear outside entry. *LB*

The descent towards the ground floor rear entry makes it possible to see the thickness of the reinforced concrete roof. *LB*

1942: Double staircases connecting the ground floor to level 1. *LB*

After the War, the National Navy condemned one of the two staircases as well as several passages where we can see a metal beam above the framing. *LB*

The "Bunker Bar" of the 10th Flotilla, with the drink menus on the table and counter. *LB*

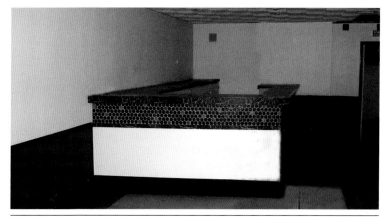

The bar renovated by the National Navy in the bunker that joins the sailors' hostel building. *LB*

BUNKER-BAR

10. U.-FL.

IM WESTEN

The Bunker Bar's card showing the selections available. *UBA*

The Art Deco lamps from the walls of the Bunker Bar in 1944 had been taken down and stored in a part of the bunker until 2010. *LB*

BUNKER FOR OFFICERS OF THE 10TH FLOTILLA

Sliding reinforced door that could be closed in the event of an air or poisoned gas attack. *LB*

Reinforced hinged door used for the same purpose. *LB*

Boiler in the basement for heating the radiators. *LB*

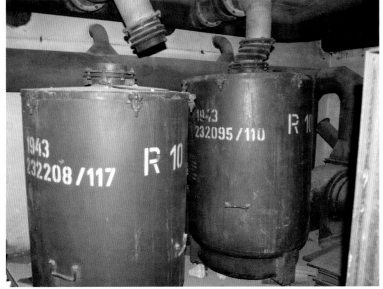

Large filters for ventilation in the event of attack. *LB*

"*Auer*" brand filters dating back to 1943. *LB*

Dumbwaiter for sending up food between the two floors, from the kitchen to level 1 and the bar on the ground floor. *LB*

Plate on the dumb waiter of the authorized maximum weight. *LB*

Skoda (Czech) brand power generator; *LB*

War correspondent Kurt Esmarch types his articles in one of the bunker's 138 individual rooms, each equipped with a bed, a desk and a small wash basin. He has decorated to his satisfaction, a door with a lock ensures his privacy. *UBA*

The bunker's floor was covered with parquet or tiles and the walls were entirely panelled, which gave off more heat than bare concrete walls. Below the bar on the ground floor was a mess on level 1. *LB*

One of the four tubs in the bathrooms. A true luxury at that time! *LB*

Names engraved in the concrete on level 1 dating back to 1942. *LB*

Names engraved in the concrete on level 1 during construction. *LB*

One of the sixteen individual toilets entirely tiled and equipped underneath with a ventilation system and above with a pressure relief valve. *LB*

One of the six medical blocks, the showers in the front, four toilets in the back. *LB*

Access doors to the individual showers. On the right, the remains of some wash basins. *LB*

Reinforced door with a Cross of Lorraine drawn on it after the Liberation. This gigantic two-story bunker was entirely destroyed in 2011. *LB*

BUNKER FOR THE CREWS OF THE 10TH FLOTILLA

This large bunker, of 1,250 square meters, sheltered eight submarine crews from bombardment. In 1943, it was camouflaged under large nets to protect it against air raids. On the right: the maritime hospital surrounded by three bunkers. *LB*

The bunker for the crews in 2009, with concreted ventilation outlets on the roof; on the right: the rear wall of the *Haus Mugler Hundius Kaserne*. *LB*

The double-door entry was used as a decontamination chamber. *LB*

One of the corridors giving onto the dormitories equipped with reinforced sliding doors. Everything remains as it was at the epoch from the floor tiles to the air-distribution pipes above. *LB*

One of the eight submariners' dormitories. *LB*

The bathrooms. *LB*

Communal showers. *LB*

The power generator could provide electricity for the bunker in the event of an exterior rupture. This bunker was entirely destroyed in 2010. *LB*

One of the two boiler complexes; the ventilation filters are still in place. *LB*

A few days after the arrival of U-160 in Lorient on August 24, 1942, an awards ceremony is held in front of the huts built on the *Place d'Armes*, opposite the Gabriel House pavilions. Aided by his warrant officer, Günther Kuhnke, the chief of the 10th Flotilla hands out the Iron Cross 2nd Class, watched by Commander Georg Lassen. *UBA*

Recent view.

After the bombardments in mid-February 1943, the Germans moved surviving furniture out of the Maritime Prefecture. On the right, one of the protected entries leading to the bunker buried between the Gabriel House pavilions' two back wings. The huts built over the bunker were destroyed by bombs. They were quickly rebuilt. *UBA*

The concrete entry has disappeared. The only access to the bunker is reached by the basement in the Maritime Prefecture. *LB*

The staircase leading to the bunker of underground command, built between the two rear wings of the Gabriel House pavilions. *LB*

Access passage to the various parts of the bunker; the ventilation outlets are still in place. *LB*

Access passage to the various offices that housed the administrative section of the 2nd and 10th U-boat Flotillas. *LB*

The bathrooms are still intact. With the destruction of the two, large, two-story shelters in the center of the Péristyle barracks in 2012, this bunker is the only one still remaining in this sector. *LB*

MARKINGS IN THE T5 DOM-BUNKER

Kriegsmarine gray-wood, double-door cupboard—still in place in 2008—in a room on the ground floor of the *T5 Dom-Bunker. LB*

Inscription "U-511" written in chalk on the first floor of the *Dom-Bunker*, on the frame of a door of a storage room housing the personal effects of submariners on mission. *LB*

Inscription painted on a concrete beam on the ground floor indicating the storeroom for the personal effects of U-68's crew. *LB*

Plate reading "U-510" on the grille in front of a storeroom on the second floor. *LB*

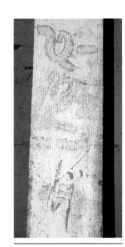

Crayon inscription in three colors on a concrete beam on the first floor reading "U-123" with the 2nd Flotilla's inscription below it. *LB*

Inscription in chalk behind a latticed door of a storeroom on the ground floor belonging to the U-129. *LB*

Plate and inscription reading "U-155" on the second floor, indicating storeroom reserved for this U-boat. *LB*

"U-155" painted on the concave interior walls on the second floor of the *Dom-bunker*. *LB*

Inscription "U-507" in chalk on a doorframe. *LB*

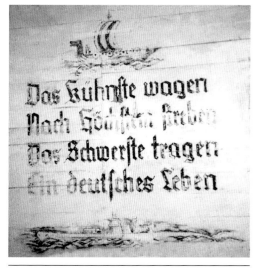

In the torpedo bunker *Jaguar* in Kérolay, a framed maxim with a Viking ship and a U-boat reads: "To dare to be the most audacious, to seek to reach the highest limits, to carry the heaviest load is the German life." The bunker was destroyed at the end of the 1980s. *Alain Chazette*

Torpedo bunker *Iltis* (polecat) in Kérolay before its destruction in 1996. *Alain Chazette*

During March 1943, the submariners of U-382 are billeted in Kernével Point, in one of the three blockhouses reserved for the crews. On the right: the Kernével redoubt with a concreted projector shelter. *LB*

Recent view.

The crew of U-382 in their bunker in Kernével. With those presented in the chapter covering March 1942, these are the only known photographs at this time of a U-boat crew at rest in a blockhouse in Lorient. *LB*

Recent view.

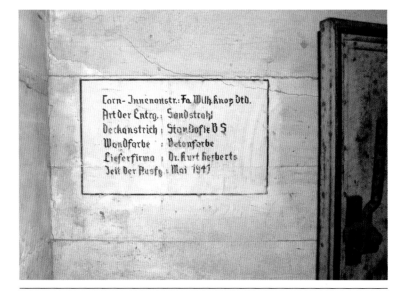

Cartouche of the German firm Kurt Heberts that built this bunker in May 1941. *LB*

The vertical bars for the tubular beds are still in the bunker. *LB*

A submariner drew this small landscape that perhaps reminded him of home. *LB*

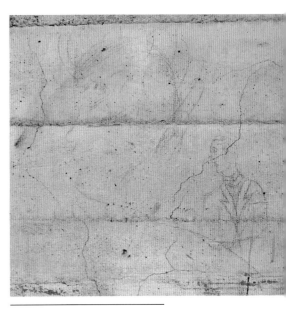

Another drawing is of his fiancée. *LB*

KERENTRECH CEMETERY

The German military section in Kerentrech Cemetery. In the center, a stone monument was built with a German helmet and a large, black granite cross. In the background, the house on the left is surmounted by a wood platform for an anti-aircraft gun. The holes in the roof of the house on the right, obviously caused by shrapnel, were repaired with metal sheets. *DR*.

These three houses survived the war. *LB*

Large black granite cross dedicated to the victims of the trawler *La Tanche*, sunk by a mine on June 19, 1940. *LB*

Allied military section in Kerentrech Cemetery, mainly for aviators who died during combat missions. The building in the background was built on the site of the former German military section after the graves were moved to Pornichet in 1959. *LB*

Kerentrech Cemetery: a wooden cross for *Matrosengefreiter* Herbert Hering, the nineteen-year-old cook aboard U-526 that was sunk by a mine off Larmor on April 14, 1943. He was a former cook in the canteen of a company in Dresden. *Robert Maschauer/Uwe Stachelhaus*

Block 9 of the German military cemetery in Pornichet filled with the tombs from the German military section in Kerentrech Cemetery. *LB*

Tomb of Herbert Hering that was transferred to the German military cemetery in Pornichet: block 9, row 26, number 732. In all, 1,519 remains of German soldiers were transferred from Kerentrech to Pornichet in 1959 by the German War Graves Commission. *LB*

Tomb of *Matrose* Kurt Kunze of U-171. The U-boat was sunk by a mine on October 9, 1942. Block 9, row 17, No.419. *LB*

Tomb of Masch.Mt. Otto Hollemann of U-103 who died in Pont-Callec on April 10, 1943. Block 9, row 25, No.697. *LB*

Pornichet: tomb of Hans Möglich, commander of U-526. Block 9, row 26, number 723. This cemetery has two tombs for submariners from U-171, and twenty-six from U-526. *LB*

2002: Meeting between the author, Uwe Stachelhaus, and Robert Maschauer, veteran of U-526. The latter returned to France to see the two fishermen from Lorient who pulled him out of the water on April 14, 1943, when his U-boat was sunk off Larmor. He had a bad leg wound and it had to be amputated at the hospital. *Uwe Stachelhaus*

Ring with the 10th Flotilla's insignia. *Benoit Senne*

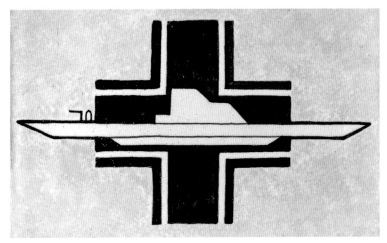

Earthenware tile of the 10th Flotilla manufactured by Henriot Quimper. *LB*

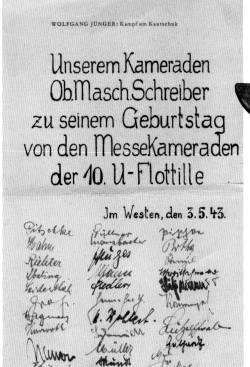

A page from a book offered to a member of the 10th Flotilla for his birthday on May 3, 1943. *LB*

Metal insignia of the 10th Flotilla, sewn on the garrison cap. *LB*

Card signed by Günther Kuhnke, chief of the 10th Flotilla on the fourth Christmas at war in December 1942. Offered to the members of his unit, it was probably accompanied by a package full of gifts. *LB*

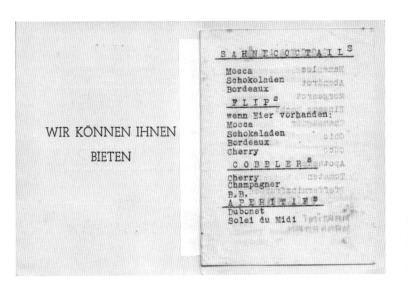

Back of the drinks menu from the Bunker Bar, in the 10th Flotilla's officers' bunker. *UBA*

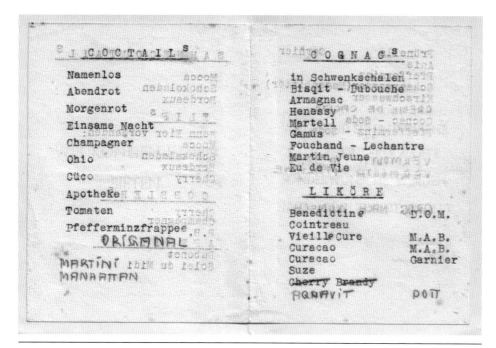

Choice of drinks. *UBA*

Rear of the drinks menu from the Bunker Bar. *UBA*

SOUVENIRS OF GERMAN SUBMARINERS STOPPING OFF IN LORIENT

U-boat depth gauge going from 1 to 25 meters. *Pascal Theffo*

Greeting card, Christmas 1942 from Viktor Schütze, chief of the 2nd Flotilla, indicating that his flotilla's U-boats had sunk five million tons worth of Allied ships since the beginning of the war. *LB*

Diary of the 2nd Flotilla for the year 1943. *UBA*

Book written by U-123 Commander Reinhard Hardegen about his patrols along the American coast, published in 1943. *LB*

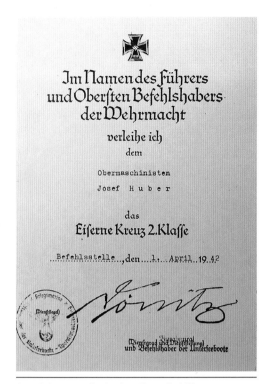

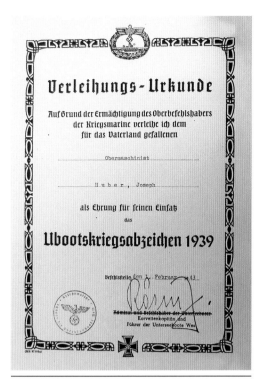

Award document for the Iron Cross 2nd Class to machinist Josef Huber of U-158, on April 1, 1942. *UBA*

Award document for the U-boat Combat Badge, awarded posthumously to Josef Huber, on February 1, 1943. *UBA*

Dcoument, "Died in the Field of Honor," awarded to Josef Huber on February 1, 1943. The date attributed is July 1, 1942, but in reality the U-boat was sunk by a plane the day before west of Bermuda, along with its fifty-four crewmembers. It is signed by Kuhnke, chief of the 10th Flotilla. *UBA*

Calling card of Ernst Kals, chief of the 2nd Flotilla promoted to the rank of *Fregattenkapitän* on June 1, 1943. *LB*

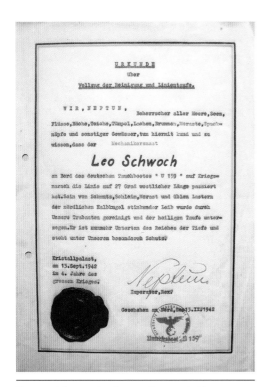

Document for crossing the equator awarded to submariner mechanic Leo Schwoch of U-159 on September 13, 1942. This U-boat then joined the *Eisbär* Wolfpack in direction of the Cape for the first attack in this sector. *Serge Lhotellier*

Book written by U-69 Commander Jost Metzler published in 1943. Its French translation, under the title *Sous-marin Corsaire*, was published by "*J'ai lu*" Editions in 1956. *UBA*

Cover of the *Soldbuch* of Rudolf Mollinger, submariner aboard U-527. The first page carries the words written in pencil: "Lost at sea." *LB*

Pages from the *Soldbuch* belonging to *Masch. Obergefreiter* Rudolf Mollinger, barred with a red line and notated, "disappeared since July 25, 1943." Actually, this U-boat was sunk during an air attack two days later at a supply rendezvous south of the Azores; this crewmember was among the forty dead. The commander and twelve men were fished out of the water by an Allied ship and taken prisoner. *LB*

On August 24, 1943, Kals, chief of the 2nd Flotilla sent a gift to Wolfgang Lüth, a member of his flotilla when he commanded U-43. The accompanying letter said that he hoped that the commander would think of his old flotilla when he drank from the gift. It was an engraved silver goblet (*Ritterkreuzbecher*), manufactured in Paris and reserved for commanders awarded the Knight's Cross. *Andreas Dwulecki*

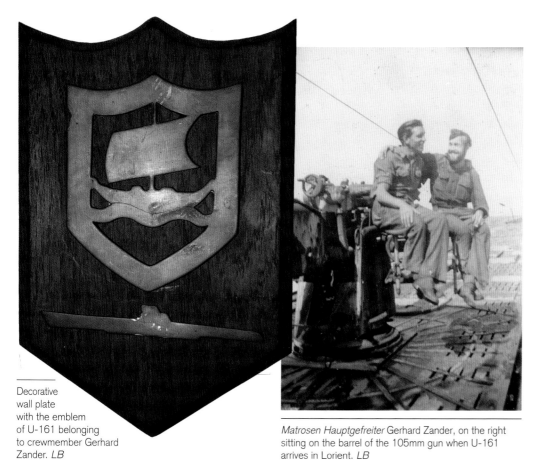

Decorative
wall plate
with the emblem
of U-161 belonging
to crewmember Gerhard
Zander. *LB*

Matrosen Hauptgefreiter Gerhard Zander, on the right
sitting on the barrel of the 105mm gun when U-161
arrives in Lorient. *LB*

Gerhard Zander with his U-boat Combat Badge awarded
after three combat patrols. He was lost at sea with
fifty-one other crewmembers on September 27, 1943. *LB*

EARTHENWARE TILES WITH THE INSIGNIA OF THE U-BOATS THAT CAME TO LORIENT

Insignia of U-126: the Queen of Hearts. *Pierre Pennanech*

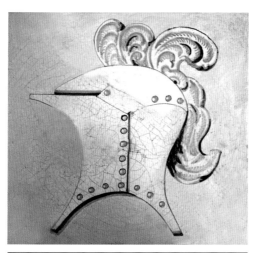

Insignia of U-130: A knight's helmet. *UBA*

Insignia of U-156, the blazon of Plauen, the U-boat's
patron town. *LB*

Blazon of U-163. *LB*

Insignia of U-504. *LB*

Insignia of U-507. *LB*

Blazon of U-521. *LB*

Insignia of U-522. *LB*

INSIGNIA WORN ON THE CAPS OF SUBMARINERS WHO CAME TO LORIENT

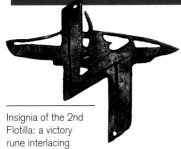

Insignia of the 2nd Flotilla: a victory rune interlacing a U-boat. *LB*

Insignia of the 10th Flotilla, designed by Commander Günther Kuhnke. *Private collection*

Insignia of the 10th Flotilla. *Benoît Senne*

Insignia of U-67. *Eric Miquelon*

Insignia of U-103: victory rune. Its former Commander Viktor Schütze, after he was named chief of the 2nd Flotilla, adopted it for all the U-boats under his command. *Marc Braeuer*

Insignia of U-124. The Edelweiss was adopted during the campaign in Norway in 1940, following contacts between U-64, sunk off Narvik, and the *Chasseurs Apins.* The crew of U-64 was later affected to the new U-124. *LB*

Insignia of U-128 having belonged to *Masch. Mt.* Günter Lorek. The insignia of the U-boat's patron unit, the *Todt Organization Officers' School* based at Chateau Pont-Callec (*OT-Lehrlager – Frontführerschule*). *UBA*

Insignia of U-161, having belonged to radio operator Gotthard Hoffmann. It is the Viking blazon of the U-boat's patron, an army unit that in 1940 was supposed to be part of the landing forces during the Invasion of Britain. *UBA*

Insignia of U-172: Poseidon. *UBA*